SO THIS BABY SEAL WALKS INTO A CLUB...

DRUNKEN THEODICIES AND HALFWAY STORIES ABOUT SELFISHNESS AND SCHADENFREUDE

By Your Mother

Cover and interior design by SW, KK, EK, RW & JH

Library of Congress Control Number: 2008942406

ISBN-13: 978-0-578-00043-5

Printed in the United States of America via LuLu Press (www.lulu.com)

Author's contact info: RE.Woock@gmail.com

The crackhead sulks in the middle of the rehab's lobby, his arms crossed, facing us. He's bitching at me and my coworker. The flaking paint and busted chairs lining the wall behind the crackhead amplify his complaints of neglect. Under the baggy tent of his wife-beater you can see guy's ribs. I could improvise a xylophone recital on them, and his arms are about as thick around as my dick.

(not a compliment to either of us)

He rocks back and forth, heels to toes. There's no rhythm to the crackhead's movements, just urgency. After running for so long on coke and baking powder he can't relax. He can't shut up. The crackhead grits his teeth between sentences and glares, like he wants to show how much the communication is costing him. How it's my fault he's nailed to the cross of his own drug-wrecked body.

The crackhead is the epitome of decades of proud black defiance whittled down into a sickly, whining form. The sullen archetype of a people brought low. Think Malcolm X, if he'd stuck with dealing drugs and just used the preaching as an outlet for his persecution complex.

Twitching in the ruins of the lobby, the crackhead's like the Ghost of Drug Epidemics Past, Present and Future. Generations of chemical coping, all rolled into one repulsive package. His words whistle from the space where his front teeth should be. The vowels dribble out like a pervert drooling over little girls. I have to actively decipher his gruntings before he sounds like something other than Charlie Brown's teachers.

The crackhead's speaking to me and my coworker. Haranguing us as we slouch behind the front desk. A target is needed for his anger. In rough translation, he says: "If y'all so great, what *y'all* fuckers do all day? 'Sides just sittin' around on your asses?"

Well, there's the rampant sadism and pill-popping, but…"We sit around some more," I answer. "It takes a well-trained ass to handle this job."
The voices in my head agree that the crackheads all resemble Muppets. *Angry Muppets.*

I think of Kermit smoking rock and start giggling. It's tough to stop.
"Us Techs run the place," my coworker clarifies. The crackhead isn't satisfied with the answer, so Jack gives a broken smile to show that he's been there, too.
"We in charge of emergency counseling and stuff. We deal with the clients after they counselors spend the day getting 'em all riled up. Talk and listen to 'em."

Actually, me and Jack talk *at* the clients and *pretend* to listen to them. We give them abuse and neglect and call it healthcare. Good enough, in my opinion.

But, it's not like anyone's going to care what you think when you're as stoned as I am...

Yeah, so:

This is about a bunch of stuff that happened when I worked at a rehab.

Some of it's funny.

Some of it's not.

Some of it's horrific.

Some of it's not.

This is a book about crackheads and bums. About junkies and losers. About what it's like to spend all your time around sick people.

This book is a 100-percent true work of fiction. And that's all it is.

It is not an extended allegory for the futility of human existence. Segments of it don't correspond to the cantos of *Dante's Inferno* or *The Tibetan Book of the Dead*. There are no secret allegories or cabbalistic correspondences hidden within it. I'm not a writer. I don't have an English degree. This book was not written to impress the other no-talent jack-offs in my Creative Writing class.

It's not even a novel. There is no building action, no plot, no first, second, or third act, no climax, no dénouement.

This book is essentially the account of a year at a rehab/halfway house for recovering addicts, told in the form of random vignettes.

It's all set up non-chronologically, you should be warned. Characters reminisce about events that occur later in the book, and anticipate things that you, the reader, have already encountered. Events that take place in December are followed by a chapter from the previous March. Think of it as a jumbled slide show from a vacation you'd never want to take. Keeping things straight shouldn't be any trouble for a literate and seriously sexy individual like yourself, but giving a friendly warning seemed like the nice thing to do.

You're welcome.

The people you meet in this book are all real people with real problems. Only the names have been changed to protect the guilty. No one is imaginary or a composite. There are no tidy morals here. No warm feelings that will tickle your heart. No one in this book learns a lesson by the end of it, and neither will you. This isn't fucking *Sesame Street*. If you still need moral guidance at your age there was something seriously wrong with your upbringing.

Everyone in this book ruined their lives because they have a disease or because they are weak, unlucky or stupid. One excuse is just as good as the next.

The fault for these ruined lives lie squarely at the feet of the people living those lives. No one forced them. No one else could stop them. That they also frequently destroyed the lives of those who loved them is just part of the tragedy of addiction.

Part of the tragedy…and maybe part of the comedy, as well.

Hope you like your humor black.

P.C. DISCLAIMER

The dialogue of the clients at the rehab is not structured to make them sound ignorant or like classic stereotypes, though some of them certainly can act like stereotypes. It's structured to make them sound *coherent*. Your average crack-head does not talk like a Harvard-educated banker. In "real life," most of their speech resembles a long, mumbled slur of vowels. What you're getting is a decent approximation that actually makes them sound a lot more intelligent and intelligible than they do in person. If some of the characters sound like stereo-types straight from a latter-day minstrel show, it's because there happens to be a significant population in this country that refuses to talk like they just shoved a finger down their throat and ralphed up the King James Bible.

Sho 'nuff!

One Mɔ' Thang

Always remember: *"New Start Rule #1*: Never Trust a Junkie."

MORNING SHIFT
(8am-4pm)

PROLOGUE:
THAT'S ALL WELL AND GOOD FOR SHEEP,
BUT WHAT ARE WE TO DO?

My name is Ray, and I'm a Substance Abuse Technician.

The sun is failing to break through the petrochemical clouds of downtown Pasadena, leaving the world hazy and gray. I push my bike through the front door of *A New Start,* the local drug rehab/halfway house. It's an Ozone Warning day, and the Terror Alert level is at Orange. This means the young and elderly are to stay inside, and the rest of us should remain scared.

The door closes behind me as I transition from one toxic environment to another. The vomit on my tires rolls itself onto the linoleum of the lobby floor. It's drippy and brown, like rotten syrup. The ink for the world's most disgusting notary stamp comes from a puddle of stomach juices blocking the front door.

Maybe the acidic broth I'm trailing is the fault of one of the three bums slumped against the outside wall. Maybe it had been a collaborative effort on all their parts. Maybe not. All that matters to me is that Lake Puke represents the moat separating my work from the rest of the world. The helplessly sick isolated from those who can hide it. This lets the human wastes here know that they're in their element. It's as much of a calling card as that big-ass cross we've got out front. And a lot more honest.

That's right: *Symbolism.*

I'm a psychology major, but I did sleep through English 201 last semester. Picked a few things up by osmosis. This is one honky whose college education won't go to waste.

The front lobby's small and cramped, lined with rotting chairs and a cracked leather couch. A smell that drifts between burnt garbage and a sewage martini sulks in the air. Somewhere a radio talks about dead children and U.S. bombing raids. There's a busted telephone on a table by the door and a bookshelf stacked with spotty encyclopedia collections. An L-shaped desk cordons off the back-right corner of the lobby. Behind it stand two filing cabinets and a middle-aged black guy.

"Ray!" My coworker cheers at the sight of me. Weasely little man. Huge forehead and small body. He looks like the sole survivor of an auto mishap between a short bus and mobile neutering station. Bastard's ratted me out for misconduct twice before, but I don't hold it against him. He's just another person whose open coffin I'll piss in some day.

I nod in his direction. "Hey Regg," is called back with less enthusiasm. My bike leaves a slime trail as it's maneuvered through the lobby and into the side hallway. The tires print a pattern of indigestion as they roll, like they're laying the red carpet for a bulimics' convention.

Someone else will clean it up.

My backpack is shed behind the front desk. I stretch out one shoulder, then the other. It's a short ride here from my girlfriend's place, but I'm so out of shape that any exertion takes a toll. Having a job that consists of sitting on your ass for eight-to-sixteen hours will do that. Had I arrived only an hour later, I'd also be drenched in sweat from the subtropical East Texas climate.

So, it could be worse. It could always be worse. It's remembering those little things that can help with maintaining an attitude of gratitude.

"Anything to report?" I ask.

Reginald shakes his head. That means none of our clients got fucked up on crack, huffed Scotch Guard, attacked another client or any of the usual things that make working here so amusing. "Quiet as can be," he says.

"That's the way I like it," I say back to him. It's the same verbal exchange every time I show up for work. Our little ritual.

Reginald finishes packing up his things and heads to where his car's parked in the back lot. He calls out a final, *"Take it easy!"* as he departs.

I wait till he's out of range before shouting, "That's what your mom says when we do anal!"

Immature, but satisfying. And also a part of our little ritual.

There's no one else in the lobby. I settle behind the desk, slap a Pixies album on the CD player and pump up the volume.

"Wanna grow up to be…!" Frank Black screams at me, *"Be a Debaser!"*

My feet thump on the desk as I adjust myself through my shorts. In a little while I'll go raid the facility's fridge to see what's left over from breakfast.

My name is Ray, and I'm a 23-year-old white boy plugging his way through college. I work as a Substance Abuse Technician at the rehab since I'm too lazy to have a real job. Being a Tech just means that I baby-sit a bunch of grown-up failures. Drug addicts stay at *A New Start* after they've gone through detox. The junkies, the alkies, the pill-poppers and crackheads all live in this dreary little place and spend their days attending 12-Step meetings at outside locations. It's an all-male establishment, which at least keeps the sexual harassment charges against me to a minimum.

The rehab is also an expensive place, about three grand a month. You'd be right to suspect that the average addict doesn't have piles of cash just lying around, so most of them are funded by a state program. Most of *New Start's* income is derived from government handouts. Money is taken straight from your paychecks to be used on sorry-assed junkies. It's one of the last remaining examples of our society helping the less fortunate.

That, or just another way the government funnels your tax dollars to private businesses.

There's a banging on the front door. I lean over the desk to scope it out. The lobby's got a glass front, and through it I can see some bum with his face busted to hell and back, like he got tag-teamed by a hammer and ginsu knife. He hits the door again. Blood's caked on his face and down the front of his jacket. Apparently under the impression that our secret knock involves punching the glass as hard as possible, I watch him smack the door a few more times. Then he notices me watching and gives it an extra kick.

Somebody wants in.

Somebody is shit-out-of-luck.

I give him a slow shake of my head, and he responds by smashing his face against the door and smearing a bloody streak across the glass. Then the guy turns and stalks off.

He'll be back.

My employers share a building and its lobby with a Methodist Homeless Assistance Ministry. It's called *Christ in the Gutter*. Cute name, though vaguely unflattering. As if having a bunch of junkies and crackheads here wasn't bad enough, for half the day the downstairs is packed with piss-soaked bums and crazed transients. Once again, there's nothing in this world so bad that we can't find some way to make it worse.

This is probably the most educational job I've ever had. Pushing T-shirts made by Indonesian slave-labor at The Gap might pay more and offer health insurance, but at least working here guarantees me something interesting to say when I'm at parties and somebody asks me: *So, what do you do?*

Well...I tell them:

I catch people using dirty needles to inject urine into their bladders to cheat a piss test. I hang around homeless families where the parents use their kids to stub out cigarettes. I see alcoholics chug vodka and drive their trucks off the side of elevated highways. I watch hookers get thrown from moving automobiles.

I tell them: My name is Ray, and I get to see the worst that humanity has to offer. I watch people go ten hard rounds with life and, trust me, *life always wins*. I see where the American Dream said '*fukkit*' and decided to go back to blowing its dealer for a fix. I witness despair, pain, insanity and the human spirit getting its spine broken in half, only to drag itself back up for one more shot at survival. I spend hours each day around people whose biggest accomplishment is not slitting their throat or the throats of everyone around them.

I catch the shit and the filth and the shame. Every horrible thing we try to hide from each other gets broadcast in fucking Technicolor right in front of my face. I meet all the monsters you double-bolt your doors against, and it's funny how they're just as frightened as the rest of us.

My name is Ray, and I love my job.

7:52am
SIMPLE MACHINES

Solomon waddled into the lobby and shouted a hello at me. In addition to being fat and AIDS-ridden, Solly was also stuck talking at several-dozen decibels louder than needed. The headphones permanently attached to his ears probably had something to do with this.

Solomon shouted at me, "WHATCHA KNOW, BOSS MAN?" as he wrote his name in the sign-out sheet on my desk.

"I know a lot," I said. Such are the useless benefits of higher education. "Especially about *your* crazy ass."

And I did:

I knew that Solly was in here for his crack addiction. I knew that it took a small pharmacy of pills to keep his liver, heart and immune system from imploding. I knew that he stored his own urine in cranberry juice bottles. I knew that he had two felony counts of statutory rape and one for the sexual assault of a child. I also knew that he'd spent fourteen years in jail and that he wasn't the first multiple rapist I'd met at work.

I was in charge of filing the medical records and legal papers for the clients. There was no way I could resist reading the stuff. Having grown up around nothing but middle class white folk, the job was really expanding my horizons. It was as educational as it was horrifying.

What I *didn't* know about Solomon was to how many of those little girls he had spread his disease. It was a small detail, but I couldn't help but be curious.

Solly hummed to himself as he wrote, tossing his head from one side to the other. Back and forth while I watched the fat rolls on his neck bunch up on the right side then the left. He looked like the world's most harmless black man. Pudgy and content, like a harem eunuch. Nothing about his appearance suggested the guy was a crackheaded kiddie-fucker.

Solly coughed once, and I instinctively held my breath. Irrational AIDS fear.

It's so easy to be judgmental towards people. It's also against company policy. As if any of us limited little robots have much control over the fucked-up shit we all do. I'm sure that we'd like to think otherwise, especially when other people do stuff we disapprove of. But, most of us seem to be little more than the unwitting combination of our genetics, imprinting and early conditioning.

Solomon squinted up at the clock on the wall behind me, pondering what the hell the big and little hands were trying to say.

I had to wonder: are we all helpless, or just weak and lazy?

Does it matter either way?

"Did you like it when they screamed?" I asked him. "Or was it the pre-teen tightness that did it for ya, Solly? Maybe you're scared of body hair?"

Solomon looked up from the sign-out sheet and blessed me with a gap-toothed smile. "THAT'S GREAT, BOSS MAN." Guy hadn't heard a word I'd said. "GOIN' TO THE STO'. YOU NEED ANYTHING?"

I thought for a second before suggesting, "Something young and unable to fight back?"

"*Huh?*" Solomon reached up and lifted a headphone away from his left ear. A deep, thudding bass told me that Solly was pulping his eardrums with some kind of rap. Hopefully it was also making him impotent.

I shook my head and smiled back at him. "Fine, thanks."

He lowered the headphones back over his ears. "YOU ALRIGHT FOR A CRACKER, RAY."

Sol gave me another smile to go with the compliment and turned to leave. I waved at him as he walked out the door.

Friendly motherfucker.

7:56am
FORGET IT WITH PEOPLE

I sat at the front desk and picked at the powdered eggs and sausage on my plate. It's what was left over from the clients' breakfast. It's what was *always* left over from the clients' breakfast. A fourth of my bodyweight was probably comprised of this shit.

Horrid stuff. As one of the clients had told me: '*It like prison food, but ain't nobody gonna shank you while ya eatin' it.*'

I wouldn't have been too surprised to find out that a steady diet of the stuff caused cancer in lab rats. It seemed like everything else did. Hell, maybe those furry little bastards were just naturally prone to cancer. Why should humans be the only species weighted towards destruction?

The doorbell rang. I clicked the unlock switch under the desk without first checking to see who wanted in. Wouldn't have been too difficult; the door was about fifteen feet in front of me and made of glass. And, in case I was incredibly near-sighted, a security camera pointed at the door, broadcasting its image onto the small monitor on my desk.

The *Christ in the Gutter* signs taped to the door (like the one stating that free handouts don't start till 9am) obscured the face of the person seeking entrance. Made it damn tough to see who was banging on the door unless you were willing to go to the trouble of lifting your fat ass from your seat for a look. So, like most of us, the security camera was both extraneous *and* useless.

The sound of feet shuffling on linoleum announced the entrance of two people into the lobby. I glanced up to see a tall, scruffy black man and a fat old bum in a tattered overcoat. Their size differences made for a nicely mismatched pair. The stereotypical odd couple. Hell, in a better world they could've been a classic comedy duo. Imagine the matinee title: *It's Laurel and Hardy in: 'Will Knife You for Food*!'

The two homeless men were shaking from the cold. East Texas winters might not have the low numbers that make for impressive viewing on The Weather Channel, but the cold has a way of seeping right into you. The guys, shivering in unison, looked at me expectantly.

I sighed. Time to deal with the homeless. Time to take care of stuff that wasn't even my problem. Time to let these people know that they were going to have to go wanting for just a little while longer.

I put on my patient/friendly face. "Can I help y'all?"

The tall one was the more in charge of the two. He lacked that submissive crouch that most of the homeless acquired after a short while of living on charity. "We hungry," he stated, looking first at me then down at my sumptuous meal.

Christ in the Gutter typically gave out free crap like hand-me-down clothes and toothbrushes. The occasional bus passes, maybe. Free food for the homeless was a rare thing around here. Sometimes restaurants donated their nearly spoiled excess, but not often.

I looked up at the guy. He stared back. "Too bad this isn't a Luby's," I said.

6

My sarcasm didn't go over well. "*Whatchu* say?" He glared down at me. Hands planted firmly on my desk. His compatriot hung a few feet back, satisfied with letting him do the heavy work.

I leaned back in my seat and let out another sigh. *Jesus.* As if bullying was required to get the handouts they were after. I guess that living too long in a capitalist society makes us think that we always have to stomp on somebody to get what we want.

"You heard me," I said. "They don't start giving out the free shit till nine. Right now this is an entirely different business."

The homeless always had the hardest time understanding that I didn't have a damn thing to do with free socks or sandwiches or whatever. I was just an innocent bystander, unlucky enough to be in the same vicinity as their handouts.

"Think you can talk to us like that?" The tall guy was getting angry. Well, he'd actually started out kind of angry, and was now rapidly moving towards *pissed*. Someone would have to work on their panhandling technique if they were going to keep from starving. '*Friendly and passive*' tends to be a lot more effective. It lets the people helping you feel powerfully magnanimous.

"*Look*," I said. "The only food we've got is what's right here on my plate."

The fat bum jumped to attention. "I take it!"

It hadn't really been an offer, but...

I shrugged and handed over the food. He rushed up to the desk, grabbed the plate, then hauled ass out the door. Me and Captain Pissed were left alone.

I looked back up at him. "You might wanna go tackle your pal if you're expecting him to share." What was this guy still hanging around for? Waiting to see if I whipped an emergency breakfast stash from my pants?

He leaned across the desk. "You keep talkin' to me like that and there gonna be consequences." We exchanged stares, angry energy in his eyes, boredom in mine. "You do know what *consequences* means, don't you?"

"Why?" I asked. "That your vocabulary word for the day?"

You're still on top of a situation so long as you can keep making smart-ass remarks.

Never ceasing to stare at me (guess it was supposed to be intimidating), he growled, "I just got outta jail, and I ain't goin' back for you."

I rolled my eyes. Why did I have to put up with these people when it wasn't part of *my* job? So the rehab shared the building with a bunch of religious do-gooders; so fuckin' what? It would be like the employees at the Cookie Bouquet having to fold towels just because they shared the same mall with Bed Bath and Beyond.

Where were the goddamn Christers? *Their* charity organization, let *them* deal with it!

"No one's making you go back to jail..."

He reached into his back pocket. Out came a knife.

"I just sayin' there be *consequences*." On the last word he flicked out the blade. My heart revved up several gears. "I slit you open before I go back." My mouth went dry. My balls tried to hide in my stomach. I could feel the pulse thrumming in my ears. It was too early in the morning to have my life threatened.

A definite word would be had with those Methodist motherfuckers about me having to put up with this kind of shit.

"Y-you need to leave," I said, looking around the desk for something heavy to hit him with. Hopefully something with a decent reach, so I could crack his skull open before he had the chance to carve his initials in my face. The facility's key ring was attached to a large hunk of solid oak, but it was nowhere in sight. Had I left it in the kitchen? Panic was beginning to seem like a viable alternative. "*Please?*"

He smiled. They may not teach too much about social rehabilitation in prison, but apparently you do learn the finer points of submission and dominance. Mr. Switchblade saw that he had the upper hand on an uppity white boy, so he wasn't going anywhere. "*Consequences,*" he said again. His verbal needle was stuck, and from the look in his eyes, I might get stuck, too.

I tried to speak. Tried to tell him to take a fucking hike, to go play in traffic, but my tongue picked that moment to freeze in my mouth. The rest of my body thought that seemed like a great idea, and I was riveted to the spot. I wasn't going anywhere, and neither was he.

"*Consequences.*"

Not until my boss rounded the corner. At the sight of Gim, my new playmate folded his blade and headed for the door.

"*Consequences!*" he called back to me.

"*…fuck you…*" was all I could think to say. My legs started shaking and wouldn't stop.

8:01am
THE COURAGE TO CHANGE THE THINGS WE CAN

My boss is a monster. Not morally, like Hitler or myself, but physically. The man's around seven feet tall and used to play for the NFL. Biggest mammal I've ever seen outside a zoo. Two steps were all it took to carry him from the edge of the lobby to the side of my desk. His handshake smothered mine like an envelope.

Gim was the director for the rehab/halfway house. Bigger and blacker than anyone I've ever met. Friendlier, too. He had the body of a linebacker and the personality of a PR agent, all smiles and warmth. And since respectability is half the battle in today's world, Gim had a wardrobe that consisted of nothing but plaid golf shirts and slacks large enough to house a Cub Scout troop. The Big and Tall store apparently had a pretty limited selection. Not that I'd really know; I'm so all-over average that you could lose me in any decent-sized crowd of honkies.

Gim's job was to oversee all the clients, counselors, and—beneath the counselors—the Techs like me. It wasn't the easiest job in the world to manage a bunch of intellectual lightweights and slackers like me and my coworkers.

8

There's only so much idiocy and sloth that one man can try to compensate for. But, Gim was a pretty likeable chap, so no one held it against him when shit went wrong. Someone as big as Gim, you're just glad the man didn't feel like stepping on you. He totally could, if the urge ever struck.

"How're you doing, Ray?" Gim stepped around the side of the desk to give me a hug (my boss *hugs* me; how many people can say that? And not just during sexual harassment hearings?), and engage me in the sort of small talk that's all a part of his outgoing personality and such a big hit with potential clients. *Chat chat chat, smile smile smile.* How am I doing, how's school, how's my cold, how's life in general? And all the while, a look of *'genuine'* interest on his face. Still haven't figured out how he fakes it so well.

With most folks I wouldn't have even pretended to care, but since Gim's my boss (and signs my paychecks), I reciprocated the pleasantries. How's his life, how's the family, how's the old football injuries, *etc.*

He told me about his recent trip to Rome. Saw the sights, acted like a typical tourist, and endured a guide whom never stopped talking about himself the entire time. According to Gim, the guy kept mum about anything of historical interest and just blabbed about shit that had happened to his own Italian ass; like getting arrested for disorderly conduct in the Trajan Market, taking acid at the Vatican, how he nailed his cousin in the Coliseum, *etc.*

Personally, I could identify with that sort of egocentrism. My reaction to stuff was always more important than what's actually going on around me, but Gim was the opposite. He actually seemed interested in other people.

It made him stand out around here almost as much as his height.

A nice perk of being so huge was that Gim never needed to form all the defensive complexes that make the rest of us so edgy, uncomfortable and introverted. Nothing could hurt him, so he could be as open as he wanted. It's like being physically imposing gave Gim the ultimate *'Get Out Of Your Self-Imposed Jail Free'* card. The only thing that could lay the man low was himself, and that's probably why he used to be such a huge cokehead and drunk.

"Did you see that sunrise?" Gim asked. "We came out of our morning meeting, and I don't think anyone had ever seen such a shade of russet in the clouds!"

"That's the pollution," I said.

Nobody, and I mean *nobody*, sneaks into this place through the back door. Every employee here was a resident at one time or another ('cept for me, of course). Every one of my coworkers used to be an alcoholic or crackhead or junkie or just sniff way too much glue. They're all the walking wounded, but I guess that's what makes them interesting.

Even Reginald, the pud-whacker that I relieve on Thursday mornings and a couple different nights. *Christ,* I've heard the craziest stories about that guy stealing cars while cracked out of his skull. Heard about it taking four cops to beat him into submission. To look at the guy now, you'd never believe that he was capable of anything beyond stamp collecting and sniffing bicycle seats.

Or, I don't know, maybe he's full of shit.

New Start Rule #1: Never Trust a Junkie.

Done hugging and talking to me, my boss walked back to his office. Once he was out of sight I patted my back pocket. The wallet was still there.

8:13am
BALLAD OF A COMEBACK KID

The lobby's CD player skipped and stuttered over the latest Locust Ghost recording. There was enough time for the band to get a decent jam going, and then the disk would start tripping over itself again. I was cursing a sincere *"Goddamnit!"* when one of the clients came by to say hello. They lived on the second level of the building. It's a narrow hallway lined by dormitory rooms, all crammed full of clients. We pack them in four or five to a room.

The med room is up there, too. Filled with the legal drugs that the clients now used to get through the day in lieu of their preferred pharmaceuticals. The money made from this socially-approved form of chemical coping flowed into the righteous coffers of Big Pharm companies instead of the smaller pockets of local businessmen.

Across from the med room was our other narcotic dispenser, our ultimate in addict pacification technology: the TV lounge. Seventy-six channels and twenty-four hours of mindless distraction. The junkies spent hours basking in its benevolent rays, starring slack-jawed and vacant like all good Americans should. That's what we in the healthcare industry call Progress.

The Methodists used to house the bums up on the second floor. This was before the rehab moved in, and before they had two murders and one overdose during a single week.

I was hitting the CD player when, "Hey *nigga!*" was shouted at me from across the lobby.

"Hey *honky!*" I called back. Robert strolled toward my desk. He'd survived a five-year addiction to crack-cocaine, four marriages and six years in prison only to come down with throat cancer last Christmas.

If there is a God, I think He hates us.

"Whaddup, Ray!" Robert reached across the desk to give me a real *brutha*-style handshake. Our fingers made a snapping sound as we pulled our palms away. After a few months of working here, I'd become expert at twelve varieties of exotic handshaking. All I needed now was to join the Masons, and I'd have a full set.

Robert asked how I was doing, how was my Tuesday (or whatever day it was), same as he did every time he saw me working here. When he talks I can see the gap where his front teeth used to be. Just about all the crackheads have this. I used to think that part of crackheadedness was that you were too high to care about proper dental hygiene, but then someone told me that the smoke rots your teeth.

Sexy.

When Robert shifted his head the lights changed their refractive pattern on his skull. The chemo had left him an utter cue ball. This was actually something of an improvement for the guy. He used to have a wild, Jheri Curl-style *do* like Samuel Jackson's in *Pulp Fiction*. Looked cool on Samuel Jackson, but that's why he's a millionaire and Robert's dying in a halfway house.

"I tell you I goin' to the VA today?' Robert asked. He had, but I said nothing. "Doc gonna check me out; see how my cancer doin'."

Utterly Terminal was how his cancer had been doing, but Robert was one of those oddly irrepressible souls. Always smiling, or willing to fake it, at least. That's a rare trait in the world, and an even rarer one around here. Most of the people between these walls were Officially Crushed by Life and seemed to have grown to accept it. As far as attitudes go, that's a pretty contagious one.

Even so, Robert's glaring exception wasn't all that inspiring. Saintly cancer patients are hoary clichés, thanks to network television. So, besides thinking of Robert as anyone to learn a valuable lesson from, he just made me feel like my work was a crappy Made for TV movie. I'd seen the plot a million times before; Robert would die horribly, but, in those brief flashes of programming between all the car ads and beer commercials, the story would give us viewers a warm glow about the resiliency of the human spirit or some such crap.

If Robert weren't such a nice guy, I'd almost resent him for it.

"I know I be all right," Robert said. I slid low in my seat to adjust myself once, then again for the fun of it. "Had a dream 'bout my *momma* last night. She tell me I gonna be fine."

A few other clients came up to my desk to sign out from the building while Robert and I were yapping. We keep track of these guys' comings and goings like overprotective mothers. All clients use the sign-out sheet upon exiting or entering the building. They have to log the date, where they're going, what they're going to be doing there, expected time back and then the actual time when they return.

Pike, an alcoholic and compulsive philanderer from New Orleans, signed out first. James, a crackhead resembling a black version of Sloth from *The Goonies,* was next. Then Paul, a lanky, twitchy pill head with a drooling problem. Those broad strokes were all I knew about any of them, and all I cared to know. Statistics said they'd be gone and relapsed soon, so why bother with details?

Upon signing out, all three reached across the desk to slap palms with me. A mental note was made to wash my hands.

James asked, "Wassup, uhhh...*Einstein?*"

I answered, "Hey, uhhhh...*James.*"

Wiping the drool from his chin with the back of his hand, Paul said he'd see me when he got back from hauling freight to Louisiana. Yeah, our program lets some of the clients keep working their jobs while they're in here. No lengthy sabbaticals from the outside world required. I mean, God forbid that any programs of self-change affect too much of your life.

I dug around in my backpack and tossed Paul a handmade card. "Happy belated birthday, man."

He'd told me yesterday about turning 50, and so I'd spent five minutes making Paul a card celebrating how half a century had seen him manage not dying of an overdose. Someone pretending to give a shit about your existence is just one of the many perks offered by *A New Start*.

Paul looked embarrassingly grateful for this small gesture that had been nothing more than a product of my boredom, so I turned back to Robert. "Couldn't your mom have used the phone?" I asked. "Or does nothin' say lovin' like showing up in someone's dream?"

Occasionally my sarcasm gets the best of me, but the clients seemed so used to life shitting on them that a little more abuse didn't make a difference.

The smile expired on Robert's face. "My momma *dead*, Ray."

"Oh, *fuck*," I said. *Open mouth, insert foot.* "Sorry to hear that, man."

"That's okay," he said, leaning on the front edge of the desk. "I ever tell you 'bout my momma?"

"Don't think so." I made myself comfortable. My *faux paus* obliged me to listen to him ramble for a bit.

"My momma had a special power," Robert said (*What*, I thought, *bitch could fly?*). "She do that healin' thing, ya know? Heal people with 'er hands."

"Your mom was a *faith healer*?" This was a little more interesting than expected.

Robert could tell that he had my attention. "She always say that she didn't do it. She say that *God* do it through her. She just lay her hands on somebody and start praying and then they get better."

Interesting.

Curious for first-hand details, I asked, "She say what it was like?" As a psychology student, I'd gotten used to unscientific mumbo-jumbo. And hell, it wasn't like the 12-Step programs the clients used were built on a firm foundation of double-blind laboratory testing.

"She just always say that she start prayin', then step aside and God take over. That's all. She say she don't do nothin'. It all from God. She ain't even there while it happening." Then he nodded at me, like that was all the explanation needed to scientifically duplicate the experience.

Translating Robert's none-too-helpful description from *ignorant-old-lady-ese*, it sounded like his mom went into a sort of healing trance, using prayer as a trance-inducing mantra. Textbook case, basically.

"Think your mom could get rid of my jock-itch?" I asked.

Robert laughed. "I don't think I want my momma goin' anywhere near yo dreams or yo dick!"

"Let ya borrow my sisters for yours," I offered.

He cackled. "For my *what*?"

"Your call," I said. "But they're related to me, so *caveat emptor*, man!"

I laughed alone.

Robert tugged his ear. "*What*?"

8:27am
BEWARE THE RELIGIOUS:
THEIR GOD WILL FORGIVE THEM FOR ANYTHING

There was an uproar among the Methodists at the Homeless Assistance Ministry. Apparently, some miscreant had defaced property of theirs in a highly disrespectful manner. Actually, make that disrespectful *and* amusing.

The property in question was a large headshot photo of the current American president, eyes raised to heaven, looking properly pious. The Head Puppet-in-Chief was posed for the photo as if he had just concluded his bedtime prayers by asking Jesus—in his best Shirley Temple voice—to '...*bless all the little kittens and puppies and the bunny rabbits, too!*'

Taped next to the photo on the chapel door was a written statement circulated by the Methodist hierarchy. It reminded all their minions of the great necessity to pray for our Good and Christian leader in *his* time of need. The prez, at the time the picture was posted, was busy trying to rally support for the slaughter of yet more dark-skinned folks halfway around the world.

(In the fucker's defense, there's plenty of precedent for that sort of thing.)

Apparently someone, tired of seeing that glaring example of religious hypocrisy every time they came to work, had added something to the photo late one night. It was a word balloon, like the kind you see in comics, pointing to the president and bearing the words, ' Thou Shalt Not What?"

The seriously religious are even less tolerant than your average moron when it comes to having the contradictions in their belief system pointed out. So the Christers were pretty pissed when the affront was discovered the next morning. Threats were issued every which way. Heads were promised to roll, and it would have surprised no one had they started crucifying people at random until somebody broke down and confessed.

Since I had been on duty the night it happened, I was called in and confronted.

Chatting with the Head Christer seemed unavoidable. I steeled myself for the meeting. "If you don't hear back from me," I told my girlfriend over the phone, "I want to know that I've loved you more than anyone else I've ever just used for sex."

Christ in the Gutter had their offices in a separate hallway from the one *A New Start* used. More towards the back of the building. I usually tried to avoid that hallway since the sewage smell got stronger around there. Reminded me of Ezra Pound's great line: *"shit and religion always stinking in concord."*

I was stopped on the way back there by a client. The guy's tall, blonde, handsome and looks so out of place here. JDZ pointed at me and laughed. "I heard you're in trouble with the Methodists," he said.

"Apparently, someone killed their god," I said. "And you know I get blamed for everything around here…"

JDZ pulled a switchblade out of his back pocket, flicking it open with a smile. I took an involuntary step back. Bad memories. "Want me to knife that fuckin' cunt for you?"

13

He might have resembled the average junior executive, but JDZ was just a thieving, scheming, and probably dangerous junkie like the rest of the clients. The guy was nice to me, though, and that's all I really cared about.

"I'll shove this right up her and twist." He held the blade out for my inspection. "You like it? I got it off some crackhead for real cheap."

JDZ was his own social blight, no doubt, but it's best to keep all of your options open. "I'll let ya know how it goes," I told him. "And don't go waving that thing around in here."

In her cross-covered office was Selma, the whale of a minister in charge of *Christ in the Gutter*. The majority of the people working at *C.i.t.G.* were homeless volunteers. They did all the dirty work. The people who actually got paid were mouthy white folk in charge of not too much else besides ordering the volunteers around. Sounded like a pretty cushy gig.

Considering that she didn't employ me, since we only worked in the same building and were at best neighbors, I wondered if the Good Reverend really had the power to call me on the carpet. Bitch wasn't my boss, after all, and there's only so much I would take from *him*. Did she let Gim know that she would be interrogating me?

Maybe. Since the Christers owned the building (and *A New Start* was just renting space), Gim had probably given her *carte blanche* to do whatever she felt. Us bottom-rung Techs were easily thrown to the lions.

I popped my head around the corner into her office. "Hey! How's it hangin'?"

Selma was wearing a purple sweat suit with the customary minister's collar somehow attached. Sitting behind her desk and overflowing the sides of her chair, she had her scowl in its usual place. Curly gray hair framed her angry face. I wondered how long it had been since the last time she had smiled. During church, perhaps? Or maybe then she just turned her frown in the direction of the nearest cross.

She glared at me and I did my best not to glance back at her for too long. Selma looked like the result of a liposuction gone horribly wrong, like during the operation someone had kicked the machine in reverse. She was puffiness stretched to the limit. So, I stared instead at the crosses that covered her office like a dead forest.

Pretty fucking morbid to plaster your workspace in ancient torture devices. It'd be like decorating a nursery with guillotine wallpaper. Still, they were easier on the eyes than Selma.

I wasn't avoiding the sight of her just for aesthetic reasons. Whenever my gaze flickered in Selma's direction, I got a horrible mental image of her wearing nothing but her minister's collar while working the Tijuana donkey show. Christ knows where that thought came from, but it made me feel bad for the donkey.

She pointed at the chair in front of her desk, but I chose to stand. Thankfully, Selma was pretty quick to get to the point with me. Did my heathen ass have something to do with the desecration, she wanted to know.

Did I?

DID I?

"Course not," I lied. "But, ya gotta admit; it *does* make a pretty good point."

9:20am
OMNISCIENT, OMNIPOTENT, OMNIBENEVOLENT

A shriek cut through the general murmur of the lobby.

"My stepfather's outside!" Mary screamed. She tore through the lobby, pig-tails flapping in the air. "Call the police!" Her face was tattooed with the boundless fear of a child. "My stepfather's outside!" She pushed her way through the hordes of homeless waiting for handouts.

"Call the police! He's gonna get me!"

It's hypothesized that Dissociate Identity Disorder can be caused by extreme childhood sexual abuse. Mary was such an obvious D.I.D. case that whoever did the abusing in her long-ago childhood must've stuck it to her good and hard.

"My stepfather's outside! He's gonna get me! *Please!* He's gonna get me!"

Dressed in pink overalls like a four-year-old (but actually closer in age to forty), Mary and her hysteria were starting to excite the herd. Waves of agitation swept the room. Feet shuffled faster. Tongues ran over chapped lips in quicker and quicker repetition. Nervous twitches multiplied, and a few additional shrieks answered Mary's like the response to a particularly unhinged mating call. A worker for *Christ in the Gutter* led Mary into a back room before she started a stampede of homeless hysteria.

"*My stepfather's right out-*" Mary was cut off mid-shriek by the slamming of a door. The entire lobby was still turned in her direction. I held the phone loosely to my ear. On the other end my girlfriend asked what the screaming was all about. The momentary excitement Mary provided had dragged us all from our own problems, and we returned to them grudgingly.

Mary was a common fixture at *Christ in the Gutter*. She even volunteered sometimes. That got her preferential treatment of a sort. Like being taken into the women's bathroom to be calmed down instead of getting tossed out onto the street.

I had watched Mary's freak-out from behind the front desk. Just another nutcase in a job full of them, as far as I was concerned—or, as Mother Teresa had phrased it, *Christ in His most wretched of guises.* Hanging around the needy and pathetic had been a divinely mandated hobby for ol' Teresa. To us less-charitable types it was an unfortunate part of an otherwise easy job.

"Yeah, the crazy-o-meter just hit 11," I said into the phone. "I'll call ya back later."

I lit another scented candle—the homeless fucking reek—and stepped out from behind the desk for a look. Figured I'd catch a glimpse of Mary's demonic stepfather.

Hiding behind my protective shield of potpourri and scented candles was bad enough; venturing out into the mass of vagrants was like swimming

15

through a garbage dump. Your average middle-class citizen, living in their per-fumed world of colognes and deodorants *cannot* imagine the noxious fumes the human body is capable of producing. Scents that ooze their way into your de-fenseless nostrils, cling to your sinuses and repeatedly rape your basal ganglia. The human wrecks surrounding me radiated vile bouquets containing weeks of sweat, piss, vomit and recycled booze.

And if that wasn't your dollar's worth of gagging, there was also the build-ing's pervasive scent of sewage mixed with rotten eggs. It's a real classy joint they run here. After months of exposure you'd think the nose would develop some kind of immunity, but each day was still an extended exercise in the sup-pression of the gag reflex.

I picked my way through the living sea of the desolate that clogged the lobby. Stepped over trash bags full of aluminum cans that never left their owner's grasp. Dodged dirty children that ran underfoot while their mothers sat slumped, unconscious and drooling against the walls. Elbowed my way through drunks too slow to move aside. Strode past the young mulatto girl with a swollen belly and frightened eyes.

Every Monday through Friday, from nine till four, *Christ in the Gutter* opened its doors to the homeless, the crazy, and the dispossessed of downtown Pasadena. *C.i.t.G.* wasn't a homeless shelter, merely what they called an Assis-tance Ministry. This meant that handouts were plentiful, nothing besides tax write-offs were asked in return and the homeless came in droves.

Wouldn't you?

I told myself, as I shouldered through the crowd, that I only had to put up with them and their stench and crazed ramblings for a few hours a day. After that I had nothing to do but sit on my ass, feet propped on the desk, and collect an hourly wage for the simple act of existing. Just a few short hours. Chill with the *'homelies'* for a bit before my company was upgraded to nothing but junk-ies, alcoholics and crackheads.

I finally made it out the door and peered down the street in one direction, then another, scanning for Mary's step-bogeyman.

The street, of course, was deserted.

9:54am
LEVENDIS

"1. We admitted we were powerless over alcohol—that our lives had become unmanageable."

I was browsing through *The Big Book*, which serves as the AA bible. They call it *The Big Book* to distinguish the thing from *The Good Book*, a.k.a. the Christian bible. That they took such care not to impugn the Bible's space kind of put the lie to the AA line about not being a Christian organization. Not to mention how most of the meetings ended with the Lord's Prayer.

16

I'd occasionally call my girlfriend and read her some of the more amusing case studies from the book. She didn't find them as funny as I did. Guess you had to be there. Or here.

"3. Made a decision to turn our will and our lives over to the care of God as we understood Him."

Nicely submissive stuff. Good and weak. Exactly what I'd expect from an organization started by a couple Protestant drunks. Of course, in official AA terminology, the term *'God'* is replaced by the more ambiguous phrase, *'Higher Power.'* It keeps the organization open to people with more brain cells than the terminally religious. Guess it's also a concession to 21st century social reality. These days, it's best to keep nice and vague about delusional terminology: once you're off the drugs you no longer have an excuse for thinking that invisible monsters watch your every move.

(Unless you live in America, where a vast majority of the population believes they have an all-powerful imaginary friend. Every time they cut federal funding to schools I'm reminded of that.)

I flipped though a few more pages, tried to read, got bored. My original plan had been to finish all of *The Big Book*. I figured that it'd help out on the job; give me some insight into the stumbling wrecks around me. Besides, there's not much else to do around here on the weekend. It'd be more entertaining than just sitting and scratching myself for the entire shift (left nut for the first four hours, then start with the right). The reading was turning out to be a lot more difficult than I figured. The Big Book was about as thrilling as sitting through church, was full of embarrassing stereotypes and probably about as helpful as suntan lotion in a burn ward.

If I couldn't get through the damn thing, how'd they expect a bunch of semi-literate crackheads to manage?

"Hey, Ray!" Robert limped into the lobby, a huge smile on his face.

Leaning forward in my seat so he didn't have to reach too far, we slapped palms. "Thought I could smell the evil coming down the hallway," I said.

"Naw," said Robert, "That's just the cancer." We both threw our heads back and howled with laughter. Robert laughed because that's how he was dealing with his impending death, me because I hadn't a clue how else to react to something so morbid.

Robert pointed at the blue hardback in my hands. "You reading the Big Book?" he asked. "You ain't an addict like the rest of us, is ya?"

I shook my head, stifling a yawn. The girl from *Christ in the Gutter* had been over way too late the previous night. It'd been pretty tough getting rid of her. Guess I should've known that someone with nowhere else to sleep would be reluctant to take a hint and leave.

"Just too lazy to have a real job." I said. "Thought it couldn't hurt to get familiar with the thing."

It was tossed onto the desk. "Boring as fuck, though."

Robert nodded. "Never could get more than a chapter or two in," he said. "Guess I should keep trying."

I hadn't worked at the rehab long, but the Big Book already struck me as extraneous to one's sobriety. Either you were going to do it, or you weren't. If books really made that much difference in peoples' lives, everyone who owned a Bible would be canonized.

"If you wanna," I shrugged.

Robert walked over to the sign-out sheet. "I gonna go hit me a meetin'," he said, "But I wanted to let ya know that I goin' in for more chemo tomorrow, so I ain't gonna be here."

I wasn't going to be here the next day either, and Robert knew my schedule. There was also a listing of his chemo treatments in Gim's office, so the reminder was doubly unnecessary. But if Robert wanted to share about his life, who was I to stop him?

"Good luck with it, man."

"Thanks, Ray," he said. "They got some real pretty nurses there, so I gonna be fine."

We both laughed. "Bring me back one," I requested.

"I get you a skinny one," Robert said. "You white boys like that."

"Not *too* skinny," I told him. "It's a real fine line. You like 'em larger?"

Standard guy talk.

Robert made a face like a chef sampling the perfect soufflé. "You know it! They *gotta* have somethin' in the back!" He cupped his hands around his butt and did a weird little *bump 'n' grind* dance. It was like I had just stumbled into an oncological burlesque club. "Somethin' in the back!" I wondered if having chemo-bald men shaking their butts at me would be a standard on-the-job occurrence.

"*Somethin', somethin', somethin' in the back!*" he sang and danced. "*Somethin', somethin', somethin' in the back!*"

Laughing like he was going to hemorrhage, Robert strutted to the front door and swung it open. "Don't forget to pray for me!"

Now *there* was something to request from the local atheist. "Sacrifice some kittens?" I offered.

Robert laughed. "Couple squirrels, too!"

"You *wish* you deserved squirrels," I said. "Now get outta here, you weird bastard!"

Still laughing, Robert shook the booty one last time and leapt through the open door.

10:01am
LIVING WITH SICK PEOPLE
MAKES ME FEEL SO STRONG

In a lobby crowded with homelies, two bums fought over an old flannel jacket. Their struggle danced from one side of the room to the other. Grunting and cursing, one hand fought for a better hold on the jacket, and the other struggled for a tighter grip on their opponent's throat.

The entire lobby watched, enraptured. Now *this* was entertainment. I watched, the homelies watched, and the black guy writing his name in *A New Start*'s sign-out sheet stopped to watch the spectacle. Two people had their hands on each other's throats over a faded piece of cloth, and the rest of us couldn't have been more entertained.

The bums would careen into a chair-lined wall, and the chairs' occupants would shout and push them away, leading the opponents to stumble into another group of on-lookers. The *New Start* client wedged himself into the corner where the desk met the wall, his hands out protectively.

"Left hook!" I shouted encouragement to no one in particular. The clothing given away by the Christers didn't strike me as anything worth paying for, let alone hurting another human being over, but the homelies were welcome to their own value system. When staying warm each night was a struggle, one's appraisal of the relative worth of clothing probably underwent drastic changes. Hell, under the right circumstances, it'd probably make sense to kill for a hoodie.

The bums kept shouting a '*muthafucka*' this and '*gah-damn*' that as they tore at the flannel between them. "I fuckin' kill you!" one screamed before a left hook caught him upside the head.

He staggered, but never let go of the flannel. "Now go for the right!" I shouted. Instead of manifesting as a follow-up, this advice was taken by the bum who'd just been struck. He let go of his opponent's throat long enough to switch hands on the flannel, then lashed out with a right hook. Spit and blood flew from the other bum's mouth.

"*Oooh*!" said the crowd.

I was apparently coaching both sides of the fight and doing a decent job of it. "Now kick!" I shrieked. "*Kick!*"

Both bums tried this move at the same time. One kick went wild, the other landed firmly in the nearest crotch. The recipient of the crotch-busting doubled over, still gripping the flannel. He gasped twice, each louder than the other, then let out a long groan. This was followed by an even louder moan that seemed to drag on forever as he waited for his balls to drop back into place.

I waited for another kick to land, a punch at the very least. This would seem to be the ideal time for some additional violence, now that one party was unable to resist, but none was forthcoming. The winner was just as intrigued to see what further course the reaction would take.

Would the bum start to cry? Would he vomit blood? Would he scream '*Eloi, Eloi, lema sabachthani!*' and breathe his last?

Then, as if to spite us, the loser just fell over backwards, his grip on the flannel finally loosening. He lay on the floor, on his back, unwilling to move.

It was pretty anticlimactic. I could swear I heard a disappointed sigh escape the audience. TV and movies had accustomed us to things ending with a bang. Violence that didn't conclude in explosions always fell short of expectation.

It was then we all noticed dark stain spreading from his crotch. It started small, then quickly consumed the front of this pants. As if to make up for the low level of violence we'd just tolerated, nature rewarded us with some degradation as the bum submissively pissed his own pants.

There was a collective "*Ewww!*" from the crowd, despite how many of them reeked of their own fluids. It's funny how our tolerance levels tend to stop with our own squalor.

I watched the winner of the bum brawl take a running start to deliver a game-winning kick into his opponent's side. This elicited another "*Ooh!*" from the crowd and still more urine into the loser's pants. Then, clutching the torn flannel, the victor rushed out the door.

"Man, I been there," said the *New Start* client standing in front of the desk. He shook his head. "Been there and worse."

I looked at the client. Glanced over his gut and bald spot. Imagined him piss-stained on the dirty carpet of some crackhouse. Wondered if he'd looked as pathetic as the bum on the lobby floor.

"Not me," I said. "But I'm still young. Give me time."

10:39am
JUNKIE DRAMA

When I arrived at work Saturday morning one of the clients was missing. JDZ had relapsed. He'd disappeared, robbed his family and friends and had taken to the needle with a vengeance.

Junkie-relapse S.O.P. Nothing too original.

Other clients were informing me of this when JDZ walked in. He looked like shit. He smelled like shit. He had the same scruffy five o'clock shadow that all the guys here seem to acquire when they relapse. It was like their drug of choice stimulated hair growth. His pale face and long, scabby fingers looked greasy, as if he'd wiped them on the bottom of a bucket of fried chicken.

"Speak of the devil," said one of the clients (I've stopped expecting anything clever from these guys).

JDZ had come for his clothes, which were stuffed upstairs in the med room along with the personal items of other junkies who'd relapsed or simply left with nowhere else to put it all. We usually kept their crap for a month before donating it to the Methodists.

Walking up the stairs with him, making friendly small talk (*how's life on the needle treatin' you, price of the stuff fluctuate much since the last time you did it?, etc.*) I couldn't get over his stench. "*Good Christ*, you fuckin' reek!"

"Really?" he asked, like the possibility had never occurred to him.

I assured JDZ of his smell, comparing it unfavorably with that of the combined homeless odors that filled the lobby on crowded days. He shrugged it off. Who cares about body odor when you got an armful, right? It took a little prodding (I made it a condition of him getting his stuff), but eventually he came to see bathing as his civic duty.

JDZ took about twenty minutes to gather his things and shower. I was never more than ten feet away the entire time. Not like I suddenly felt the need for proximity to someone who had an even harder time being human than myself. Nor was I hoping for a glimpse of him toweling off. It just would have been a *bad* idea to leave JDZ alone upstairs with everybody else's stuff. Like that famous line from *Sid & Nancy* (and *New Start Rule #1*): Never Trust a Junkie.

Especially one who'd spent the past week ripping off everyone he knew.

Walking back downstairs, JDZ enlightened me on the panhandling technique that—along with petty theft—was earning his daily smack. Apparently, aggressiveness and dogged persistence play a big role in successful begging. Looking vaguely threatening doesn't hurt, either, and I bet the knife I'd seen him with played the occasional part.

This went against all the ideas I'd ever had about using a submissive air when you're trying to convince people to give money they'd worked for to some skuzzy stranger...but JDZ had practical experience to my mere theorizing.

I couldn't explain why I had always liked JDZ, besides how he was such an unrepentant degenerate. The guy seemed to recognize that his purpose in life was to make the world an uglier place, and he was cool with that. If people crossed to the other side of the street when they saw him coming, if he blew every job he ever had, if all he knew how to do was steal and get fucked up, if he couldn't stay sober for more than a month at a time, if he always destroyed his life and the lives of those around him, then So Be It. That seemed to be his attitude. Hard not to admire such a perverse sense of self-acceptance.

When we got back to the lobby his old girlfriend was waiting outside the front door for him. You'd think she'd have learned her lesson about JDZ by now, but who was I to argue with somebody else's co-dependence? This was the same lady whose credit cards he'd ran off with last week, and similar acts had been performed at least twice before. She was apparently the forgiving type (and absolutely perfect for that special someone on your Xmas list who wants not a companion, but a talking doormat they can hump). I waved *adios* and closed the door behind them, leaving the two lovebirds alone on the front steps.

I figured, now that JDZ had stopped wearing his alluring *Scent of a Junkie* All-Natural Cologne, that their dysfunctional asses would go reenact their American version of *Trainspotting* somewhere else.

Admittedly, it wasn't like they were affecting the property value by being in front of the building. Now that JDZ had showered and changed clothes, the pair of them could have been mistaken for any other urbanite couple in their early thirties.

Still, I wanted them gone. Illusions that profound never last long, and I wanted JDZ and his woman to get lost before the mirage faded.

Yeah, them leaving and taking their sickness with them would have been nice, but first they felt a need to indulge in that pastime shared by couples everywhere: fighting.

I had gone back to my desk to call my girlfriend. I'd figured on telling her JDZ's story as a reminder that she could do a hell of a lot worse than me. Then the plan was aborted like a prom-night pregnancy when I heard angry voices coming in from outside. It was JDZ and his woman. Her hysterical shrieking and the bass of JDZ's counter-screams made a charming fugue of our basic inability to all get along.

Jesus, I thought. *Time to go play the authority figure.*

I went outside to tell them to take their bullshit elsewhere. Not only because it looks jank to have people scream at each other in front of your establishment (even in a part of town with a large bum population), but because I hated listening to couples fight. It made me feel like a little kid again, watching my parents trying to draw blood in front of me and my siblings. I couldn't force my folks to stop it at the time, but I could sure as hell get rid of the human wastes shouting in front of my workplace.

"*Hey!*" I shoved the door open between them. "Go play '*Springer*' somewhere else!"

Having been told to fuck off and do it promptly, JDZ started leaving. But, his girlfriend stood where she was, faced me (she had been pretty at one time, possibly still was from a distance, but life—or life with JDZ—had worn her down around the eyes) and stated that she needed to speak with one of the other junkies.

"I need to talk with Jamie," she said.

The name didn't ring a bell (like I'd waste time memorizing over fifty constantly changing names). I was about to say so when a greasy white kid pushed up from behind me. He looked to be late teens, early twenties; heavily tattooed and with a posture like he was constantly cringing. The kid was taken by the girlfriend around to the side of the building. JDZ followed behind them, shouting.

"Hope they don't kill each other on my shift," I said to the other clients watching the drama with me. "Fuck knows there'd be lots of paperwork to fill out."

We all laughed at this, and made a few more jokes at the expense of whatever the hell was going on outside. I thought about what a great anecdote this would make to tell my girlfriend.

The door shook. *BANG!BANG!BANG!BANG!BANG!*

I jumped at the noise. It was a quick, frantic pounding on the glass, mixed with a desperate ringing of the bell. It felt frightened, as if ignoring the banging and ringing ensured that blood would start seeping in under the door.

I turned around. There was the kid. Jamie's head swiveled back and forth, looking through the door, then back at the far side of the building. His eyes pleaded for entrance.

I contemplated leaving him there, just to see what would happen if his fears—whatever had him so shaken—were allowed to come true.

The small part of me that still feels compassion won out, and I opened the door. Jamie scurried in like a Ritalin baby chased by an alcoholic father.

"He tried to hit me!" the kid said, chest fluttering with adrenaline rapidity.

"*Shit!*" we cheered, our combined maleness excited at the prospect of a fight.

Jamie was shaking like a freezing epileptic. "He tried to hit me, but decked his girlfriend instead!"

There was a pause while we decided how exactly to respond to this news. Actions require more contemplation than usual if they fall outside our usual *stimulus-response* repertoire.

We all decided on explosive laughter.

But once we got the rest of the story out of the greasy little chap, it turned out to be no laughing matter.

(Well, nothing to laugh about in front of the people it affected, at least.)

JDZ and Jamie had known each other for a while. They used to shoot up together, share needles and all sorts of other healthy behaviors. This would be uncool enough on its own, even without the kid having recently discovered that he's got…Hepatitis C (*dum Dum DUM!*).

Apparently, JDZ didn't want his girlfriend to find this out. As all of us disease-literate types know, not only is Hepatitis C terminal, it's also communicable in all the same ways as AIDS. That includes blood transfusions, sharing needles and sex. So many different ways to transfer it, so many different ways to pass on the love.

Ripped off by a loved one, fed a right hook, infected with a terminal disease…goddamn if somebody's girlfriend didn't just have the worst week imaginable.

It's tough, but junkie dramas rarely comes with happy endings.

10:58am
ALWAYS MORE BOTTOM TO BE SCRAPED IN YOUR BARREL

Sitting on my desk, Cassandra handed me a post-it note with the number to the assisted-living apartment she shared with her dad. Her old man was also on federal assistance. Counting the baby on her chest covered by a nursing blanket, that made three generations suckling on the welfare teat.

The thought of that may outrage some hard-working folks in the heartland. But, if the government just *had* to steal my money, I'd prefer the taxes go to help people rather than hurt them. The way the politicians and press had been howling for foreign blood these past few months, I knew that it wouldn't be long before we were all paying to kill dark-skinned babies instead of feeding the little bastards.

"Give me a call," she said over the rumble and shrieks of the homeless. The downstairs of the facility was filled with just about every variety of hard-luck story imaginable. It was like a discount emporium of human suffering. In my imagination, I caused all of their heads to explode.

"Any time before nine is okay."

It's so easy to hate the helpless. The loathing's in our blood. There's a million years of social biology behind the repugnance you feel when you pass a bum on the street. It's instinctual to abhor the weak and the failed. Primates and other mammals loathe vulnerability to the point of attacking any group member that becomes disabled, that can't take care of itself. Birds do it, too. Why would people be any different?

It's so easy, so natural to hate the helpless. Any excuse will do, and it's not like they're capable of stopping you.

"Okay?"

Temporary vulnerability is one thing. We'll all help somebody change a flat tire or walk a little old lady across the street. But when you're permanently and consistently unable to care for yourself, most people just want you to stop being such a burden and crawl off somewhere to die. Some folks can admit to these feelings. Some can't.

Don't think I always felt this way. Did I? It was tough to recall when my thinking changed on the subject of charity. Probably sometime after I started working here.

"Okay," I said to Cassandra, having no intention of doing what I just agreed to. Sure, she might have been a volunteer rather than a recipient of *C.i.t.G.* charity. Sure, she might've been looking rather nice in her tight blue jeans and the tan shirt that matched her skin tone. But, it wasn't too long ago that Cassandra had been big and pregnant and sitting in the lobby with the rest of the homelies.

Making a Homeless Assistance Ministry into my own sexual hunting ground was something that I'd have to be a fuck of a lot more desperate to even consider. Maybe if I broke up with my girlfriend, or found myself on the other side of the desk, or if I just got bored, or *whatever*.

But, even then, I couldn't imagine hooking up with a welfare mother. From a mile off, my paranoid ass can smell a plot to make me the surrogate daddy to someone's ugly little baby.

"This where I sign in?" interrupted a bum, about to write his name down on the *New Start*'s sign-out sheet. The bum, in the increasingly filthy jogging suit he wore every day, never failed to ask this question.

"On the pink paper." I pointed to the glaringly obvious sheet of hot pink paper on the adjacent side of the desk. "Write your name down there and they'll call it eventually. *Then* you can go get your free shit."

"Right here?" he asked, starting to write in the same place.

"Pink paper!" I repeated, pointing with more emphasis.

"You got change?" He kept scribbling in the same spot.

I slapped my palm on the correct sign-in sheet. "*Here!*"

"*Oh...*" the bum shuffled on over. Just like he had the day before and the day before that.

"*Oooh...*" Cassandra carefully slid down from where she had been sitting on top of my desk. Suckling sounds drifted from under her nursing blanket. "You gettin' a little upset? I thought you were more laid-back than that."

She gave me a smile that I guess was supposed to be flirtatious. Seeing her in full-on maternal mode didn't quite do it for me, though. Cassandra was an ex-stripper, hiding down in Pasadena from her abusive baby-daddy. She was

24

on welfare thanks to having quit dancing out of fear that she'd be killed if the guy ever found her.

Love's a pretty fucked up thing, isn't it? I can't ever imagine hitting my own girlfriend, but maybe that just shows my lack of commitment.

I returned Cassandra's smile with a faked one of my own. She beamed at this, showing that she was just as starved for attention as the rest of us. "Just feelin' a little thirsty," I said, nodding towards her mammary glands. "You weren't planning on letting that other one go to waste, were ya?"

Cassandra ducked behind her hair and smiled. If her skin was lighter she might've blushed.

(Yeah, I flirt back. It passes the time.)

"You racist!" someone yelled. I turned to look into what had once been a woman's face. Now it was distorted, angry and unnaturally sallow to the point of caricature. Her lips were ruined with herpetic sores and heat blisters.

(I swear; the first crackhead to invent a pipe with an insulated mouthpiece would make a fortune. Of course, you know they'd just blow that fortune on more crack.)

"Racist!" The woman's look of triumphant outrage said that she'd just found an outlet for some of the shit life had been dumping on her. "I wanna file a complaint. You a goddamn racist!" While the woman shouted variations on that theme, all four of her kids were scampering around the lobby. They fought and screamed and got underfoot while Mommy busied herself with more important matters. The entire scene was a living advertisement for those involuntary sterilizations the government used to conduct.

I sighed. *God*, I was tired. Too tired for anyone's persecution complex. I was on the third leg of a 24-hour shift. There was probably some kind of labor law against making workers do such things, but it's not like that shit ever gets enforced. Companies do what they like in America, and the rest of us can play along or starve.

"Racist honky motherfucker!" Calling me several kinds of bigot was something of a hobby with the homeless. Just something to say when they were pissed off in my general direction. Even the white ones did it. Accusing me of racial bias apparently passed the time better than reading the donated magazines they had lying around here. *And* it wouldn't rot the brain like TV does.

I was tempted to ask the woman: '*Don't you see me flirting with this mulatto girl? Isn't it proof of what an open-minded chap I am if I'm almost considering shagging someone who's halfway like you?*'

Hated to give Cassandra false hope, though.

"They don't pay me enough to discriminate," I assured the woman. I wondered what had set her off. We hadn't exchanged a single word before her accusation. Maybe I had a bigoted aura. "You can be sure you're getting the same crappy treatment as everyone else."

She started yelling again as Toni showed back up. I had been covering at the front desk for the guy while he grabbed a smoke in the back lot. Toni was a swishy little ex-crackhead (of the Caucasian variety) who worked for *Christ in the Gutter*.

I told him, "Customer for you," and Toni got busy ignoring the woman's complaints.

It was actually *his* job to sit at the front desk and deal with the transients. I was just there to hang out and make sure that the junkies didn't need anything. They usually didn't. Not during the 8-4 shift on weekdays. Or, if they did need something, they usually couldn't be bothered to come downstairs to ask me for it.

As long as I hung out in the lobby, I was safe from responsibility. Probably had something to do with all the homeless down here. The junkies were scared of them. They tended to see the homelies as Ghosts of Xmas Future, *This Could Be You!* warning signs.

Personally, I was beginning to see them as proof that maybe euthanasia shouldn't be limited to the elderly. But, that's just the kind-hearted sort of fucker that I'm finding myself to be these days.

11:23am
TECH TAX

"Ya can't have fuckin' nothin' in this fuckin' place without some fuckin' addict stealing it!"

Curtis was on a little bender of outrage. The fists at the end of his skinny white arms were waving like antennae towards the heavens, and his hair stood straight up from either indignation or static electricity.

I didn't really care about whatever of his got lifted. Jesus was boning Mary Magdalene in the book I was reading, and that was a hell of a lot more arousing than anything Curtis had to say. Toni wasn't busy with anything, but he ignored Curtis, too.

Curtis repeated his gripe a few more times, talking into the air and indirectly at me. A few of the homelies stared at him, then they too lost interest. Curtis was obviously just waiting to hear the magic question, so after making him wait a few more seconds, I asked.

"My fuckin' dinner's gone!" With a faded iron-cross tattooed on his arm, he was now the white-trash version of Job. "*Ah* ate at *Pappadeaux's* last night, took most of it back here and stuck it in the fridge, put my *gah*-damn name on it, and this mornin' it was gone!"

Oh. I went back to my book. "Life is indeed suffering," I said, after searching for an appropriate phrase of commiseration. "If ya wanna make sure no one's gonna munch your stuff, just ask me and I'll stick it in the back freezer, the one with locks on it."

"Can I put my lunch in there?" Toni asked.

"Sorry," I told him. "Can't risk your Christian food infecting the rest of the grub, turning the sandwich bread into dead carpenter or whatever. For all I know, you people said grace over the stuff."

Toni folded his arms in a dramatized pout. "*Bitch.*"

I had considered the matter with Curtis closed, but he apparently didn't. "And I had twenty bucks that disappeared outta my wallet! *Motherfuckers*! No one respects anything 'round here!"

My interest in Curtis and his grievance had expired about two seconds after it'd started. Still, I managed to mumble, "What'd you expect from a bunch of addicts?"

"Not too much," he said. And that's our species for you; we're all covered in shit and complaining about everyone else's smell. "*Ah* wonder who the hell took it? One of them niggers, *Ah* bet!"

Apparently it takes one piss-poor example of a race to know another. "*Watch* that word," I told him, while Toni said "*Oooh!*"

Curtis was lucky that no one else seemed to have heard him. A bunch of ignorant white and black guys (not sure where all the Hispanics are) living in relative peace under the same roof in the Deep South was one of the few real miracles about this place. It'd be a pity for the delicate balance maintained here to be toppled by something as stupid as an angry hick saying the wrong word.

"*Ah'm* not racist," Curtis protested, like they always do, "But *Ah* bet that—"

"Zip it, *honky*."

Conversation over.

Curtis did have a legitimate complaint, even if I hadn't felt like listening to him voice it. Stuff here does do a good job of walking off on its own. The theft rate's high enough that, if I was unlucky enough to ever live in this shit hole (*please god no*), everything I owned would be under lock and key. Christ knows I don't leave any of my own stuff just lying out on the desk. Not unless I'm sitting behind it.

Still, it's probably asking a bit much to live in a building full of people who used to steal from everyone they knew, and not expect a few of them to slip back into their old ways. That theft was only *common* and not *epidemic*— considering the client population—was yet another of this place's mundane miracles.

I guess that's just the optimist in me talking. Work here long enough and the sunshine can't help but pour out of your ass.

But, all that was beside the point. Not a clue about his money, but I knew exactly who had stolen Curtis' dinner. I knew who had snuck into the fridge in the middle of the night and microwaved then munched his shrimp etouffee, hush puppies, and 'slaw, but I'd be goddamned if I was gonna turn them in.

I'm no snitch. And besides, those all-night shifts make a man hungry.

11:35am
SETTLING FOR HALF THE TEA IN CHINA

The woman was hunched over like a gorilla, ratty orange hair in her face. "I'm tired of you assholes stealing my money!" she screamed at me and Toni.

The rest of the lobby watched intently. Sometimes I suspected that the homeless took turns flipping out to keep each other entertained.

"*Yeah*," I said to Toni from my usual seat on the filing cabinets. "Give her back the money, you fuckin' thief!"

"Give me back my money!" the woman echoed. Every time she opened her mouth to screech I could see the blackened ruins of her teeth.

"Shut up," Toni warned me. "Don't encourage her."

This was the third time the woman had flipped out about her money this month. No one had stolen it. She was just nuts. The aggressive sort of crazy that likes to share its fucked-upness with the rest of the world. Whatever had set her off in our general direction was a mystery to everyone but her. Toni spoke in a gentle tone, "Dearie, you're going to have to calm down or leave."

The woman had a better idea. "I oughtta kick the shit outta both you faggot asslicks!"

"*Faggot*?" I played shocked to Toni. "Have you been telling everyone about our Friday nights?"

"Ray, shut up!" He spoke more firmly to the woman. "You're going to have to leave now, before I call the cops."

"Fuck you!" she screamed, making the only possible response to a world that had given her a damaged brain and bad temper. "I want my fuckin' money! I'm not retarded!"

"Nope," I agreed. "You're just crazy." Work brought out my compassionate side. Earlier in the shift I had to chase several of the homelies out of *New Start*'s kitchen, where they had been trying to eat the clients' lunches. They screamed and fussed, called me a racist, and I was left there to reflect on how I earned eight bucks an hour denying food to starving people.

It's pretty apparent why some professions don't attract groupies.

"Faggot asslicks!" the woman screamed.

"How do I keep getting lumped in with you people?" I asked Toni. "It's 'cause I'm such a snappy dresser, isn't it?" Old t-shirts with shorts and sandals were due to come back into fashion any day now. I could feel it.

"We're calling the cops," Toni informed the woman when she showed no sign of ceasing her newfound hobby of calling us *faggot asslicks*. I couldn't blame her. Not only was she a few carbs short of a water pipe, but *faggot asslicks* was actually pretty fun to say.

"*Faggot asslicks*," I repeated to myself and chuckled.

Toni picked up the phone, and the woman shouted, "You go ahead and call the cops!" She rushed to the desk, grabbed the phone base unit, and heaved it at us. Toni shrieked and jumped back. I had no time to duck. The phone flew straight at me. My eyes closed.

It stopped a foot short, jerked back by its cord.

"That does it!" Toni shouted. "Get the hell out now!"

The woman screamed, "*Faggot asslicks*!" one last time before running out the door. I gave her a cheerful wave goodbye.

"Ray?" Tony put a piece of the phone back on the desk and continued fishing for the rest of the broken bits. They were scattered all over the floor. "Ray? You mind giving me a hand with this?"

"Do it yourself," I said, then had to add, "*Faggot asslick*."

28

11:55pm

...MONKEY IS THE GATE. MONKEY IS THE KEY AND GUARDIAN OF THE GATE. PAST, PRESENT AND FUTURE, ALL IS ONE IN MONKEY...

I came to the realization that, during the few times when I was actually called upon to do my job in the morning, the task usually involved little more than the opening or closing of doors at the behest of clients.

Open door. Shut door. Open med room door. Unlock TV room door. Lock med room door. Unlock offices. Open back gate with remote. Close back gate with remote. Talk to junkie. Ignore junkie. My college education was really coming in handy.

(The whole Open/Close binary did get a little confusing at times, but I tried my goddamnedest to keep it all straight.)

My job therefore got a failing grade for the R.M. Test. This means that it officially could've been done—and possibly done better—by a Retarded Monkey. Possibly one that was drunk, as well. Maybe even crippled.

Of course, I'm convinced that a neurologically challenged, disabled primate with a drinking problem wouldn't appreciate the Selbyan nuances of the job like I did (or like I enjoyed pretending that I did). Nor would it have figured just which pill combination to take from the med room in order to have as interesting a shift as possible.

It was going on the fourth hour of a midweek workday, and my big accomplishments of the shift were flirting with homeless girls, arranging a post-work meeting with my girlfriend and heading back to the kitchen for that second bowl of Lucky Charms.

I love my job.

12:03am

BABY-BUTT ASHTRAY

When one member of the homeless couple would leave the lobby to smoke outside, the other would get stuck holding their infant offspring. The second the smoke break was over, the kid was passed off, and the previous holder would be free to go outside and smoke. I watched this process recur for over seventy minutes.

The couple, a weatherworn man and woman here for the handouts, took turns holding their baby during the other's nicotine breaks. The kid, a skinny little thing dressed in what was probably its father's white T-shirt, was traded off with all the tenderness typically reserved for a frozen turkey.

During one of the pass-offs, as the baby was plopped from one lap to the other, the kid's shirt/gown slipped up to reveal its little ass. The Anne Geddes

29

potential of the moment was somewhat ruined by the circular burn marks that pocked the baby's butt. No one was going to make a sunblock ad out of something like that.

Then the parental hand came and pulled the shirt back down. Not in haste or worry. There was nothing in the action that could have been construed as: *'gosh, sure hope someone doesn't notice that I often mistake my offspring for an ashtray!'* Just the typically languid motion of a parent straightening out their child's ruffled apparel.

The thought of calling Child Protective Services never crossed my mind. Growing up homeless would fuck the baby up enough as it was. The kid was already a lost cause. Worrying about the other stuff its parents might be doing was like worrying about wetting the ocean by pissing on it.

Look at it this way, kid, I thought as I watched it being passed from one unhappy parent to the other, *Your folks putting out cigarettes on your ass could one day make some pretty decent fodder for your public defender.*

The shirt slipped up again and I caught a second glimpse of the baby's scarred backside. I quickly averted my eyes. *I'm sorry, kid.*

Jesus, I'm sorry.

12:21pm
THE WINNER AT CANDYLAND GETS A FREE LOLLIPOP ENEMA

There was a weird bacteria covering my hands. They were peeling in discrete flakes that came off only when ripped by a firm application of front teeth. Looked like a light version of leprosy. Hopefully temporary.

I had probably picked it up here. Fuck knows that this place was crawling with germs and bacteria. A terminally toxic environment. It's filled with homelies who wash themselves on a monthly basis. Who pick their meals out of dumpsters. Who consider sink-baths to be adequate hygiene. They're joined by all the junkies and crackheads who have the luxury of hand washing but no inclination to use it.

Filthy, *filthy* fucking place. From now on I'd use a shirttail over my hand to touch anything.

After work I'd go home and masturbate with latex gloves.

I made a mental note to steal some from the supply room, and that was when Toni handed me the pills. Five Vicodin for sixteen bucks. Not a great deal, but not a bad one, either. There was nobody else in the lobby besides a few homelies staring at the floor, but Toni passed them off to me using that totally obvious druggy handshake.

I laughed at him. "You hokey motherfucker." Christ knows from where that bacteria on my hands had come, but now Toni had it, too.

Drool lurked at the edge of his mouth. "Ray-*baaaaby*," he sighed, "They are *gooood*."

I believed him. Toni was having trouble keeping his eyes open, and even more trouble keeping his words from slurring. He looked fucked up in a way that you really shouldn't look in a rehab.

Everyone who worked here was trained to catch people trying to hide just how high they were. I would've detected Toni blindfolded at a hundred paces. The guy was going to get himself busted, but it wouldn't be the first time. And I'm sure it wouldn't be as bad as the time he got caught dealing coke. That little infraction had landed him in prison from the time he was seventeen till his mid-thirties. Just another casualty of the American War on Some Drugs.

"*You should try one,*" Toni urged in an exaggerated whisper. He seemed ready to kiss linoleum at any moment. I crossed my fingers for something interesting.

"Try one…"

"I'll wait, thanks." Work wasn't too intolerable, yet. Not quite enough to warrant being fucked up during it. Maybe some day, but not right now. The pills would keep until I figured out something to do with them. Maybe slip one into my girlfriend's drink the next time I felt like trying anal. The possibilities were endless when it came to substance abuse.

Our hands had just parted contact when the phone rang. I picked it up, and a solicitor on the other end asked for Mr. Neil Young. About once a week here we got a call for "*a Mr. Neil Young.*" I was pretty sure that we don't have any client here by that name. Celebrity monikers tend to stick in the mind like any other form of advertising. And none of my co-workers could recall anyone by that name from the past five years. Somehow the name and this phone number got stuck on a phone solicitor's list, and now—sure as death, taxes, and dysfunctional relationships—I could always count on fielding the weekly call for Mr. Young.

Since my main goal in life is to amuse myself, I always told the solicitors, "Sorry, but Mr. Young is currently touring in support of his new album while nailing a groupie, mainlining heroin and feasting upon the remains of his former band mates. He's old but spry."

That, or I'd offer to go fetch him, and Toni would burst on the phone a few minutes later with his own rendition of *Rockin' in the Free World*.

That's not humor at its sophisticated finest, but we always enjoyed it.

1:11pm
COMES IN TWO NEW SCENTS: WINTERGREEN AND CRACKHEAD

Said one of the junkies, "I feel like I about to go crazy, living here with all these guys. Need me some titty."

There was a general round of agreement from the other junkies. We were all shooting the shit in the front lobby. The day was crawling by. Anything to pass the time.

My work is a place of inaction, a place where people cease to do things and focus on *not* doing them. My English teacher last semester said that F. Scott Fitzgerald claimed action to be character. We are what we do, right? At the time, I didn't get what the professor meant, but here at the rehab the maxim designates our clients to be even bigger nobodies than before. Their presence is based upon a cessation of previous actions, quitting the things that used to define their days. Their personalities seem to fade into generalities without the drugs to back them up. Their individual identities couldn't be asserted without the framework of the things from which they were fleeing.

That let me feel fine about not remembering the clients' identities, and so, they mostly just become *junkies* to me. What the hell, it beat having to memorize all those names.

"I fuckin' bet," I said. "I don't see how y'all live in such a purely dick-filled environment."

"We jack off constantly," one said, and the others laughed and shouted agreements.

I shrugged. "Hell, I do that anyways."

I do at home, at least, when the girlfriend isn't around. Still haven't sunk to the level of masturbating at work.

Someone asked, "Ever do it in the *downstairs bathroom*?" and there was another round of shouts and laughter, like someone had just named the secret word on *PeeWee's Playhouse*. "Go in there, lock the door, *bambambam*, tug one out real quick?"

"Here?" I asked, thinking that *bambambam* as a masturbatory sound effect reminded me how the Victorians used to call it *self-abuse*. "Not while I'm on the clock, thanks."

That doesn't mean I've never been tempted to, but... "I mean, I piss in it, but isn't that the *ladies'* bathroom?"

Big smiles and nods of acknowledgement all around. "Yep," said one of the guys. "Jes' somethin' about that sweet potpourri smell..."

1:56pm
THE UNKINDNESS OF STRANGERS

The buzz of a poverty-filled lobby surrounded us while Toni shared prison stories with me. I sat on the filing cabinets above him, scanning the lobby in hopes that I'd recognize someone from high school. Anything was better than looking Toni in the face. Not from close up. Toni had a mug like he shaved with a sand-belt. Like he'd hit a second puberty and started developing into a reptile. Like every year spent in prison had counted for double on his face.

One horribly wrinkled motherfucker. And all of thirty-six years old.

Which isn't *too* young, but *Jeeezus...*

"I just munched Xanax and Valium every day," he said, and I nodded like I actually gave a shit. "And by the time my seventeen years was up, I was all, *what, finished already?*" Toni had a voice like a Southern Belle. High-pitched, twanged with Dixie inflections and terminally infected with camp. He sounded like Blanche Dubois's effeminate male twin.

It's tough ridding your mind of stereotypes when you're surrounded by them.

Everyone starts getting to me by the middle of a shift. Even the people I can usually tolerate. Toni's stories about enjoying being a prison bitch were wearing thin. If he said the phrase, '*all the meat I could handle*,' one more time, I was going to tump the filing cabinet over on him. Just get it rocking back and forth before hopping off at the last minute. Watch it fall forward and flatten him against the desk.

It was probably the annoyance of being stuck in a single location for so long. I liked to be able to move around. Having to stay in the same place for hours on end started to wear on me, especially considering the fine specimens of human potential with whom I was stuck.

"I heard about your guys' parties getting busted." Now that Toni had something bad to say about other people, he could finally stop talking about himself.

Some of the clients had been throwing coke parties upstairs at night. They'd do huge lines off the tables in the TV room and chug beer till the early hours.

The people I'm supposed to be watching during nightshifts? That's what they do while I'm asleep.

"Too bad about Sam and Pike," Toni said. "They were cute." I shrugged in reply. Not my types, really. He followed up his evaluation with a stage whisper that I heard just fine over the noise of the lobby. "*Had them both*."

"At the same time?"

Toni waved me off. "Oh, don't I wish!"

Scott shuffled up to the desk. He kept his eyes mostly on the floor, but threw occasional side-glances at the homeless. Looked like a shy man at a freak show. Entranced and horrified by what he saw, but not wanting to admit to his car-crash fascination. "Is my counselor in today?" he asked in a quiet voice.

I made Scott repeat himself twice before answering with a shrug. That's service the *New Start* style!

He spit out an exasperated huff. "I've been here two weeks!" Scott said, like it was my fault he couldn't handle the outside world.

"And?"

"Two weeks and I've only seen them once!"

I shrugged again. It's the expression I've found most useful in my job. Eight in the morning to four in the afternoon *was* the time when the entire staff was supposed to be available for the clients. Office doors *were* supposed to be open and inviting. That's what the brochures claimed, at least. But, the counselors never told me how to do my job, and I was determined to reciprocate.

"State law says your counselor's only gotta see ya twice a month." Although, considering how many times Scott had been here, and in every other treatment facility in Pasadena and neighboring Houston, he should've moved his bed into his counselor's office. And then maybe chained himself to the headboard.

"That's *bullshit*," he whined, and I was about to agree with him when Toni cut in.

"Hey, Mr. Grumpy," Toni said. "Somebody's *awfully* cranky! I bet you just need a little reciprocation, huh?"

Scott blushed like a klieg light and mumbled something about checking on his counselor himself. Toni smiled and gave a fingers-only wave as Scott hurried off into the side hallway. Then Toni turned to me and said, "Don't even bother asking, 'cause I'm not going to tell."

He didn't need to. It was already old news to me. Last week I'd been upstairs grabbing something from the med room when I'd heard a weird sound coming from the community bathroom. Not the usual theatrical grunting. Something else. More like a loud sigh. Loud and happy. I'd stopped and listened for it again. Heard it a second time. Curiosity piqued, I tiptoed in to investigate. Crouched to peer down the line of stalls.

What I saw were two occupants in one stall. A pair of legs with pants crumpled around the ankles, and a second pair kneeling before the first. More happy sighing. And then even more happy sighing. Didn't take a genius to figure out what was going on. Or going down. We all had different ways of relieving the tedium of this place. I'm sure there were plenty worse than getting sucked off in the men's bathroom.

Toni and Scott had walked out from the bathroom a whole five seconds apart, as if that was going to fool anybody. I smiled at them both and admired the dirty knees on Scott's pants. It was tempting to ask him if Toni had mentioned his Hepatitis, but I decided to keep that question to myself.

2:22pm
SOMETIMES MEANING WELL JUST ISN'T ENOUGH

Knowledge isn't exactly power, and ignorance isn't always bliss. But on some occasions they're close enough.

Troubled by the number of clients I'd seen relapse in my first few months at work, I did a little research on Alcoholics Anonymous and the 12-Step programs that went along with it. Researched the history, used the databases at school to search medical journals for studies and turned up an interesting fact or two.

Now I just had to figure out whether to tell the clients.

The first controlled study on AA took place in San Diego in the '60s. A group of "chronic drunk offenders" was used, and no statistically significant differences were found between the ones who went through AA, the ones who had clinical treatment and the guys who had no treatment at all.

How about that? Listening to how the clients and the counselors blather about "The Program" (as they called it) and the importance of going to meetings, you'd almost think AA was the only thing standing between human decency and a world of crazed drunks.

The second controlled study was in Kentucky in the '70s. They slapped the chronic alcoholics in the study into five different treatment groups. The AA subjects had the highest relapse rate, about a third more than any of the other treatment groups. Things like Rational Behavior therapy and even Freudian therapy whipped the crap out of it. Hell, the AA folks had an even higher binging relapse rate than the fucking control group.

Pretty goddamn sad, in my opinion.

Made me wonder why anyone would base a recovery establishment on a program that obviously didn't work for shit. Did they want people constantly coming back, or what? And, like most things in our ruthlessly capitalist society, was money involved? A revolving-door clientele would definitely put more cash in the coffers.

I thought about this possibility for a while. I hoped that plain ol' human stupidity was more to blame than avarice, but with our species it's usually something of a toss-up between the two.

Herman interrupted my pondering as he waddled into the lobby, slow and arthritic. I set the Xeroxed articles down and gave him a half-assed salute.

"How ya doin', old man?"

He looked up from the sign out sheet to squint at the clock on the back wall. "Jes' blessed," he said to me. "Jes' blessed, boy. Off to a meetin'!" Herman gave another squint at the articles spread over the desk. "You readin', boy?"

"Yep," I said. "If you're nice, I'll teach you how some day."

"Fuck you," he said. Chances are Herman was probably either borderline illiterate or totally so. A lot of the old black guys here were. Modern schools in Texas are bad enough. I can't imagine what the segregated ones were like. "What you readin' about?"

I stared at his withered face and considered spilling the beans for a second. Just to see how he'd react to the revelation that he was placing all his hope for improvement in something that was ineffective at best.

Would he soldier on, regardless? Would he relapse? Would he tell the other guys and there'd be a keg party upstairs before the day was over? Would they care that, thanks to the program's worthlessness, all their hopes had been conceived stillborn? How would everybody react if they knew how useless were all their dreams of a better life?

I swept the papers off the desk. "It's nothing," I said.

Herman gave a smug nod. "That's why I never bother with that shit."

3:11pm
PEOPLE LIKE US WERE PUT HERE TO MAKE THINGS WORSE

"Y'all do realize," I said to the other guys sitting on the sidewalk, "That our gawking and jeering's probably ruinin' what's supposed to be a very beautiful day."

One of the junkies bothered raising his fist at me to extend the middle finger. "Shut up and get me some popcorn," he said.

Across the street from the rehab/halfway house stands a large colonial mansion. The bleach-white facade and thick, Doric columns made it stick out in this part of town like a Matisse painting in a field of broken syringes. Inside the mansion was a bridal boutique, and on the left side was a lush garden and flower-covered gazebo.

They held a wedding reception there today.

The valet parking covered both sides of the street in either direction with SUVs, sports cars, and limousines. The only empty space for fifty yards was where we all dangled our feet in the gutter, refusing to move and lose our front row seats.

Or maybe *front row* was too complementary of a term. The wedding was not only across the street and behind a wrought-iron fence, but also guarded by three large men with blue suits and guns. It was a clear message that the riff-raff so prevalent in this area should stay the hell out.

The junkies hooted, hollered, and pointed freely at the wedding guests, especially those of the young and female variety. We watched a family walk through the front gate. "Whenever I see a hot-ass bitch with a baby," said Frankie, "I always think to myself, *Damn, somebody done had the same idea as me!*"

Everyone laughed, and the woman's husband glared back at us. We weren't more than twenty yards away. It was myself, Robert, Pike, Frankie, Warren, Solomon of the Eternal Headphones, and a host of other characters that would have most people keeping an eye on their wallets. With the rehab's door propped open, we sat and cooked in the East Texas heat, our profuse sweating a small price to pay for the entertainment.

Everyone was *just chillin'*. Just enjoying the show. It couldn't have been too difficult for the wedding guests to hear us; the idea of yapping at less than full-blast was an alien concept to most of the junkies.

"She *is* attractive," I agreed; studying the woman's retreating figure in its tight, gray dress. "But I could do without the marriage or the kid."

"You ain't married, is ya?" Frankie asked me.

"*Jesus Fuck, no!*" I cried in horror, prompting laughter from the junkies. My folks had three kids and a twenty-year mortgage by my age; I'm determined to learn from the mistakes of others. "Can't imagine being dumb enough for something like that."

"Whuz so dumb about marriage?" he asked. Frankie was a huge, 'fro-ridden bastard. Like somebody had forgotten to inform him that the '70s were over and his side lost.

"*Muthafuka*." Robert said. "Ask a stupid question like that, I know yo' ass ain't never been married."

I asked Robert, "You've been married, haven't ya?" He'd told me before, but my listening skills could do with some improvement. I decided that the amount I listened attentively to people should be directly proportional to how close they were to death. Robert, being cancer-ridden, deserved an open ear.

36

Then again, Solomon had AIDS, and there was no way he was going to say anything worthwhile.

It had been well intentioned, but another policy quickly bit the dust.

"*Shit*," Robert said. "I been married fo' fuckin' times, and each time I like, *nigga, what was you thinkin'*?"

Pike chimed in with, "I bet they asked themselves the same thing!" and we all cracked up.

Each time we laughed, a few wedding guests would look over in our direction, certain that their sacred event was being mocked by the collection of white trash and street niggers across the road.

"*Fuck dat*," Robert said. "I always marry fat bitches. They just grateful to have a man."

Well, he was half-right, at least. Robert had shown me pictures of his ex-wives once, and sure enough, none of them could even make it through the entrance of a *5-7-9* store.

How *they* had felt about having a husband who was first a crack dealer, then an addict of the product he once sold, all the while in and out of one jail after another…well, Pike's remark probably summed it up nicely.

"*Man*," said Frankie, "My wife get a restraining order 'gainst me last week. Can't go within a hundred yards of the bitch."

Maybe he was expecting consolation. No one offered any.

"Wait till you're paying alimony," Pike said. "Costs me seven-hundred a month to my ex."

The other junkies chimed in with their respective sums: *three-fifty, two-hundred, five-twenty-five…*

"Reason two-billion-and-thirty-seven why marriage is retarded," I said. "Can't imagine giving money to my ex-girlfriends. Once you're off my dick, you're also the hell outta my wallet."

"Goddamn right," said Pike. "Judge at my hearing called alimony, *the fucking you get for the fucking you got*."

We all found this hilarious. Even Solomon started laughing, though I doubt he could hear anything through his headphones. Made me wonder what he was chuckling about. Probably some fantasy involving the little kids across the street.

The garden next to the mansion was slowly filling up with wedding attendants. Resplendent in their formal wear, the guests laughed softly and socialized among themselves. Proud parents balanced spotless children on their hips. Everyone smiled, everyone was polite, everyone had sizable bank accounts. It was a priceless scene of White Protestant America as brought to you by *Reader's Digest*, *Nick at Nite* and the Klu Klux Klan.

"Why the restraining order?" I asked Frankie. Not like those were rare around my work. Addicts have a lovely habit of dragging everyone down with them, and sometimes their spouses found sacrificing the family to one member's sickness to be an unacceptable option. Couldn't say I blamed them.

"Ah, I used to get a bit rough with 'er," he said with a shrug. "Ain't touched the bitch in months, though."

A pair of binoculars circulated among the guys. They were passed from one sweaty pair of hands to another for a closer examination of all things feminine across the street. The off-duty cops watching us from in front of the fence were obviously displeased by this. So were the members of the wedding party standing further up the driveway, but nobody wanted to draw more attention to what we were doing.

Solomon boomed, "HURRY UP WITH THEM GLASSES!" and I bypassed my turn to speed the binoculars to him before boredom led the guy to start molesting people at random.

The binoculars had passed to Solomon, still jamming on his headphones, when the bride and groom emerged from the mansion's front door. They stood arm in arm, framed in the doorway. The wedding guests all stood at attention. A reverent hush fell over the crowd.

"*GODDAMN*, THAT MOTHERFUCKER OLD!" Solomon shouted. "SHE YOUNG ENOUGH TO BE HIS GRANDDAUGHTER! YOU JUST KNOW THAT FUCKER RICH AS HELL!"

Sound travels. The entire wedding turned around to gape at us as one shocked and outraged entity.

Shit! All the guys ran inside the rehab, leaving me and Solly alone on the curb.

Solomon watched the guys bolt inside. "THE FUCK'S THEY PROBLEM?"

A quick look across the street explained things. The crowd stared pure anger. A hundred or so eyes were still on us, the wedding utterly forgotten in light of the tremendous *faux-paus*. Murmurs swept back and forth through the crowd. They all stared at us. Stared and probably wondered; who *were* these sad little creatures daring to desecrate their magical day? All those eyes belonging to the happily wed and comfortably loved, now focused on an AIDS-ridden child molester and an increasingly cynical white boy.

Being on display got old quick. I stood up and raised my arms at the crowd.

"Fuckin' *WHAT*?" I screamed. This didn't cause a single person to turn away, but it did make the cops decide to cross the street to pay us a visit.

Solly and I scampered inside. They rang the buzzer repeatedly, but on my orders no one answered the door.

3:25pm
GOD IS PUNISHING YOU
...OR WOULD BE, IF HE THOUGHT YOU WORTH THE EFFORT

"...and then my dad jumped on my back and my sister grabbed my arm, and gosh, I don't like to be touched, so..."

Warren was telling me and Old Herman about beating up his family. Apparently, they had tried to stop him from going out and buying more crack. Warren gave his dad a concussion and knocked out four of his sister's front teeth.

The lesson here is to *never* get between a man and his rock.

Warren was the kind of guy you'd expect to get picked on by cripples. He'd have to bulk up to be a ninety-seven pound weakling. It was hard to imagine him beating up anyone. He looked too timid to even throw a punch. You'd expect him to shit himself at the very thought of violence. Maybe I could see Warren roughing up a few prostitutes. It's always the impotent types who get caught doing that shit.

Warren sighed. "I paid for their medical bills, for my sister's dental surgery, but they still won't talk to me." He seemed genuinely confused by their obstinacy. It's always a shock to realize that there isn't such a thing as unconditional love.

Herman, sitting on the lobby's couch next to Warren, shook his head sadly. I propped my feet up on the desk. This was definitely a story I'd be sharing with my girlfriend. Christ knows if a constant supply of disturbing anecdotes were enough to keep someone's love, but it wasn't like I had too much else going for me. "I'm sure they'll come around eventually," I said. "Just give 'em a few years or maybe a death in the family or somethin' else to make this not seem like such a big deal. Or, for twenty bucks, I'll set ya on fire."

"What?" Warren took off his glasses and squinted at me. Why he thought that'd help his hearing is one hell of a mystery.

"Deal of a lifetime," I said with a straight face. I had seventeen copies of a newspaper clipping that I had just taken from the Xerox machine. Per Gim's orders, I was supposed to tape one to every door upstairs. "You give me twenty bucks—fifteen 'cause I like ya—and I'll set you on fire. Family's sure to visit you in the hospital."

"Forget that shit." Sensing an opportunity to make light of another's suffering, Herman joined in. "I'll do it for twelve dollars, boy."

I wadded up one of the newspaper clippings and threw it at Herman. I said, "Stop underselling me, you old bastard!" and we both laughed.

Warren put his glasses back on and squinted again at both of us. Then he coughed a few times, and Herman started coughing, and I resisted the urge to do the same. We were all sick, of course. Hard not to catch the occasional cold in this place, but it was a great excuse for coming to work wrecked on Nyquil.

"If they don't visit," I said generously, "I'll give ya half your money back."

Herman laughed. "It's double your money with me, boy."

I laughed, too. It seemed like Herman and I finally had something we could bond over. Maybe next we'd go mug a cripple together.

Unsettled by our mocking of his trauma, Warren just said, "Let me think about it," and got up to leave.

I held one of the clippings out to him. "Tape this up on the fridge if you're headed to the kitchen." He took the clipping from me and looked it over as he walked off.

"Where does 288 connect to Highway 59?" Warren asked. I pointed in a vaguely southeastern direction towards the elevated on-ramp. "Is that a long drop?"

"Oh yeah," I said. "It's *way* up in the air. Go over the side there and you've got plenty of time for a decent scream. I used to live by there, and I always wondered what that would be like."

Warren gave a slow shudder. "Guess Gerry found out the hard way." Herman slowly shook his head.

My response was a wave of dismissal. "Fucker was probably too drunk to even appreciate it."

We all laughed, but only Warren and Herman looked guilty about it afterwards.

3:33pm
QUALITY TIME

A blur of a little kid ran from the back hallway into the women's bathroom. I caught it as a flash of movement out of the corner of my eye. Thought it was just my imagination. I used to get that back in the days when I did a lot of acid. Some dark movement in the peripheral vision that vanished when the head was turned for a better look. We called them the *Black Acid Cats*.

I thought this was just another long-delayed manifestation of the BACs, and went back to scanning the newspaper. Then a second little blur repeated the feat.

A New Start is an 18-and-Up establishment. *Ergo*, I couldn't have just witnessed two little kids running around in here.

"Did you see that, too?" I asked Frankie as he bent over the sign-out sheet.

He shook his head. "Ain't payin' attention to nothin' but my recovery," Frankie said. "Gotta look after me, now. Caring 'bout other people's problems what got me here."

He earned a disgusted look. Nothing made me want to retch more than self-pity. Fuck knows it flowed in rather copious amounts around here. It was just another reason why every shift was an exercise in the suppression of my gag reflex.

"You poor, wounded soul," I said.

My peripheral vision caught the two small blurs racing from the women's bathroom to the back hallway. I turned to catch a better look, but they were already gone. We either had an infestation of children or an under-aged pair of apparitions on the loose.

Poltergeists wouldn't have been so bad. Our building's already filled with addicts, the homeless and a pervasive smell of sewage. It'd be hard for things to get much worse, but I'm sure we'd manage to find some way.

I heard the back door swing shut with its usual squealing protest and went to investigate.

Out in the back lot, where everyone congregates to smoke inside a barbwire fence, Curtis sat on a plastic chair. Surrounding him like a solar system of impoverished planets were his wife and five children. Two boys, two girls and a baby.

His buck-toothed kids were all dressed in ragged clothes. The wife might have been pretty in the days before Curtis turned her into a walking incubator. Now, she was a skinny mess of worry lines and moved with an irritated slowness. Just a little extra stress was probably needed before shotgun swallowing became a viable option.

"Are *all* these yours?" I asked. Someone had snuck an entire family past me. It just went to show how much attention was paid to my job.

I glanced over the rotten fruit of Curtis's loins. The thought that anyone would have so many offspring baffled me. The oldest one looked to be about twelve, and had done the usual overblown adolescent job of painting her face. The baby was being carried by the second oldest girl. Two boys chased each other around the back lot. The baby and both of the boys were barefoot.

I meet way too many stereotypes at my job.

"Got another two at home," Curtis said. His mustache rippled as he talked. It was so large I almost didn't notice that he was one of the few crackheads I'd met with all his teeth. Considering how popular it was in the hinterlands, it surprised me that someone as rural as Curtis wasn't more into methamphetamines than crack. Guess we all like to think that we're different. "They've come on down to visit me for the weekend...that okay?" He waved his boys on over towards us. They stopped tempting tetanus and shuffled over to join the rest of the brood.

I looked over Curtis's spawn again. Portrait of the American family as misery machine. They all stood by or around their dad. No one actually sat *with* dad, or *on* dad's lap, and no one looked particularly thrilled to be there.

Couldn't blame them.

"So, where y'all from?" I was so surprised by my feelings of pity for Curtis's brood that I was making small talk. Poor fucking kids. As if being so obviously shit-poor and numerous wasn't bad enough. Now they were spending their Saturday watching Daddy detox in a trash-strewn back lot. The theological theory of God's omnibenevolence wears really thin around here. "Anywhere close?"

None of the kids responded to the question. They just stared at the ground. I seemed to be making them as uncomfortable as they were making me. They stared at the ground, kept quiet, and I could feel them wishing me gone. Probably didn't want me witnessing their embarrassment of a family life.

That was fine. I didn't really care what pocket of rural poverty they spent the rest of their week infesting.

A childless front desk was beckoning to me when Curtis's wife answered for her unresponsive litter. Said they were from a small town (name unimportant) about five hours west of here, and did I have any coffee?

The question sounded like such a desperate plea that I volunteered to go fetch her some (getting away from the palpable misery of the Trailer Park

Posse comprised the real motive). She insisted on coming with me. Apparently, someone felt the same way about being around her family as I did.

The oldest daughter asked if she could have some coffee, too. When her mom said no, she muttered that common reply of childhood desire thwarted by maternal authority: "...*bitch*."

Her mother spun around and backhanded her face. Her head whipped to the side. I jumped. "*Jesus Christ!*"

The mother strolled right on inside. Kept going, like she hadn't just assaulted a child in front of me. I didn't follow her. My gaze was locked onto her daughter, who hadn't given much of a response to the recent meeting of cheek and knuckles. Blood seeped from the corner of her mouth.

The girl didn't make a noise. Didn't cry, didn't do anything but stare in the direction of her mother with a hatred that could have burned holes through steel.

"You okay?" I asked the girl.

Curtis chuckled. "Sure she is."

3:45pm
FORGIVE YOUR OWN TRESPASSES
AND LEAVE MINE THE HELL ALONE

I watched in fascination as the fat old bum puked blood all over the desktop. One retch, two retches, three retches worth of stuff meant to stay on the inside. "*Jesus Christ!*" Toni shrieked as the blood splashed and started spreading. It soaked the sign-up sheet and began dribbling over the edges.

"*Oooh g-g-god,*" the bum moaned before collapsing onto his own fluids. His head bonked on the desk and blood splashed again as his upper body collapsed into it. Then he was dragged off the desk by his own weight, wiping a clean swath in the middle of the blood pool.

Everyone just stared. Myself, Toni, the other homelies, all transfixed and silent. No one moved to help. The homelies stared at their compatriot on the floor. I stared at the blood flowing back into the space wiped by the bum's torso and face. Toni stared at the splotches of blood on his shirt. We could've stayed that way forever if the human blood dispenser hadn't given a quiet moan from the floor.

Everyone snapped back to life.

The homeless started shouting. Toni screamed for someone to call *9-1-1*. I went back to reading the paper's Help Wanted section, commenting, "*There's somethin' you don't see every day,*" because it's more of an every-other-week thing around here.

It had been a slow morning, so something interesting was long overdue. If that '*something interesting*' ended up costing some bum his life, *well*...plenty more where that came from.

"*Jesus Jesus Jesus*, he got blood on me," Toni whined. "He got blood on me. There's blood on me."

42

There sure was. Toni's shirt was pretty ruined, unless bloodstained button-downs were back in fashion. I ignored his wardrobe complaints and pointed at the desk phone.

"You gonna call *9-1-1* or what?"

The homelies crowded around the dying bum like their favorite TV show was playing on his chest. Wouldn't have surprised me if they poked him with a stick. '*Give him air! Back up!*' a few shouted, but of course no one did.

"What?" Toni asked.

I pointed at the phone again. "That *9-1-1* shit you were yellin' about. Looks like you're the only one able to do something about it."

He gave a slow nod and picked up the phone. It was halfway to his ear before he shrieked again and dropped it. "There's blood on it!"

Big surprise. There was blood everywhere on the desk, spreading across the top and dripping over the sides. Toni made a few aborted grabs for the phone, dangling by its cord. Blood flowed down the curly-q path to drip from the bottom of the earpiece. "Ray, give me your shirt!" Toni said.

"Use your own damn shirt," I countered. "It's already ruined."

Toni was frozen by disgust and a desire to not further sully his clothes. One hand reached towards the phone, the other held his shirt away from his skin. Figuring this distraction had used up its novelty after only thirty seconds (my attention span sucks), I slipped off the filing cabinets and headed for the door.

My boss stuck his head out from his office. Gim asked what was going on. I answered with an exaggerated shrug as I edged between the mob and the lobby's Xmas tree. The homelies were giving their fallen comrade as little breathing room as possible. Not that he would've been able to use the air, anyways. Not with the gurgling sounds he was making.

I caught a glimpse of curly gray hair poking out from the back hallway where the Christers kept their offices. It was a rare appearance by the infamous Reverend Selma. She apparently wasn't going to expose more of her massive bulk until the situation was safely under control.

"TELL ME WHAT'S GOING ON!" she demanded.

"Y'all just got one less tax write-off," was the only decent response to make. Not that religious institutions even pay taxes, but hell, it sounded good at the time.

I went and sat outside in the smog and autumn heat, fending off demands for spare change or free cigarettes. Cars drove past on their way to someplace nicer. Bums watched the cars and provided incentive for them to keep driving. The front of the building always swarmed with the homeless during *C.i.t.G.'s* regular business hours. I thought about how the bum had face-planted into his own blood. There had been a look of realization in his eyes before he hit that said, '*Well, that's me fucked.*'

I chuckled at the image. There's so much suffering in the world that we'd be stupid *not* to find it funny. I hoped my own demise would be equally chuckle-worthy.

At the end of the street another victim of modern life stood screaming at no one in particular. He wore two different army jackets in spite of the heat, and emphasized each word by jabbing his finger at the sky. His dreadlocks jerked with each stab of his finger. The flecks of blue paint on his face meant that he'd recently been maced.

"OUR FATHER," he screamed hoarsely, "HALLOWED BE THY NAME!"

This was the guy's seventh go at the Lord's Prayer since I had been outside. Each time he got more incoherent and louder. Maybe he was worried that his god wouldn't be able to hear him over the traffic. "GIVE US THIS DAY OUR DAILY BREAD!"

Religion and the mentally ill: like they were made for each other.

"He's not listening!" I shouted at the street preacher. An ambulance pulled in front of the building. The lights and sirens were off. There was no hurry. It was too little, too late, and we all knew it

3:59pm
DEAR CATASTROPHE BABYSITTER

"The party in yo mouth, *bitch*, and everyone's coming!"

Julian's belly shook as he laughed at his own joke. Despite his threats, he hadn't killed himself after being booted from the rehab a few days back. It was by far the most disappointing thing to have happened to me all week.

How the kid had managed to talk his way back in here was beyond me. I'd busted Julian and thrown him out, myself. For most folks, failing a piss test meant that we evicted you and kept your money. But, here was this smarmy little bastard still giving me crap after I'd already sent him packing. I bet his parents had talked Gim into it.

Well, if they could talk to Gim, so could I. A serious word was going to be had with my boss about this crap. This job was for sitting on my ass and laughing in the face of other people's suffering. Not for playing babysitter to fat Hispanic kids.

Julian was eighteen, though. A legal adult. He just acted like a brain-damaged child, a side effect of his mom's reproductive system not picking the right fetuses to spontaneously abort.

Just about the entire shift had been spent stopping him from doing one thing or another. I'd caught him at property damage and starting fights with the older clients and hustling stolen goods.

It was apparent which of us was enjoying this more.

"Look, kid," I said, and felt uncomfortably old for having said it, "You can't go around acting like a stupid-ass motherfucker for the rest of your life."

Hearing myself talk in crude, but slightly paternal tones was another reason to get my hackles up. Made me sound too much like my old man. And calling a client '*stupid-ass motherfucker*' was probably one of those things they had talked about in that training seminar I'd slept through.

Calm the fuck down, I told myself. *You're not really letting some fat kid get your goat, are ya?*

44

I took a deep breath. Don't strangle the little shit. Don't play those games. Grow up. Be mature.

Julian smiled from across the lobby. He winked and grabbed his balls at me. Sorry little bastard. In his mind I'm sure he was the cool and rebellious Thugg defying The Man (as portrayed by the uptight cracker sitting behind that eternal symbol of authority, a desk).

He's not a goddamn kid, I told myself. *Fat little fuck's 18-years old, and when you were that goddamn age you were...well, doing a lot of drugs and being obnoxious. Still, you weren't in a goddamn rehab, and you sure as hell weren't fat or Hispanic. The hell with this little shit playing Vato Without A Cause with you in the role of the joyless authority figure.*

"I got fifty G's in the bank," Julian said. "How much you got?"

Bastard was a Trust Fund baby. His family was loaded enough to buy him his own rehab. Try as he might to pretend that he was one *hard-livin' gangsta* from the Mean Streets, Julian was just another punk-ass rich kid. The young ones at the rehab always were.

"Bet I own yo bitch ass."

The pudgy little fucker wasn't the first client to try an economic pissing contest with me. Usually the clients who did were middle-aged business own-ers who had built their own companies only to drink it all away (never '*smoke it all away*;' alcoholics seemed to have the best luck climbing the corporate ladder; crackheads never made it beyond assistant manager). Having them flash their old bank statements at me was an obvious ego-defense reaction caused by being in the rehab, by having fallen so far. Julian, on the other hand, hadn't done shit in his life besides chose the wrong male archetype to emulate and then failed at everything accordingly.

High school dropout. Claimed to have done every drug under the sun, but his file only read marijuana and alcohol. He'd call the front desk from the up-stairs phone and play some crank call that ended with the phrase, '*deez nuts.*' Then he'd hang up and call back thirty seconds later, asking to speak to himself as if anyone was going be fooled.

I took another deep breath and reminded myself that the biggest challenge in life was to love the unlovable.

This crap thought was replaced two seconds later by the decision that I'd trade all the self-righteous sanctimony in my body for the chance to throttle the mouthy little fuck while bashing his head into the linoleum.

The desire to keep my job wrestled with my urge for temporary satisfaction.

"How much you got, *bitch*?" He threw his chubby arms up while saying that. Fucking retard.

"What you got?"

All this flashed through my head the next day when I arrived at work to find an ambulance and several cop cars in front of the building. They had blocked off three lanes of traffic, and in the middle of the mess were five cops and Julian. They all knelt with their full weight on him, knees jammed into sensi-tive parts of his body while a paramedic strapped him down to a gurney. He writhed and screamed an incomprehensible mix of fear and pain.

Somebody had smoked some bad shit. Or huffed it.

I stood on the edge of the gawking crowd and watched him being loaded into the ambulance—still struggling, still screaming—and found myself filled with the sort of gleeful satisfaction to which we're not supposed to admit in polite society. There went my biggest work-related headache. Today's shift would be much quieter.

Julian kept lifting his head and smashing it back into the gurney. "*Heeeeelp!*" he screamed.

I gave into temptation and waved a heartfelt goodbye as the ambulance doors closed. Good fucking riddance. A silent prayer was offered up that someone in the mental ward had a thing for fat boys.

Whistling a happy tune as best I could, the door to the rehab was knocked on. Still trying to whistle through an irrepressible smile, I opened the door when it clicked unlocked. Yeah, I might have been too atheist to think that Somebody Up There liked me, but at least They seemed to dislike the same people I did.

SWING SHIFT
(4PM-MIDNIGHT)

4:04pm
MORE THAN YOU CAN CHEW

All the homeless were supposed to be cleared out of the building by four. That's when *Christ in the Gutter* closed its doors for the day and the place became 100-percent rehab/halfway house. Goodbye bums, hello addicts. It was *something* of a step up, or close enough that it was hard to complain.

Personally, my uncharitable ass didn't see why they let the homeless hang around after they finished giving out free shit at noon. All the homelies did was pass out around the lobby, beg for change and stink up the place. Maybe Selma owned stock in a potpourri company, I don't know.

It was a few minutes past four and, as usual, some of the homeless were still loitering around the building. When I worked the swing shift on the weekdays, it was up to me to send them on their way. That kind of sucked, since I wasn't the one who invited them here in the first place. It was hard enough to clean up my own messes, let alone problems created by other people.

Hunched over the lobby's phone, and smelling strong enough for me to get a whiff of him from behind the desk, was a thick black guy in a poncho. Just a poncho, no undershirt. He kept his bag of flattened beer cans tucked between his legs, and thumbed through the complimentary phone book on the table next to the phone. He'd flip to a random page, run his finger down the list of names without even looking at the page, then punch a couple numbers into the phone. The guy would mumble a few incoherencies into the receiver before hanging up and repeating the process. It was like a bizarre pantomime of a hard-working secretary, the kind who probably phoned the cops when this guy wandered into their office.

I watched for a little while, amused, then called to him, "Time to pack it in and head on out!"

He looked up at me and barked, "I busy!" then went back to his routine.

Great, I thought, *Semi-retarded AND surly.*

Figuring that he might get tired of his little game after awhile, I went back to reading. A few pages later I looked back up and, seeing that he was still there, called out, "Hey, *Christ of the Crap* is closed, man! Time for you to head out."

He put his hand over the receiver and growled, "I said *I busy*!" then went back to his mummery.

I was pulling an 8-to-12 double shift. After having already spent a few hours around the homeless, my daily allotment of 'tolerating-the-eccentricities-of-the-less-fortunate' was at a low point.

You can mouth all the pious, compassionate bullshit you want when you're speaking it from the freshly scented comfort of your own home. But, spend enough time around the folks that you're supposed to feel so enlightened about, and your feelings change a bit. You start out feeling bad for them, then you get sick of your own pity and start despising the folks who make you feel that way.

Compassion fatigue, I think it's called. How Mother Teresa tolerated those fucking lepers for so long, I'll never know.

Personally, at this point I would've given my left nut to work a job that didn't involve humanity's rejects. Then again, I'd give my left nut for a lot of things. Most of them nowhere near what you'd expect a testicle to go for in an open market economy.

Still...even though I was miffed at being saddled with problems created by the Christers' charity hard-on, I thought I'd stay on the polite side of things:

"No, *really*. Get the hell out."

The bum slammed down the phone and turned, mouth agape that anyone would speak to him like that. Eyes wide with disbelief, he shook his head like I had just made the biggest, most incredibly stupid mistake in the world.

Then he stood up.

Mr. Bum was One Huge Motherfucker. Nearly seven-feet tall and stocky as hell.

Oh...Jesus, something squeaked in the back of my brain. He hadn't looked half this big sitting down.

"Somebody need to kick yo ass!" he thundered.

Oh, shit.

"Somebody need to," he repeated, "But I ain't gonna...not today." Then the Amazing Colossal Bum grabbed his sack of flattened cans and marched out the door.

Except that he missed the handle, and the door failed to open. The entire door shook as the bum walked face-first into it, bumping his forehead against the frame.

Usually not a fan of slapstick, I found this hilarious.

"Really fucked up your exit, huh?"

The bum turned, face red with hate. "THAT DOES IT!" he roared, and came for me.

Panicking, I reached back for the solid oak cudgel attached to the building's key ring. I'd always suspected it'd be needed for something like this. Hopefully I could get in a few good whacks at his skull while he slowly crushed the life from me. I reached back and—

Nothing.

I was grabbing for the cudgel but there was a big fucking *Nothing* where my salvation should have been. Spinning around I scanned the desk for it. Where was the goddamn thing? I kept it right behind my chair in case of emergencies. *Dear fucking Christ*, where did it go?

He lunged across the desk. I shot my chair back and almost fell out sideways.

My eyes scanned the desk: nothing, nothing, Nothing!

Shit!

Where did it fucking go?

I backed up against the filing cabinets. Contemplated climbing on top of them. The bum headed around the desk to pulp me up close and personal.

Was this how it was going to end? I wasn't going to die of cancer? A traffic accident? Nor a horrible sexual mishap involving cocoa butter and trained capuchin monkeys, but from a bum-induced mangling? *Shit!* Where the fuck was everybody when I was about to get killed? The clients? My ex-NFL boss?

Where had the cudgel gone?

A voice in my head whimpered, *My only regret is to die without ever having 'shroomed with the Pope.* The bum rounded the desk and reached for me.

"That's enough!" shouted a squeaky voice. "That's *quite* enough!"

A small, skinny body wedged itself between me and certain death. *"You* need to leave," Toni instructed the bum. "Time to go. Time to get out. *Shoo! Shoo!"*

The bum was herded out of the building by my favorite *C.i.t.G.* employee. Still flattened against the filing cabinets, I watched in relief as the door shut behind him.

Toni came back to inspect me. "Don't you worry," he said, taking the opportunity to pat me repeatedly on the chest and help me back into my chair. "Don't you worry; he won't hurt you."

Toni patted and fussed over me for a short while longer (a little groping was better than the previous option). Then he grabbed his bags, took a cigarette from its pack, and headed home for the day. The cigarette was lit as he walked out the front door. Despite having just finished an end-of-shift cigarette break, touching me apparently called for a celebratory smoke.

"Fuck...me," I sighed. A poncho-wearing minority from a lower tax bracket had almost killed me. It was exactly what all those conservative pundits had always warned would happen. But where the fucking hell had the cudgel gone? Where was my one means of defense when I had needed it?

The question was answered when my boss strolled past the desk, carrying a plate of food that he had just liberated from the kitchen fridge...the *locked* kitchen fridge.

Gim smiled at me as he passed. "Keep up the good work, Ray!" Then he tossed the cudgel-mounted keys onto the desk.

I stared after him in disbelief. I had almost gotten killed because someone's oversized ass couldn't wait to hit a drive-thru on the way home from work? Thanks to him I'd had to suffer the agony of expecting my life to flash before my eyes while only getting reruns of *Friends*?

Bastard!

I made a plan to wait till my boss was gone and then piss in one of the potted plants he kept in his office. It wouldn't threaten Gim's life in a similar manner, no. But, the week or so he'd spend wondering where *that smell* was coming from would go a ways toward evening the score.

4:08PM
JOE HILL DIED IN VAIN

Gim was hanging around longer than usual. Most days he'd be already gone, but at a little past four he walked out of his office and handed questionnaires to myself and Jack.

As head Tech and my immediate supervisor, Jack was manning the front desk (and thus stuck answering the phone and clicking the door unlocked) while I lay on the lobby's leather couch.

State law dictated that two Techs always be on duty whenever the client population exceeded thirty-five persons. We had fifty-plus clients at any one time. My employers broke the law every morning, night, and weekend by only having one Tech on duty (and thus, only one on the payroll). To make up for this, on weekday afternoons there were two people sitting around for a job that barely required one of us.

Gim towered over me, tall enough to block out the lobby's florescent lighting. He handed a sheet of paper first to Jack, then myself. "It's from the head office," Gim explained as I hurriedly sat up on the couch. Reclining like I was discussing my Oedipal tendencies was all well and good when Gim was gone, but otherwise I did try to *look* busy. Awake, at the very least.

I examined the paper. "The hell's this?"

It read:

FROM THE DESK OF GEORGE FRIST, CEO:

LET'S WORK TOGETHER TO MAKE OUR COMPANY BETTER!

Our company, huh? So why didn't I ever get an invite when the board of directors convened for a meeting?

ONLY BY WORKING TOGETHER CAN WE MAKE THIS THE BEST CHEMICAL DEPENDENCY REHABILITATION SERVICE IN TEXAS! ANSWER THE SIMPLE QUESTIONS BELOW AND SHARE WITH US WHAT YOU CAN DO TO IMPROVE A NEW START, INC.!

As far as I was concerned, I was doing my part for the company by working for shit wages with no medical benefits. What more did the guy want from us plebeians? Effort?

1. WHAT CAN YOU DO TO HELP OUR COMPANY CUT DOWN ON EXTRANEOUS COSTS?

For starters, I could probably stop stealing office supplies. It wouldn't be easy to kick my monthly stapler habit cold turkey. Maybe if I switched to something less addictive, like paper clips.

2. HOW CAN YOU INCREASE OUR COMPANY'S BUSINESS LEVELS?

What the fuck? When did I get drafted to work in the advertising department? Did they want me to suggest installing a giant-sized Junkie Magnet outside our building?

It began to dawn on me that our cheap-ass CEO just hadn't felt like springing for a consulting firm. He'd apparently hoped that canvassing his employees for ideas would save a few thousand bucks. Considering how most of my co-workers could barely alphabetize (sad, really, but it gave an accurate view of the American education system), I'd have to say that the fucker was majorly shit out of luck.

Served him right.

I took my pen and wrote under the second question: '*I'm going to get all my friends hooked on crack.*'

Gim cleared his throat. "By the way, guys, George's birthday is coming up, and everybody's pitching in five bucks for a present."

Our boss looked at me then Jack, expectantly. I stared right back.

"Is this the asshole that gives us ten-cent raises? Or is it the prick that refuses to pay us for overtime?" Two purely rhetorical questions.

Gim shrugged and turned to my coworker. "Jack?"

"Fuck him," said Jack. "I had a birthday, too."

4:13pm
BLACK HISTORY MONTH: ABRIDGED

February was Black History Month. I was surrounded by living Black History. There were guys here old enough to tell me what it was like to live in Pasadena during segregation. They could give me a first-hand appreciation of what it felt like to be legally recognized as a second-class citizen.

Fuck knows why I cared. Possibly it was intellectual curiosity, but the smart money would've been on boredom. Time passed damn slow around here, just like it does at any job.

I decided to ask Jack about it. He was my coworker for the four-to-midnight shift. An ex-crackhead like Toni. He looked like an aged version of the actor, Danny Glover, if only Glover had shot Mel Gibson in the back midway through the first *Lethal Weapon* movie then stolen his wallet.

Jack was the shiftiest fucker I'd met in my life. And I admired the hell out of him for it. Whenever something went wrong during our shift he'd blame me like it was a natural reflex.

Tap the knee. "*Ray done it!*"

And yeah, I'd shrug and take the blame. What the fuck; like I was going to make a career out of this shit? Jack, on the other hand, was in his 70s, already retired, and worked the rehab as a way of augmenting his social security or something. Maybe they paid him under the table, I don't know.

Jack had lived in Pasadena all his life. He'd remember what it was like to drink from '*Colored*' fountains. How it felt to address every white man with a polite '*Sir*' and downcast eyes. Jack would be able to tell me what it was like to spend his youth in the back of the bus.

If all those years of smoking crack hadn't eaten up that part of his brain.

(the hippocampus, isn't it?)

"What was it like back then?" I asked him as he sat at the front desk making up the chore list. I was on the couch, thumbing through the *Help Wanted* section of the newspaper. "What was it like living in Texas back during segregation?"

"What was *what*?" Jack's old, but not hard of hearing.

"What was it like to live here in Pasadena back during segregation? The water fountains and separate dining areas and shit. What was it like?"

52

Jack kept staring down at the chore list. I thought he wasn't going to answer, but then he said, "It sucked."

I waited for elaboration.

None was forthcoming.

"Yeah, I figured that much," I said. "But what was it like? What was the sucking like?"

Jack just shrugged. "It sucked."

Obviously this was as informative as the guy was going to get. I guess as a white boy I didn't have the proper security clearance to hear about it. Or maybe he didn't want painful memories to be used as entertainment fodder by someone who could never understand what it had been like to be born on society's bottom rung.

Or was I just indulging in the sort of liberal bullshit that I usually despised?

A strong dose of cheap cologne hit my nose, and then Corey walked into the lobby. He was done up in a purple dress suit with a striped yellow tie. The word '*natty*' came to mind, for some reason. The suit made him look even smaller than usual, and Corey couldn't have been more than a few inches over five feet. No wonder his wife wouldn't talk with him anymore. How could you take someone so diminutive seriously in the sack?

Corey and I had gotten off to a rough start earlier that week, so I decided to be extra nice with the guy. "Off to church?" I asked.

"Sure am," he smiled broadly as he signed himself out. "Gonna go give some praise to the Lord with my brothers and sisters."

"You got brothers and sisters?" Jack asked. "Figure yo' parents woulda known to stop after you."

Corey stiffened for a second, then said as sweetly as possible, "I'm ignorin' you today, Jack."

"Lucky me."

"You ain't gonna get my goat, today," Corey said.

Jack loved giving Corey shit. *Reverend Leroy*, Jack called him. It was the same name he gave to every client with only a few days' sobriety and a mouthful of Jesus. '*Yo' mouth the first thing to heal*,' Jack would always say. '*Yo brain may still be sick as shit, but that don't stop yo' mouth from flappin'*.'

Corey was the third Reverend Leroy I'd known here. They never lasted long.

"Don't want yo' goats," Jack said. "Just you *gone*."

Picking on the junkies was a hobby of Jack's. Fuck knows how he got away with it, but nobody had fired him yet. Corey looked like he was about to lose his cool—and right before church, to boot—so I changed the subject.

I asked, "*You* live down here during segregation?" He nodded.

"*Hell yeah*," Corey said, then made an obvious display of crossing himself for having cursed. "Course, I wasn't born till sixty-two, and by that time the Good Lord was already leading our people from the Valley of Shadows into the Prom—"

"*Reverend* Leroy!" Jack slapped the desk. "Shut the *hell* up!"

For a second it looked like Corey was actually going to say something back. "*Jack*, I don't…"

Jack stared him down. "You don't *what*?"

Corey gave up and stormed out the front door.

Jack went back to the chore list. "Stupid *muthafucka*," he said. "Let's see how full of God he be when I put his ass scrubbin' pots and pans."

4:16pm
THANKS FOR THE CONTEMPT

Late getting out the door, my boss passed by the couch to give me a small plastic box. Another was placed on the desk next to Jack. It was transparent, wrapped in pink ribbon and filled with confetti. An envelope was nestled inside.

"The head office thought morale was getting low among you Techs," he explained with a *not-my-fault* shrug.

"There better be a raise in here," I said. I'd just learned about the scam the management at American Airlines pulled on its employees while giving a humongous bonus to its CEO, so I wasn't in the mood to get jerked around by ours. "Or some health insurance."

Gim never stopped walking as he passed, just handed the package off like we were playing Hot Potato. "It's a $10 gift certificate to *Einstein's Bagels*," he explained.

"That's perfect!" I shouted at his retreating form. "Since I can't *fucking* afford groceries!" Not receiving shit for a salary meant that even on my days off I'd sneak back up to work and eat dinner with the junkies. The food got shoveled down my throat fast enough to give me indigestion. Not even free grub made me want to spend time around here without getting paid for it.

There's a theory that if you hang around *anything* long enough you'll start to emulate it, and I'd hate to ever find myself blowing strangers for a fix.

(Oddly enough, even though I can't afford groceries, I *can* afford to go out and hit the clubs on my days off. Prioritizing can be a bitch.)

I would have yelled something else, but Gim's enormous stride had him out the back door before my brain could devise anything angry enough to express my displeasure, yet safe to yell at someone twice my size.

"Can you believe this shit?" I asked Jack, who answered with a shrug. "I haven't had health insurance in almost a year, our CEO lives in a River Oaks estate, and their thanks for us working on starvation wages is a fuckin' *bagel certificate*?" I got up to slam my gilded piece of class warfare into the trash, then plopped back down on the couch in a sulk.

I realized that my not getting paid for shit at work was possibly related to my not *doing* shit at work, but why should I be penalized for the inherent laziness of my job?

We sat in silence for a while, me stewing in my own self-righteous juices and Jack listening to smooth jazz on the radio. "I'll show 'em," I said finally. "Just for that, I'm gonna work *half* as hard!"

Jack started chuckling and I joined in, both of us laughing at the thought of putting any sort of effort into our jobs. Then I sat around and fantasized about violating our CEO with a bowie knife strap-on.

"If somebody can get away with doing somethin' to yo' ass, they gonna do it," Jack said, "Ain't nothin' personal, just how people are."

"Whatever," I said.

At the end of the shift, when no one was looking, I fished the certificate out of the trash. I knew I'd probably need it.

4:20pm
WATCHING OTHER MEN URINATE:
FOR FUN AND PROFIT

There was a long list of names in my work mailbox, and I knew what that meant: Mass U.A.s

Urinary Analyses.

Piss tests, in the common vernacular.

It was time once again for my favorite part of the job: watching other men urinate.

Joy.

Rapture.

Yee-*fuckin'*-haw.

Time to observe the junkies as they dribbled their wastes into plastic containers. Time to seal those plastic containers and ship them off to laboratories to be searched for those naughty chemical compounds that shouldn't be there. Time to argue with the clients about who was more degraded by the whole procedure.

Fucking piss tests. I had to take one to work here. Drank six cups of water and took that crucial, seal-breaker of a first piss before the test. The result was a 'diluted specimen,' but Gim was cool enough to let me bullshit my way past that. His trusting nature was the first hint that here was the nicest boss I'd ever had. What else could I do but take advantage of it?

The waiting list to get into the facility must've been getting long. Whenever there were large amounts of people waiting to get in here, the word came down from on high to pick about twenty of the clients to test. Broad sweeps like this would always turn up a few guys whose claims to sobriety were as big of a sham as my own. The offending parties would get the boot, the facility would keep the money they'd already shelled out for the month and someone new would move into their bed and cough up even more dough. Twice the money for half the junkie.

So, like most things in America, these episodes of mass testing were basically moneymaking scams.

This mercenary bit of bullshit wasn't Gim's fault. I think my boss was actually interested in helping addicts, having once been in their shoes, himself. The fault for this crap, and for all client/employee-screwing schemes that occurred at our facility, was squarely on the shoulders of our Beloved CEO and Leader: George.

That's where I put the blame, at least. It had to go somewhere, right?

I attended a speech the guy gave once, and all he did was ramble on about money for twenty minutes. Money. Money. Money. At three-grand a month each, with more than fifty guys here, this place was lucrative as all fucking hell. And Georgie-boy happened to own about six or seven of these facilities.

Yeah, *A New Start* is basically a franchise. We're the McDonald's of rehabilitation: '*Billions and billions failed.*'

I remembered listening in horror to our CEO's lack of subtlety during his speech. Apparently, pretending like he was at least *somewhat* interested in helping people was too much effort for the asshole. It was all about the money. And then there were the ten-cent raises the guy gave. Needless to say, I wouldn't piss up his ass if his guts were on fire.

I made a large sign and taped it to the front of the desk. It read: "PEOPLE LUCKY ENOUGH TO PISS IN FRONT OF ME," and under that the names were listed. The guys could then come up to me and say: '*My name on that list*'. It kept me from having to put names I didn't know with faces I couldn't be bothered to recognize.

"Hey!" A knock on the desk wrenched me from my book. A gangly pill-head, all flailing limbs and desperation, Paul danced an urgent shuffle in front of me. "My name's on the list, big guy. Let's do this 'cause I gotta piss like hell."

"All right." I set the book aside and whipped out the complicated form that gets shipped off to the lab along with the sample. Wiping drool off his lips with the back of his hand, Paul stared at in it horror.

Sign here, sign here, initial here, birthday here, today's date here, evening phone number here, initial here, bequeath us the rights to your first-born son here, and finally, sign right here.

"*Jesus,*" Paul moaned, saliva dripping from his chin. "You're gonna have a hell of a mess if this doesn't start going any faster!"

"Suits me fine." I pointed out the appropriate locations for his signature. "Dunno if whoever's in charge of moppin' downstairs this week would appreciate it, though."

"That's me." Paul was hunched over, crossing his skinny white legs.

"Oh…have at, then."

"Don't tempt me."

I walked Paul to the ladies' bathroom. It's the one I always use since it's about ten times cleaner and less disgusting than the men's. A pair of oversized pants was lying in a heap on the floor. Homeless fodder. I kicked them out of the way.

Paul stood over the toilet and aimed himself into the plastic sample cup. I slouched in the corner and gazed everywhere except at him. "Gonna hold it for me?" Paul asked over his shoulder.

"Nope," I said. "But for an extra five bucks I'll give it a final shake or two."

He laughed and called me a sick bastard. It was the nicest compliment I'd gotten all day.

4:31pm
ACUTE MALE SYNDROME

Being possessed of a fine pair of working eardrums, I'd already eavesdropped on Pike's conversation. He was talking with his wife on the lobby telephone. I heard the pleading, heard the apologizing, heard the angry words exchanged before the phone was slammed. When he plopped down across from my desk with an exaggerated sigh, I realized that I was going to hear the story all over again.

Pike, like most males capable of it, was a compulsive philanderer. In the two months that he'd been here Pike had shagged his way through an impressive number of young ladies. They were all met through AA functions and other 12-Step meetings. As the more predatory among us know, nobody is easier to screw than the emotionally vulnerable, and few places have more emotionally vulnerable women than 12-Step meetings.

It's not a pretty strategy. Not one you'd brag about to your friends. But it works, and that's all most guys ask.

The slang term for picking up the other human wrecks you met at recovery meetings is *13th Stepping*.

Pike was king of the 13th Step.

I'm not sure how he pulled it off so well. Pike wasn't unattractive, but he wasn't about to model for Calvin Klein in his underwear, either. The guy was just your average-looking, dark-haired cracker. Vaguely Mediterranean face. The kind you could walk past on the street (or in his case, step over in the gutter) and never look at twice. Generic with a capital *G*.

The only thing surprising about Pike was his age. Pike was 38 years old. I originally took him for about 25. Considering all the poisons that had traveled through his system, I'd have to grant the guy a super-human constitution.

Pike got back up from the couch to look down the surrounding hallways, making sure they were as empty as the rest of the lobby. Everything was clear, so Pike felt safe to tell me, "I'm in trouble."

"That's why you're here." I smiled at him without getting one in return.

Pike needed someone to talk at, and like most clients, he was willing to put up with a bit of sarcasm if it meant that he could indulge in some gut spilling. The desperate human need for disclosure can be exploited by those of us with an equally desperate need to make snide remarks at the expense of others.

"There's this girl I've been seeing..." Pike began. I slapped on my listening-attentively face, waiting for the next opportunity to amuse myself at his expense. He was about to continue the story, but a horrible coughing jag cut him short. Pike was sick, of course, just like everybody else in this goddamn place. I had the start of a cold, myself. Hopefully it'd go away on its own. Being one of the millions of American without health insurance meant that I had to use community clinics. At those places I sat right next to the same stinking homeless people I saw here in the mornings. It sucked.

Having hacked his contagion all over his hand, which he then wiped on the couch, Pike gave me the clincher: "And it turns out the girl's pregnant."

"Demand a blood test," I suggested. "And if that fails, there's always the next Greyhound outta town."

He just looked down at his hands. "It's probably mine," Pike said. "We haven't been using protection."

"Withdraw, at least?"

He shook his head.

Jesus. Now, I can understand not wanting to use condoms, but *for fuck sakes…*

"Just got off the phone with my wife about it," he said.

I know the details, I thought to myself. *Your pain is nothin' but cheap entertainment to me.*

"And," Pike sighed, "She wants me to never see the girl again."

I nodded, waiting for him to hurry up and get to the juicy parts.

"That's no problem," Pike continued. "I've hurt my wife enough, as is." The guy's got four—make that five—kids. There's three with his wife, one from a previous indiscretion, and now this little bundle of trouble.

"But then, she wanted me to promise that I'd never see the kid." He was aghast at the suggestion. "*Problem.* I grew up without a dad, myself. And look at me now!" I looked at him and saw a guy with womanizing skills I'd kill for. "No goddamn kid of mine is gonna do the same!"

His righteous declaration made, Pike stood up to leave. "Don't tell anyone, okay?"

There was no real need for him to make the request. Everyone here already knew or would know soon enough. Word travels so fast around this place, it's like the grapevine's wired with fiber optics.

"*Hey*," I said, doing my best to look offended. "Don't know why I'd tell anyone, and I don't know why anyone would care." Obviously, guys enjoy gossip just as much as the alternate sex. I was already looking forward to spreading around this little tidbit.

Pike tried to smile. "Thanks, Ray," he said. "Appreciate it." His spirits seemed to have lifted slightly. The burden a little less heavy on his brow. There's nothing like hearing a comforting lie to make things better.

Telling them helps, too. As Pike left the lobby, he called back, "No more girls, man! I'm sticking by my wife, and she's sticking by me!"

"Good luck!" I called after him. It was hard to suppress a disbelieving smirk, but what counts is that I tried.

Pike tried, too. He lasted four days. It was a personal record.

4:39pm
THERE'S NO RISING FROM THE GRAVE OF STUPIDITY

In order to fund the slaughter of Latin Americans back in the 1980s, the CIA helped flood inner-city America with coke. This created such a surplus of the product that crack cocaine came into popular being. Money was made by all the right folks, and only brown people were harmed. It was Keynesian capitalism at its finest.

A New Start's crackheads, fresh off the pipe, now went around discussing their simpleton's version of religion: the god of the 12-Step and his Lowest Common Denominator theology. They had jumped straight from one White Man's Dope to another.

Easter was next Sunday, so the miracle of the resurrection was the main topic of discussion in the lobby. Today, they argued fairy tales. Sunday, they would go to church and listen to the preacher tell how Jesus hit rock bottom and made his subsequent recovery. It was just the sort of act the junkies were all hoping to emulate.

In a reversal of our usual seating arrangement, Jack sat on the lobby's couch while I manned the desk. He was moderating the discussion with a few of the clients. And by 'moderating,' I mean that he reserved for himself the right to interrupt whenever the urge hit.

"Okay, so Jesus go and descend into hell…" Frankie said.

"I *know* what yo' ass about to say." Jack had apparently turned psychic sometime during the shift. "Jesus choose to die, right? But that ain't no suicide like if me or you do it. And even though he came back to life, that still don't take back that dyin' for our sins thing."

I tuned them out. Stupid-ass, Sunday school motherfuckers. Listening to the guys nitpick about their favorite fairy tales, I decided that A.A. hadn't picked Christianity as its religious model for reasons of intellectual complexity. Most of the crackheads could barely read, let alone tell poetic allegories from a factual assertion. And so here they were, discussing a metaphor for personal growth like they'd heard it on yesterday's evening news.

Looking for a distraction, I called my girlfriend's number. Her voice mail picked up. Busting out my best Barry White impression, I breathed, "This is Christ thy Lord, baby. I died for your sins, so the least you can do is call me back, sugar."

I was about to return the phone to its cradle, but then inspiration struck and I screamed into the receiver, "*You owe me, bitch!*"

The phone was hung up. I chuckled to myself, always amused by my own jokes. Then I looked around me. The phone line might have been dead, but now so were any nearby theological discussions. There was utter silence in the lobby. I must've interrupted things with my high-volume profanity. A dozen black faces stared at me. Robert spoke for all of them. "The fuck…?"

A smile was beamed at everyone. "That's right," I said. "*Never* turn your back on a messiah."

Look, it's not that I'm trying to talk shit about Easter. I'm not even trying to mock the overall myth of Jesus. Actually, I'm rather fond of it. I've grown to like what it says about our species. What hardcore bad-asses it makes us out to be.

To illustrate:

God shows up on our planet, tries to tell us how to live, and what do we do? We *lynch* the Bastard!

Humans: 1
Loving God: 0

4:44pm
FAVORS AND (IN)GRATITUDE

There was an envelope in my mail slot. Scrawled on it in a crude and sloppy print was my name. The handwriting looked female, but with the sharp edges and lack of grace usually associated with male scribblings.

My paycheck was the only envelope I was used to getting at work. I tore this new discovery open with all the hurry and excitement that novelty deserves. Inside was a photograph.

The front of our building formed the background of the shot, and the focus was a lone subject, Cassandra. She was the single mom whom volunteered at the homeless ministry. Whom had herself recently been homeless. And whom I had shagged the other week.

No fuckin' way, I thought, not sure whether to be amused, revolted or a mixture of the two.

The picture was a close-up shot of a blue-jean covered butt. Plump and wide in that down-home Southern style. Cassandra's smiling face peeked out from behind the mound of blue that occupied most of the shot. She had bent over and grabbed her ass at the camera. Her hands squeezed the cheeks.

Never thought I'd write this about a butt-shot, but the overall effect was monstrous. Cassandra's ass swelled to gigantic proportions and loomed almost threateningly. The grin on her face looked like it was stolen off a homicidal circus clown.

Historically speaking, this was The Scariest Picture I Had Ever Seen.

Was she mooning me? Was this supposed to be sensuous? Was her ass really bigger than I recalled? And, most importantly, whom did she convince to stick that camera in her butt and snap a picture?

Hell, the answer to the last question could have been: *anybody*. All the dirty old men in the building drooled a river whenever Cassandra walked in the door. True, they tended to overreact to any female on the premises, but Cassandra's frequent presence and cute young face guaranteed her a constant male following. And undoubtedly, a starring role in the private games of pocket-pool played in the late hours upstairs.

She probably got Toni to take the picture. Who better than a middle-aged gay man to attempt heterosexual erotica with a welfare mother? It all made sense, in its own cracked-out way.

Man, what's the opposite of arousal? I wondered. And, if my girlfriend ever found this, would she be pissed at me for cheating, or laugh at me for what I had cheated on her with?

I looked again at the picture, just to make sure that there wasn't something subtle I was missing. Maybe there was some hidden pictorial key that could reassure me that I wasn't really supposed to take it seriously. This just *couldn't* have been meant to arouse me. I checked the envelope for a "*just kidding!*" note in her jagged scrawl, but there was nothing in it apart from good intentions and failed results.

Just remember, I told myself, *Nobody forced you to sleep with the girl.*

No, no one had. I saw Cassandra occasionally when I worked the 8-4 shift. She would hang around making small talk and complaining about how long it had been since she'd gotten laid (before her kid was conceived about *13 months* ago—yikes!). I always made the usual polite and commiserative noises until I realized that she wasn't just making idle conversation.

Nor was she coming on to me. Not really. Basically, Cassandra had a problem and wanted my help taking care of it.

Why the hell not? I remember thinking. *How often are people going to ask for favors like this?* If someone needing sex wasn't an obvious chance for charity, I didn't know what was.

Cassandra was friendly enough, so my lack of physical attraction to her could be placed aside as unimportant. If she needed a favor, I might as well lend a hand. Or some other appendage. Consider it a labor of…well, not love. Not at all. *Jesus*, no. Maybe lust, at the very most. As an emotion it's way more common and inconsequential than love, and therefore infinitely more trustworthy.

"It's the one corporeal work of mercy that Thomas Aquinas's celibate ass missed out on," I explained later to Robert. "He had Feeding the Hungry and Burying the Dead, but forgot all about Shaggin' the Hard-Up."

Robert just said, "Who?"

I had met Cassandra one Sunday for drinks. She'd insisted on the alcohol, being more than a little nervous. We boozed, we chatted, and we avoided talking about the purpose for our meeting. I mentioned the Lamarckian heresy of acquired traits as an explanation for hereditary alcoholism; Cassandra told me about having worn pasties as a stripper to protect the Good and Christian people of Oklahoma from her nipples. Then we headed back to my place for that thing we all love to do.

It all felt very formal and business-like. The fucking, I mean. Like each thrust counted for an extra tally on the pay-meter. As if we should've given each other a handshake afterwards, instead of that awkward kiss. She was the first mulatto I'd ever slept with, but nothing too memorable besides that.

'Not bad for a white boy,' was Cassandra's evaluation (to my face, at least).

And I had figured that to be that. Patted myself on the back, scrubbed my genitals with antibiotic soap and considered our interactions complete. Cassandra tried to phone me a few times at work, but I always managed to dodge the call.

I did, however, learn a very important lesson about shagging the recently pregnant. A lesson aside from how cool stretch marks look when they spiderweb a melanin-tanned belly. It had to do with me thinking, as I lifted her legs over my shoulders: *Jesus Christ! Maybe I should just reach up in there and jack myself off*!

It wasn't that I regretted fucking Cassandra. Not really. A shag's a shag, after all, and it had been kind of flattering to be picked for stud-service out of an entire building of willing males. Most of them weren't what I'd consider serious competition, but the ego takes what it can get.

The photograph was looked at one more time. The blue mountain of a butt still erupted at me. Cassandra's expression looked no less frightening. I guess we're all grotesques when seen from the right angle.

I stuffed the photo back in its envelope. Maybe I could sell it to one of the guys.

4:55pm
LIKE AN ALCOHOLIC ST. FRANCIS

"I'd get up all early in the mornin', have a loaf of stale bread and a bottle of Thunderbird with me, and I'd go sit in my momma's backyard. All morning I'd drink and be feedin' the squirrels and birds."

Technically, you're not supposed to look back on any part of your addiction fondly. It's one of the innumerable AA rules. But I could have sworn that while he rambled at me from the one of the chairs lining the lobby's wall, there was something like a peaceful smile on Herman's ugly mug.

From my place on the couch, I pointed and laughed. "Who the fuck are you, the alcoholic St. Francis of Assisi?"

A puzzled look. "Who's that, boy?"

Lecture time. Professor Ray on Special Ed duty. "Catholic saint. Preached to the birds and animals when no one else would listen to his ass. Personally, I think his legend's a comp from some of the pagan nature gods, just like a bunch of the other saints. With Francis it was probably either—"

He rolled his eyes. Herman couldn't give two shits about a lecture on comparative mythology. It figured. Most of the guys here were allergic to anything more than monosyllabic grunting.

As if that set them apart from the rest of the country.

"*The fuck* you talking about?" he asked me. "*Boy*, you either stupid or crazy!"

Herman grew up here in Texas. Until he was almost thirty, anyone a few shades paler could address him with a condescending '*Boy*.' The guy had to be enjoying his turn to use the label right back on white folk without fear of reciprocation. Herman probably adopted the term right after the passage of the Civil Rights Act in '64 and hadn't stopped since.

"You gotta talk real loud and real slow, Ray." Jack strolled back into the lobby. "He gettin' deaf *and* senile."

Jack sometimes even came here on his days off to torment the clients. We've all got our hobbies.

Herman wasn't going to play along, though. "You better watch how you talk to me, old man." Jack's got five years on Herman, though it looks the other way around and doubled. "I'd hate to have to take you out front and whup yo ass in front of all them bums."

You can get thrown out for threatening the staff, but Jack just sat down behind the front desk and made a fist with his left hand. "You see this?" he held it up to Herman. "Registered as a lethal weapon. And this," he held up his right hand, "I'm scared of this one, myself."

I reclined on the couch to leave the two of them to their shit-talking. A broken marionette that someone had dressed in a blue-jean jacket and cowboy boots strolled into the lobby. Flashing me a smile through a beard that probably outweighed the rest of him, Terry came and sat on the other side of the couch. I moved my feet for him, but not much.

Terry indicated Jack and Herman with a nod of his head. "What's going on here?"

"They're taking turns threatening each other."

"Old black men love to talk shit." Terry stated this authoritatively, like it was a factoid he'd gotten off The Discovery Channel. "Go to the AA meetings and it's the same thing; get two of them together and they can't shut up about how they're still bad-asses." A look of mild disgust crossed his face and decided to stay there.

"Must be the Viagra," I suggested. Jack was on the stuff, or something like it. He had shown me a handful of little blue pills. Refused to share any, though.

"And I'm pretty sick of *that one*," he pointed at Herman, "Calling me a fucking '*boy*.'"

Tired of sparring with Jack, Herman turned to walk from the lobby. He pointed at the duffel bag he had brought with him. "Grab my bags, Ray."

I took a deep breath, counted to five, exhaled. People giving me orders drives me ape shit. Worthless old alcoholics thinking that my title was *Addicts' Bitch* were an especially sore spot with me.

He's old, I told myself in an attempt to keep calm. *He's old and going to be dead soon. He's old and going to be dead soon.*

"*Ray*! I said grab—"

"Get the fuck outta here," I growled. "And next time, stop and think before you piss off someone with keys to your insulin supply."

Herman found this hilarious. "You all right, Ray," he laughed. "You all right...no matter *what* shit Jack says behind your back."

5:02pm
DON'T WRENCH YOUR ARM OUT OF SOCKET...

In addition to sharing a building with the *Christ in the Gutter*, my work also shares a phone number with them. That means, after the Methodists have gone home, there's always people stopping by for free handouts or calling me on the phone to ask about the free handouts or anything to do with the idea of getting something for nothing.

Despite my quickness in telling about the lack of free shit to be found at the time, some of them hang around past the telling. The homelies who come wandering in want to use the facilities and/or see if it's possible to bum food or money off me. They ask for spare change or spare sandwiches, whatever's available.

Unfortunately for them, assisting the perpetually helpless and stinky was no longer part of *my* ethical code. It might've been at one time, but now I figured that they could die in the street for all my uncharitable ass cared.

One of the homelies, a skinny black guy in a worn tracksuit and purple jacket (obvious charity cast-offs) took offense when I wouldn't open my wallet to him. "You hang around here?" he asked, as if I'd come to this part of town without being paid for it.

"Maybe."

He narrowed his eyes at me. "Then I'll be waitin' for your white ass. Watch yo'self."

I shot him the bird as he walked out the door. That had been my fifth threat of the day, but it'd been a slow shift.

A mental note was made to vote Republican in the next election. Fuck these people. Then I remembered that the poor are generally left to fend for themselves in this country, no matter which branch of the ruling class held office.

I think it was British wit Samuel Johnson who said that the true worth of a man is how he treats someone who can do him no good in return. This probably meant that I was getting nothing but coal in my stocking for Christmas. If I followed Johnson's maxim, I'd be going out of my way to lavish all the free crap I could on the homelies. Hell, I'd happily give them money from my wallet, the literal shirt off my own back. I'd steal them food from the kitchen.

But, maybe it wasn't Samuel Johnson who said that. Scholars are divided on the attribution.

Almost as annoying as the homelies were the folks who called for the Methodists. These potential donors always felt the need—after I'd done the Methodists' work and recited the basic info about how the donations are handled—to continue to ramble on to me about what Great and Caring People they are. How they do the Good Lord's work and help out the street folk.

And they tell me.

And they tell me some more.

And then some more.

All the Great and Beautiful things that they do in selfless service to what Mother Teresa called, '*Christ in his Most Wretched of Guises.*'

And I'm like: '*Hey, great! Spiffy for you! Just why the fuck are you telling me this? Hoping, maybe, that through me it'll get back to Jesus?*'

'*Am I in charge of redeeming the 'GoodWorks' tickets for those brownie points you're obviously expecting in heaven?*'

'*Is altruism like martyrdom; there's no point bothering with it if you don't have an audience?*'

"Them donations do help a lot of people," Robert pointed out to me.

"Maybe," I said, "But don't mistake it for altruism. Those fucks are hoping for one hell of a reward. Like, the ultimate retirement package. A post-mortem pay-off!"

Robert rolled his eyes. "Alright, Ray; I get it."

"Hell," I said, "Those folks are expecting eternal bliss in their paychecks. I'm just doing this for eight bucks an hour." And then the phone ran again with another Good Samaritan wanting to know where he could get rid of his old sweatshirts.

Yes, God bless the big-hearted folk who take care of those less fortunate. Theirs is the kingdom *blah blah blah...*

It's just that...*well*...if you're really doing that much good in the world, I figure other people will do your bragging for you. There's no need to go tell it on the mountain. No need to bother me with it. If you're really the second fucking coming of Momma T., then other people (or your god with his hard-on for volunteerism) will notice those good deeds and reward you with the accolades that you crave. Either in this world or the one that you're so goddamn sure is yet to come.

5:18pm
LIVE AND DON'T LEARN

Jack's smile pushed the wrinkles on his face into turbulent ripples of dark brown. Switching the front desk's unit to 'speaker phone,' he keyed in the number for his voice mail, then selected his saved messages and turned up the volume.

This was to be our entertainment.

Sharing the lobby's couch were myself, Robert, and Frankie. A couple other crackheads also lounged around the lobby, either gathered by the desk or slouched in the chairs lining the lobby Jack was the center of our attention, and he knew it. This wasn't the first time Jack had amused us with phone messages from his ex-girlfriends. Considering the promiscuous life he led, it probably wouldn't be the last.

Still grinning, Jack gave a little shrug as the message blared from the speaker.

It was a woman's voice. Vaguely unhappy. "*You fuckin' slime-ass nigger piece of shit!! Pick yo goddamn phone up! I know yo stupid nigger ass be there! I know you there! Pick up the motherfuckin' phone befo' I fuckin' kill—*"

From the second the voice split the lobby's air, we were all hooting loud enough to almost drown out the message.

"*Ah haw haw hoo!*" Jack cackled along with the rest of us. It seemed that by the time you reached his age, you were comfortable enough to flaunt your failures. Most of us tried to hide how lousy we were at relationships. Not Jack. His M.O. seemed to be something along the lines of: '*Hey! Come check this out! Think y'all can't keep somebody's love for shit? Look how crazy I drove this bitch! And in record time, too!*'

Jack had been on the pipe for nine years, sober now for eight. Not only had he smoked his weight in crack, he'd also gotten his ex-wife doing it. I had asked him whatever happened to her, but he just changed the subject.

Jack also used to deal the stuff, and had told me a few tricks of the trade. I now knew how to make a roll of one-dollar bills look like a roll of twenties, and how to mix baking soda, water and a little bit of Carmex to make fake crack. I knew that you only sold a few on the corner before you got the hell out of there, since nothing's more dangerous than an addict who just gave you his last twenty bucks for something that won't get him high.

What I didn't know was how the hell Jack survived nine years of all that. There had to be plenty of people smarter and luckier who ended up dead on the floor of some filthy crackhouse.

"The *Good Load* lookin' out for me," Jack had said once.

"You really think so?"

He took off his cap to scratch at the mesh of hair underneath. "Fuck if I know or care."

5:30pm
FAITH

Back when Gim was in the depths of his addiction, he had decided that enough was enough. His marriage was ruined. His sports career was over. He was estranged from his children. He'd blown his fortune on booze and coke.

Gim's solution to this was to kill himself. He took a handful of sleeping pills, climbed into his sports car and started it in his garage with the door still down.

Asphyxiation is a pretty gentle way to die, as far as those things go. You just go to sleep, never wake up and all your problems are foisted off onto your loved ones.

Gim had drifted off to sleepy land as his garage filled with exhaust, convinced that he was closing his eyes for the last time, and was damn confused when he actually woke back up. Seems his car had run out of gas.

That bit of good fortune must have blown Gim's store of luck with automobiles. He'd had three accidents in the past two weeks, exacerbating some old football injuries. It was pretty sad to see him limping around the facility, so I was almost relieved when he took off work for a while. The rehab was left under the control of us lower-level employees.

66

The rest of the slackers and goofballs comprising the staff had to be graced with a few guidelines before he left. A special meeting was called, and Gim gave us the sort of pep talk that he'd probably heard in countless locker rooms back in his glory days.

"You Techs need to remember," he said, giving us an earnest look, "You're the first and biggest example of the power of sobriety that the clients get to see. Remember that they look up to you guys."

I started to laugh until I noticed that no one else was. Laugh, and the world laughs with you. If they *don't* laugh with you, you're in danger of someone realizing just how fucking high you are.

Looking around the room at my coworkers made me wonder how low someone would have to be to look up to people like us. Reginald was semi-literate with an old conviction for exposing himself to elderly women at a traffic stop. Jack received disability payments for his mental problems (called it his 'crazy check'). And as for myself...*shit*, I was so stoned I could barely hold my head up. The beginnings of Gim's sentences were forgotten by the time he got to the end of them.

None of us were in any danger of canonization.

"Just keep setting that same great example that you all have been, and I'm sure things will be fine." Gim smiled at us. I almost laughed again, but brought myself under control. *Never* had I seen a bigger case of misplaced confidence.

Reginald started fidgeting in his seat. This meant that he was warming up his brain to talk. "We'll...*uhhh*...we'll do...*ummm*...our...our best, Gim," he said. Five words in five times that number of seconds. Jack rolled his eyes, and I started giggling and couldn't stop.

5:35pm
THE PITY LINE

Sometimes you have to wonder at times if anyone could really miss putting up with your shit.

Corey:

"Baby! Just pick up the phone! I know you there! I just wanna say two words to you! I wanna let you know I'm *Okay in Christ*! Baby! C'mon! I wanna talk to you. That's all! I miss you! Please pick up the phone! *Baaaaby-yyy*..."

The lobby phone was slammed down.

"*GODDAMNIT!*"

I didn't even bother to look up from re-reading my copy of *Hocus Pocus*. "Don't break the phone, man. Everybody else has to use it, too." *And it's not the phone's fault you're such a fuck-up.*

He walked over to the desk. "Lord, what do I do?" His eyes were raised and hands held out beseechingly. "How can I make her see the light?"

"You talkin' to me or your god?" I asked.

"Ray, I just don't know what to do." Corey adjusted his gaze. He apparently hadn't gotten much of a response from the ceiling he'd been looking up at. "She *still* won't talk to me. I wanna tell her that she my wife, that we one flesh in Christ, that *nothin'* gonna change that!"

Nothing except her apparently getting sick and tired of his crackhead bull-shit.

I just shrugged at Corey. "Don't ask me about relationships, man. I can never make the fuckin' things work, either."

Zack:

He looked vaguely Italian, vaguely everything else that someone could look and still be considered white. Zack was probably a little older than me, mid-to-late 20s. All I knew was that he came from a rich family and loved crack. Trust fund junkies tended to be more into the heroin scene, but I guess we all need to feel different somehow. There are probably better ways to assert your individuality than being a crackhead, but I had to give Zack credit for at least trying.

His whining drifted to my desk from where he huddled over the phone.

"Dad...look, Dad...I'm all out...no...*Dad!* Look, I can't find...I *can't* find a job...there's nothing around here...Dad...*c'mon*...just two-...Dad...just two hundred...I'll go out looking tomorrow...I'll find one tomorrow...no...to-*morrow*...okay, I'll go to the labor hall ...*Jesus*...why do you have to be so difficult...I'll go slave with the nig—"

Remembering where he was, Zack cut himself off with a look in my direction. I gave a slow shake of the head: *No.*

"*Jesus*, Dad," he resumed, "Do you really want me working around those people? 'Cause that's exactly what I'll go do...that's the only other people there at the labor hall...well, hurry up, then...I need it soon as possible...Tuesday's too late..."

Curtis:

I tried reading aloud to drown out Curtis' half of the phone conversation. Mumbling passages from *The Lucifer Principle*—out loud, but not loud enough for anyone else to hear Howard Bloom's anti-Muslim sentiments in case one of the crackheads had converted in jail—was hopefully all the shield needed to keep from hearing about Curtis' life. If the book wasn't so thick, it would've been torn in half then stuffed in both ears. I was too wrapped up in my own problems (stuff with the girlfriend, *blah blah blah*) to want the complication of knowing about anyone else's.

The nasal whine of his Texas twang cut through my distractions.

"Well, *Ah* was really kinda hopin' that y'all would be able to...no, but...*Ah* know how much it costs...*Ah* can 'preciate that...*Ah* underst—...*Ah* said *Ah* understand...that's why *Ah'm* here...*Ah'm* tryin' to get better so *Ah can* be there for the kids...*Ah* realize it ain't easy for ya...shit...they ain't...they ain't gonna file charges, are they?...are they?...put 'er on the phone..."

I listened to Curtis speak to one of his daughters. He gave her '*a good talkin' to*,' as they say down here in Texas. I counted three physical threats, one

68

couched in a physiological impossibility, and still the rant ended with, "Sure, Daddy loves you, too."

Getting off the phone, he wandered by my desk. Curtis was obviously desperate to tell me what his family had the audacity to burden him with while he was living several hours away, trying to concentrate on his recovery.

Curtis stalked across the lobby like a man tormented. No, make that: *like a man trying to imitate the same act he had seen various actors do as they portrayed tormented characters in movies*. He ran his hands through his thinning hair, grimaced aloud a few times, licked his lips as loudly as possible, paced quickly, *etc*.

I didn't take the bait. I refused to say, '*Gosh, what's troubling you, old chum?*' to such a hackneyed attempt to grab my interest. Having already worked here for six months, I was well versed in all the ways the desperate and pathetic tried to suck you into their dramas. I had learned the hard way how difficult it was to get them to shut up once they had the limelight.

Curtis kept mugging for the camera. Compared to all the drama-queens I had already encountered, Curtis's need for gut spilling was strictly amateur shit. It was going to take a better display than that to drag me from my book.

Realizing that his act was failing to hook me, Curtis upped the ante. "*Ah* know what she said. They wouldn't tell me, but *Ah* know what she said."

Like '*Ah*' gave a crap what somebody said that involved the guy. Curtis had not only proven himself incapable of doing anything right around here—from making curfew to mopping a floor—but had also committed the sin of passing on his Fuck-Up genes to way too many offspring.

"*Ah* can't believe she said that."

I concentrated harder on the book. My attention would be warranted only if this anonymous '*she*' had ordered Curtis's retroactive vasectomy. Then my response would be to applaud her civic-minded decision-making.

"*Ah* know what she said," Curtis repeated. "My little girl was on the bus, and she got in a fight with another girl." There you had it; the guts got spilled whether anyone asked or not. *Jesus*, our species is desperate for attention.

But...as long as child-on-child violence was involved, I decided to fake interest.

"Your kid bite the other one?" Biting had been long considered a traditional fighting technique of lower-class kids here in the Deep South.

"*Naw*," Curtis smiled once he realized that he had his audience. "Just shoved 'er on the bus."

"Oh." How disappointing.

"But they still called the cops on 'er. Took 'er to the station and everything."

"For a kid-on-kid shoving match?" *Shit*, I was glad they didn't do that back when I was in junior high.

"Yeah," Curtis made an obvious production out of clenching then unclenching his fists. "And they wouldn't tell me what the girl said. They wouldn't tell me what the girl said!" I wondered if Curtis realized that he had just repeated himself. Probably not. The guy had obviously fried a few too many synapses during his partying days.

"*Ah* know what she said," Curtis spoke through gritted teeth (he was getting unbearably cheesy). "She probably said: '*Your daddy's a crackhead!*'"

Curtis paused, waiting for my reaction.

"Well," I said, "You are."

"What?"

"I said you *are* a fuckin' crackhead. That's why you're here!"

Curtis put on an air of offense. "I'm here to take care of my family!"

He had come to the wrong person for pity. "You're takin' care of your kids from five hours away?" I asked. "Neat trick."

He shot back what he thought was an irrefutable retort. "*You* don't know how hard it is to raise a family."

I returned the volley. "Then next time don't breed so much."

A real from-the-heart sentiment. From my heart straight into his.

Curtis was knocked temporarily speechless.

It would have been nice if it was longer, but no, only temporary.

"*Ah...Ah* can't believe you just said somethin' so cold."

Did he want me to repeat it? Because proliferate breeding by poor drug addicts really burned me up.

Stupid, *selfish* motherfuckers! Too goddamn stupid to use birth control, and too selfish to think beyond how happy they were to have another little clone of themselves. It would be real fucking cute in five-to-ten years when Curtis' neglected brood were out mugging the other kids.

Hell, it's not just children raised in poverty by drug addicts that the world could do with less of. It's children, period. No one's ever convinced me that people were such a great idea that there should be more of us. We as a species can be amusing at times, but any animal that came up with shit like nuclear weapons, religion and the forty-hour workweek needed a pretty good lawyer to argue that its pros outweighed the cons.

"Every one of those kids was a gift from God!" Curtis said.

"They were a gift from your inability to use birth control," I countered.

Curtis opened then closed his mouth several times like he was going to say something, but—cursed with a burnt raisin for a brain—nothing happened. Frustrated by his own lack of verbal acuity, Curtis stormed off.

"Try not to spread any more of your seed while you're down here!" was called after him.

It was meant in the best way possible, but I don't think he heard me.

5:49pm
NO PLACE FOR THE SENSITIVE

Undercooked chicken was on the menu for dinner again. The last batch of it had resulted in a rather traumatic experience, but the clients weren't the types to learn from past experience. They just dug right in, hopefully developing their first useful cases of tolerance.

"It taste a little better this time," Robert told me, licking sauce from his fingers. "Probably just more barbecue on it."

Wanting to avoid another case of salmonella poisoning, I gave the meal a pass and decided to do a little scavenging in the kitchen.

Our high level of cuisine had resulted in three cases of mass food poisoning in the past month. Around half the clients had woken up at two in the morning last Sunday, spewing from both ends. Twenty-seven sick men in a facility with only six toilets upstairs and two down is a recipe for a particularly nasty brand of trouble.

Luckily, I'd been working at the rehab for a while, and had developed something of a cast-iron gut. I could feast on bat guano, chug pure aspartame and almost tolerate the food served here. Instead of the killer combo that had felled most of the clients, all I had was a vicious case of the shits.

Work was the last place I'd wanted to be stranded in the bathroom. For a solid hour-and-a half I rocked back and forth in bowel-churning agony in the downstairs bathroom. I alternated between worrying that whatever butt-bacteria the homeless brought in could eat through the layers of toilet paper on the seat, and then screaming *"Occupied, Motherfucker!"* at the desperate souls who wandered downstairs in search of an empty stall.

For this little bit of unpleasantness, I earned 12 dollars (before taxes).

The cook wasn't reprimanded for that case of mass poisoning. It wasn't the first time that sort of thing had happened. It wouldn't be the last, unless one of the clients cracked and beat the guy to death with a saltshaker. The cook was something of a pro at cutting corners in the kitchen. He ordered prison-grade food, then cooked and served and reheated and served and reheated and served the food long after it had gone bad.

Meat starting to smell? Nothing that a little more barbeque sauce won't fix! Why waste money on proper storage containers or luxuries like Saran Wrap when you could just leave the food sitting out on the counter overnight? Bring on the curdled milk! Pass the rotting vegetables! Have some seconds on that chicken from last Tuesday!

The cook was part of the giant client-fucking machine that took the three grand a month paid to stay here and gave them as little as possible in return. That was his job security. Three grand would score you a month's stay in a hotel room that you didn't have to share with four or five other addicts. For three grand you could find a residence that wasn't filled with bums and vagrants for half the day. And, most importantly, for three grand you could afford to eat somewhere without the fear that your meals would be considered illegal by most biological weapon treaties.

But hey, who really gives a shit how a bunch of junkies and crackheads got treated, right? Fucking scumbags. People who ripped off their own families for an armful deserved to get ripped off in return, right?

Sure seemed to be company policy.

In the back of the kitchen, I picked through crates of fruit. Figured that making a dinner out of apples would do in lieu of the poultry that I recognized from a few days back.

The apples were all picked up and turned over. There was a naive hope that at least one of them would be edible.

Three minutes of inspecting produce and not an unspoiled one in the bunch.

Thinking that maybe the cook had something edible stashed back in his office, I worked the chain off the door and flicked on the lights. The office was a narrow room, barely bigger than a closet, but still larger than the so-called 'Tech Office' upstairs.

Roaches scattered with the light, then realized that they outnumbered me and went about their business. I scanned the shelves, hoping for a spare box of cereal, when my eyes settled on a delicious surprise. A large hunk of roast beef, already cooked and resting in a pan of grease, was sitting on the shelf.

Just sitting there. Just chillin'.

Roaches scaled the thing, reached the summit, used their antennae to flick me off and then scurried down the other side. Unless I missed my guess, I was looking at tomorrow's dinner. A mental note was made to bring a sack lunch to work the next day. And, unless I kept missing guesses, that was the cook lying on the office floor.

He was an old black man, curled up in the fetal position, and still wearing his apron and hair net. The guy might've been unconscious, but at least he was still obeying a few health regulations.

"Hey, man." I nudged him with my shoe. "You okay?"

He moaned slightly and vomited. Nice.

It was at this point that I noticed the heavy reek of booze in the air. Worried, I gave myself a discreet sniff. Surprisingly, it seemed come from somewhere else.

I looked down at the cook as he managed to roll himself over onto his stomach. "Is that you?" I asked.

Not one for verbal communication, he vomited again in reply.

At a loss for anything else to do, I went and rounded up the clients. Figured I'd bring them in for a look at their food, the roaches and the guy who let one eat the other.

They were all pretty pissed off and swore justice. Management was contacted and complained to, but shit was never done about it.

Why should there be, when there was money to be saved?

6:07pm
ANOTHER ONE OF GOD'S LITTLE TRICKS

I called him *Sloth*, after the character from *The Goonies*. He looked like someone had tried to bring Frankenstein's monster to life by using crack instead of lightning. The left side of his face had started to run a bit like candle wax.

I never used James' nickname to his face. Not only because he was a giant of a man who could crush my head using only three fingers; I just figured that he'd probably heard similar remarks a million times before. It may be tough to trust people with things like your money or affections, but you can always count on them finding your weak spots with laser-sighted accuracy.

He called me '*Einstein*' because our rehab makes a pretty decent setting for the kingdom of the blind. "I likes givin' people names," Sloth explained. I decided that as long as it wasn't followed by a punch to the groin, he was welcome to call me whatever he wanted (and it had to beat Jack's nickname of '*Asshole*'). The only thing standing in his way was the challenge of remembering it.

Each time we saw each other Sloth would call out, "Hey, wassup...uh...uh...*Einstein*!"

"Yo...uh...uh... *James*!" I'd reply. Not sure if the crack had rotted his brain or if he was born sub-intelligent (or if, like most of the clients, it was a mixture of the two). One thing for certain, though, motherfucker could play the piano like somebody had shoved Chopin's ghost up his ass. He had a wide-ranging repertoire, and his execution was nearly flawless.

"What you wanna hear?" he'd bellow at me from the piano in the chapel.

I'd call back, "Gimme some Beethoven, bitch!" And Sloth would pound out something totally unrelated, like a Billy Joel song. He couldn't match compositions and composers any better than most crackheads. Asking for Bach might get you Tchaikovsky, a request for Brahms might score Philip Glass' oeuvre. Like your average philistine, Sloth didn't have a clue when it came to the labels of classical music. Or any music, really. I could've asked for *Rock the Casbah* and he would play the *Moonlight Sonata*. I don't think he even knew what he was doing. Or how he did it.

Sloth couldn't read music. The guy only knew pieces he'd heard before, which he could then play back perfectly. He was like a big, dumb, black jukebox that ate your quarters and then spat out songs at random.

It took me a while to realize how clueless Sloth was about what he was doing. It first occurred to me when I noticed how he answered every question about the song just played with a shrug and a "*Dunno*."

Sloth was an Idiot Savant in the purest sense of the word. He was thick as a fucking brick, quasi-literate at best, couldn't even speak Ebonics that well and had the social skills that God gave a crippled amoeba. But *Jesus*, that guy could play the piano better than most of us play with ourselves.

Not sure if that made up for his being short-changed in every other aspect, but it's not like life really gives you a choice in these matters.

6:16pm
RAPE THE HORSES AND RIDE OFF ON THE WOMEN

There was a bloodstain on the sidewalk in front of the rehab. It hadn't fully dried when I showed up over two hours late for my shift. The clients told me, "Man, you went and missed all the fun."

The blood belonged to Corey. He spilled it there by winning the nose-diving contest he'd held with himself. Number one in a field of one.

This was how they explained it to me: Corey had been rambling at his half-way housemates at the crack-appropriate speed of about two-hundred words per minute. Suddenly, his eyes rolled up into his head, and the stream of words petered out into a mumbled slur. Corey toppled forward, thankfully remembering to catch himself with his face.

He broke his nose, got a nice boo-boo on his forehead and scored a free ride in the ambulance for his troubles. He's probably fine, but no one's that concerned about it.

The puddle of blood Corey left behind, however, had garnered interest. It was pretty impressive. Myself and a few clients stood around the puddle, objectively discussing it's size, shape and other properties like it was a piece of coffee table art.

Not bad, but seen better, was the general consensus.

Few things can gush blood with the sheer volume of a head wound. Severed limbs, maybe. Or two simultaneous head wounds. Whatever the case, Corey had relapsed in the manner most beloved by other clients and those of us on staff: *Entertainingly*.

There's no enjoyment to be gotten from someone who packs their bags and sneaks out of the facility, filled with shame at having succumbed to their addiction. Clients who phone in to slur out a lame excuse as to why they won't be returning that night are dull. Junkies who get busted by the bad luck of a random piss-test don't make for decent anecdotes. What we like to see here, what'll keep us chuckling for days, is when somebody fails and fails *big*.

I blessed Corey's unintentionally generous heart for giving everyone a topic of conversation for the night. Five different people did their Corey impressions for me, eyes rolling up into their heads and toppling forward. They caught themselves in time, unlike the Crackhead of the Hour, who was probably still at the hospital.

I wondered if anyone had noticed that he was about to fall over. Maybe somebody saw that Corey was swaying dangerously, maybe the thought of catching him crossed their minds as he tipped over. Maybe not.

More likely, everyone sat on the front porch and watched as he got ready to kiss pavement. Why not? The closest anyone here comes to helping their fellow man is when they rat out another client for using. But, I doubt that squealing really counts as a good deed. Especially since it's usually done out of a strong sense of jealousy that the other guy is getting high and they're not.

6:22pm
SELF-ACCLIMATING SYSTEMS

I was regaling the clients gathered around my desk with the visit to my girl-friend's family the previous night.

"Motherfuckers poisoned me!" I said, and the clients laughed.

One of the crackheads replied, "I poison yo ass, too, you come near *my* daughter!" And they all laughed even harder.

It had been yet another installment of Ray's adventures in humility, guest-starring his girlfriend. I'd gotten violently ill at her parents' place. It had to be food poisoning, since I didn't feel like I could paint the walls with my own vomit until after dinner.

In the interest of not being known as '*the guy who was violently sick that one Labor Day*,' I'd done my damnedest to ignore the pain and keep smiling. That's a tough thing to do when your food is fighting just as hard to come back up as you are to keep it down.

It was a pity, since the ribs and side dishes had to be some of the best god-damn food I had eaten all year. Well-seasoned, tender enough to fall apart in your mouth, it beat the living hell out of the cereal and prison food I'd been living off of at work.

Then, about ten minutes after dining, I felt my stomach do a few spastic jolts, and had to clamp down on my throat to keep from ralphing everywhere. Projectile vomiting is typically frowned upon at family gatherings, and it would've seemed pretty ungrateful to spray my girlfriend's family with the food they had just fed me. I'm not the casual *puke-and-party* type, so I just breathed deep, kept my throat clenched, and refused to let myself be sick.

It was a real shitty way to spend the next two hours.

After a series of good-byes that seemed to last an eternity (as everything does when you're trying not to vomit on the person talking to you), we finally drove off. I made my girlfriend stop at the first gas station we saw. It was a putrid filth-hole, but you can ignore a lot of uncleanliness when you're disgorg-ing an entire day's worth of food. Apparently my system can't handle nice things anymore.

(I told my girlfriend it must have been a bug I picked up at work.)

The clients thought that me puking was the funniest goddamn thing they'd heard in months. Riotous, whooping laughter ensued. I had to keep repeating the story for each new person that walked by the desk and asked, '*Whuzzo funny?*'

We must've been on the fourth retelling when the phone rang. It was my girlfriend; she was in the area, and did I want her to bring me some dinner?

Well, *hell yes*, I did!

"*Pretty please, Beautiful,*" I said in my sappy, singsong voice. We said our cutesy goodbyes and I hung up the phone.

The clients all stared at me with huge grin on their faces. "'Dat was pussy," Robert declared. He was smiling so big you'd think that we had switched places, and I was going for his chemo treatments while Robert got blown after work.

"That was pussy," I confirmed, showing that I spoke fluent Male. "And I don't want any of you creepy bastards hanging around when it shows up."

6:29pm
BE THE CHANGE YOU WANT TO SEE IN THE WORLD

Sunday night is check-in time at the rehab. All the junkies, crackheads and alkies granted two-day passes came back from wherever they spent their week-end fighting temptation. Check-in officially occurred upstairs in the TV room at seven o'clock sharp. A minute late and your ass got locked out (of the TV room, that is).

Sunday was also the day we checked to see who relapsed over the weekend. See who fought their addiction and lost. See who got bent over and fucked by the monkey on their back. Sometimes the guys were polite enough to call ahead and let me know that they'd blown their sobriety ("*I jusht had...zhe one mardini...*"). Sometimes they tried to fake sobriety when they arrived.

And, if I'd learned one thing at this job (besides how to change a prescription for antibiotics into one for Xanax, or how to still shoot up if you're locked in a bathroom without your rig), it's that it was damn hard to act normal after smoking a fat rock. There was something about the twitching and bloodshot eyes that gave you away.

"Motherfucker been smokin' like Sittin' Bull," Jack would say. And then, of course, blame me when Gim asked who'd been calling the clients '*mother-fuckers.*'

I once had a client nod out on my desk. Mid-sentence. One second Jamie was chatting with me as he signed back into the building—talking a little slow, but coherent—and the next he collapsed onto the desktop. Barely missed dial-ing the phone with his forehead.

I just pushed him off onto the floor and laughed. No condemnation or lec-tures from me. They're not my style. And besides, that day I had downed three Bloody Marys and the same number of bong rips before coming to work.

I was laughing about a lot of things that day.

TERTULLIAN PROMISED THE PLEASURES OF HEAVEN
WOULD INCLUDE LAUGHING AT THOSE IN HELL

The bag of medication was set down on the desk next to the phone. I opened the bag and rooted through the vials. Serequel, Celexa, Trazadone, Risperdal, Adderal, and a few others. Thanks to Zack, some pharmaceutical executive was buying his kids a new yacht for Xmas.

Jack chuckled to himself as he strolled away from the desk, leaving me to count all the meds by myself. The last thing I heard as he escaped responsibility down the back hallway was a mumbled, "Motherfucker open his own pharmacy."

"Well, young man," I smiled up at Zack, "Hope you brought enough for everybody."

Zack gave his ponytail a nervous tug and tried to smile. He failed. As usual, I had succeeded only in amusing myself.

Hell, good enough.

Zack obviously wasn't too happy to leave his family after the Thanksgiving holiday. Most of the junkies seemed unenthusiastic about abandoning their loved ones to come back to the rehab. But, hell, at least they had families to visit. Twenty-seven clients went absolutely nowhere over the holiday.

Most of America was eating turkey with their families, and our cook didn't even bother coming in on Thanksgivings to feed these guys. They just sat around the building, moping and feeling even more sorry for themselves than usual. One asked me if it was true that the suicide rate went up during the holidays.

I had replied with another question: *'That desperate for any kind of company?'*

(Yeah, I'd been there for Thanksgivings, too; no such thing as a holiday at this fucking company)

This weekend had been depressing for them, but it wouldn't be as bad as spending Xmas in a rehab. The holidays lose their customary cheer when spent in our linoleum hallways, empty except for a few other people of the unloved variety. Bad enough to be a crackhead, but realizing that you're not even well liked in comparison to your fellow addicts has to be tough on what's left of the ol' self-esteem. The relapse quotient skyrockets.

The clients don't know any of this yet, but I remember it from when I'd just started here last Xmas.

The holidays produce enough melancholy on their own. Adding institutionalization into the mix was hardly going to turn those frowns upside down. Some of these bastards were in for one intensely miserable time. Xmas alone in rehab. They didn't see it coming, but I knew it was inevitable. The heavy stink of fatalism was in the air (along with that goddamn sewage smell).

Everything in this place had the weight of inevitability dragging it down. You knew what would happen, and you could see it coming a mile off.

Eventually, everyone here will leave. Eventually, everyone here will relapse. Eventually, I'll get caught looking at porn or showing up intoxicated and get fired. Eventually, I'll end up in one of these places, myself. Eventually, Robert's cancer will come back. Eventually, we'll all get old and die. Eventually, the earth will fall into the sun.

Everything's falling apart, everything's turning to crap, and all our attempts to reverse or slow the process are just band-aids on a gushing stump wound. It's the second law of thermodynamics. Give anything enough time and it'll fall to shit. The colors fade on the Sistine Chapel. Wind and rain grind the mountains to dust. The American dollar plummets in value. *The Simpsons* stops being funny.

It happens.

What happens?

Shit happens.

So deal with it. Cope. Adjust like the sentient being you are. When you know that Rome's going to burn, there isn't a goddamn thing to do but strike up the fiddle and maybe dance the Cotton Eyed Joe while the tenements go up in flames.

And then laugh like hell when they feed the Christians to the lions for it.

Consider it like watching a historical movie. Sure, everything may be going tolerably okay-ish right now, but you *know* that's temporary. Things are guaranteed to get worse. Eventually the slaves *will* end up crucified along the Appian Way. Bambi's mother *will* get shot. Everything *will* end on one hell of a down-note.

It can be seen coming a mile off, but there isn't shit to be done about it except shutting your eyes and trying not to pay attention. Stick your head in that sand and wait for the badness to end.

But, if you've got that car-crash fascination going, if you can't help to watch it all crumble, then *do* try to see the funny side of things.

It occurred to me to send special Xmas cards to everyone stuck here over the coming holidays. It would be a little something to add holiday cheer to an otherwise dismal time. The tiniest bit of light to ward off the darkness of spending the holidays in this desolate place. It wouldn't be much at all, but it'd be nice. Maybe I'd bake some cookies for everyone, too.

Twenty seconds later the idea was abandoned in favor of a much simpler plan. I would just be grateful that, out of everyone who'd be spending the holidays alone here, one of them wouldn't be me.

Instantly, I felt better about everything. Nothing was solved. Nothing had been improved. Nothing had changed but my outlook.

Hell, *Mission Accomplished.*

6:57pm
SOMEONE ELSE MIGHT NEED THE WOOD

Corey's wife walked after him into the rehab. He had a dark look on his face, and not just because his skin was one of the deeper shades of black possible. I never really noticed the subtle color gradient on people before working around a bunch of black guys. God, they can be obsessive about it.

Corey reeked of guilt and fright. Like a child caught playing with himself. Like the priest had burst from the confessional and shouted, '*Holy Shit! You'll never guess what this pervert just told me!*'

Corey's nose and forehead were bandaged from his concrete pratfall of the previous day. His damaged appearance was the perfect match for his wife. She had an angry mouth, body like an overstuffed pillow, and a face that never had the chance, even in youth, to be beautiful. Tears dripped from her eyes.

"Baby, *please*," Corey whined quietly as possible.

"You *made* me do this!" she hissed loud enough to get everyone's attention. That, we soon found out, was the point. There were about eight us in the lobby: myself, Jack, Robert, Paul, Pike, and a few other junkies. We all stopped to tune into the living soap opera. Everyone digs drama, so long as they can sit back and watch without being dragged into it.

Voice raised and cracking, she said, "I want y'all to hear what I got to say to this man." There was no way we would have missed it. This promised to be good. Nothing's more entertaining than public humiliation. "Corey," she said, as he tried to shrink into himself, "You have let me down for the last time. I have *tried* to stand by you. I have *tried* to do the right thing by you. The Lord knows I've tried."

This was her in a textbook feat of self-crucifixion. Nothing I hadn't seen my own mother do countless times, growing up. Just another variation on the endless theme of self-pity. Sometimes I think it's the only thing our species does well (except for making war, of course, and maybe French fries).

"*Baaay-beee*," he said, and the tears started seeping from his eyes.

"But you have *let me down* for the last time, Corey. I love you. Jesus knows I love you, but you too sick and I can't stand to be with you no more. *No more*, you hear me?"

Well, the speech was crap. But, considering that she had stayed with Corey after he had fucked up three times previously, the lady was obviously no Rhodes scholar. Expecting Pulitzer-quality speechwriting from her was obviously asking a bit much. It made me think that there might be a decent business opportunity ghostwriting tell-off speeches for the terminally ineloquent.

"I can't be with you no more. You outta my life for good."

Corey was blubbering by this point, and some of the junkies started to look away. Even Jack ducked his head, hiding the scene behind the bill of his cap. Watching public humiliation was one thing, but emasculation was something that no man enjoys. We're all so sensitive about our own balls that we hate to see another man lose his. Unless, of course, we're the one taking them.

It reminded me of fights back in junior high. The inflicting of pain was all well and good until one party started crying, and then it was just embarrassing.

Still, sitting on the lobby's couch, I was riveted. Something good had to come of all this emotional trauma, even if it was only a moment's entertainment for my jaded ass.

"Goodbye," she said, starting to blubber herself, and pushed past Corey to rush out the door.

It was a decent exit, or it would've been had she hopped in her car and peeled out into traffic. Instead, Corey's wife sat in her car, parked right outside the door, and wept with her head on the steering wheel.

Corey, the focus of all this unhappiness, didn't even get that far. He didn't run from the lobby. Didn't slowly trudge upstairs. He just stood in place, crying and snuffling. Still on display, but now an exhibit that everyone wished would hurry and close down.

Nobody looked at him. As much as Corey may have wished earlier for the ground to open up and swallow him, we were all wishing twice as hard for it to happen now. His suffering had turned grotesque.

The more progressive parts of the modern world have caught on to how the notion that Boys Don't Cry is unhealthy bullshit. But still, there are quite a few of us who were raised with the notion. The sight of a weeping male makes a lot of people uncomfortable. The prejudices of youth can be tougher to toss than we'd like to admit.

I watched Corey weep for a while. Why he was still hanging around after his public emasculation was hard to say. Perhaps he was waiting for some consolation, some words of encouragement. Someone to say, '*Don't worry, man; it'll be okay.*'

If so, he was disappointed. Corey had made a leper of himself, an emotional pariah, and now no one wanted to get close. We all just wanted him to vanish.

I made a mental note of this, and decided to schedule my next emotional breakdown for somewhere else. A place where traumatizing events would at least rate a hug.

7:07pm
PAVLOV'S PEOPLE

Sloth rushed up to the front desk. It's the dark center that the junkies' sick little world revolved around. "Ray!" he pleaded. "You gotta loan me a buck, man!"

I was a little scared by his agitation. "Why do I *gotta*?"

"My girlfriend outside, man!" Sloth threw worried looks out the front door. "I swear I pay ya back, Ray! Just *quick*, man! I need a dollar!"

"*Okay*," I said, thinking about how much my own girlfriends always cost me. "Long as you don't gnaw through my neck or spend it on crack or—"

Sloth yanked the dollar from my hand and bolted through the door.

"There goes one excited mongoloid," I said to Jack, who'd walked into the lobby in time to witness Sloth's exit.

"He ain't got no girlfriend," Jack said. "There's just some ho at the bus stop sucks 'im off for eight dollars."

I shrugged. "Well, the economy being what it is…just didn't realize it was affecting the Freelance Pleasure Industry, too."

Jack sat down across from me. "Shit," he said. "You imagine the kinda girl gonna give an eight-dollar blowjob?"

I shook my head. "Fuck, I can't imagine *anyone* putting Sloth's dick in their mouth, for a thousand dollars, let alone eight." The thought of someone choking on Sloth's donkey-dick was banished from my mind. At least, I hope the guy was well endowed. He needed some extra compensation for being himself, something besides the piano skills.

"People do funny shit for the rock," Jack said. "Sometimes it works out to yo' advantage."

"Really?"

"Yeah. Used to know a girl who'd let ya fuck her, then give 'er a good beating, for thirty dollars."

"By *'beating,'* you mean, like, *kick her ass*?"

"*Mmm-hmmm.*"

I considered asking Jack if he'd ever made use of her services, but decided the question was pretty unnecessary.

Smiling, Jack reached down to adjust himself. I looked the other way. "Yep," he said. "That's what you call a night's entertainment."

7:10pm
CHILD-REARING IN MORIAH

Sam rolled the creaky leather chair up to my desk. He'd gotten tired of having to repeat himself, since he had a soft voice and my hearing was shit. Having just arrived at the rehab early Friday, it was his first weekend here.

Sam was a young guy with scruffy black hair. He was scrawny and goofy-looking in a way that told me that he had, at some time in his young life, probably skateboarded. Maybe listened to *The Misfits* or some other shitty middle school band. It's just a type that one learns to recognize. Sam was now sitting across from me due to a DWI acquired during a month he described as being, "Like *Leaving Las Vegas*, but without the attractive hookers."

Sam had spent all day wandering the drab hallways of the facility before deciding that I was the best way to pass his time. For my part, I didn't mind the company. The guy seemed to be about my age and had some of the same interests. We discussed Broken Social Scene albums, the playing style of Austin drummer Dave Evans and Hunter S Thompson's connection to the East LA Chicano uprising in the early '70s. We did the CD swapping that seems to be the modern equivalent of mutual butt sniffing.

Sam checked out fine so far.

"I always try to be up-front with girls about my bullshit," he said. By 'bull-shit,' Sam meant not only the continual alcoholism and drug abuse of the past 10 years, but also the traumatic upbringing caused by his old man going schizoid.

His dad's craziness had something of a religious bent to it. The old man became convinced that he was the biblical patriarch, Abraham, and his son was Isaac (with all the lethal cultural baggage this entailed). Also, that God wanted him to take his boy to first grade orientation in his underwear. Years later, Sam still found the public humiliations more traumatic than his dad's attempts to kill him in private. That's what we get for being social creatures.

Luckily, Sam's dad was able to talk God out of modeling his BVDs at Sam's elementary. Being a shrewd bargainer, his dad compromised by amusing the other parents with screaming '*Jesus!*' for twenty minutes straight.

('*You mean like one long Jeeeezuuuuus?*' I asked. '*No,*' said Sam. '*Lots and lots of Jesus.*')

"Yeah," I said. "The less propaganda you spew when you first hook up with somebody, the less ya have to worry about letting 'em down when you get tired of keeping up the Perfect You facade."

Sam agreed.

I continued, "Like, I always tell somebody when we first hook up about my problems with fidelity."

Sam looked puzzled. "*Fidel-?*"

"Faithfulness. Not cheating."

"Right, right," he said. "I knew that." Sam gave me a look like I had just announced my candidacy for the Second Coming. "You're kidding, *right?*" He settled back in his chair with a look of pure disbelief. The chair concurred with a long, drawn-out squeak of its own. "You don't...tell them...don't really...do that, really? *Do you?*"

"Well, *yeah*," I said. "Wouldn't want somebody dating me under false pretenses."

Made perfect sense to me. Might as well pick *something* in life to be honest about.

"Man...you just...that..."

"Seems a bit on the stupid side to you?"

"Well..." Sam ran a hand through his hair. He was obviously trying to think of a polite way to phrase this. "Well...yeah. Yeah, it really, really does. Honesty's one thing, but that..."

"Really fuckin' stupid?"

He nodded at me like I was his retarded kid brother.

Something sank in my chest. Damn, was he right? Was it stupid to be that open with somebody? Was it really such a bad idea to share the truth about yourself? Was it preferable to have a relationship built on desirable lies? Should you misrepresent yourself to people so they wouldn't know that you weren't as great as advertised? I wouldn't think so, but...

Why do you know so many women? You're not sleeping with anybody else, are you? Pleeeeze don't sleep with anybody while you're on vacation. You

82

didn't sleep with anybody while you were gone, did you? You sure you didn't sleep with anybody there? You didn't pick anyone up when you went out last night? You'd tell me if you slept with someone else, wouldn't you?' etc. Etc. ETC.

I thought about my girlfriend's worried whining, and how the questions had started coming more and more frequently for some god-knows-why reason (it *couldn't* have anything to do with my sleeping around on her). But really, what else did I expect besides a whole lot of worried nagging after telling her that I had a habit of doing the one thing that people fear their partner doing above all else? I always figured that people would want to go into relationships with their eyes wide open, but what else could you expect from them once the initial buzz wore off? What else could they do when it became apparent that you would do nothing but let them down, time and time again?

What else?

"Maybe you're on to something," I told Sam. "I think my relationship S.O.P. just changed."

Sam brushed a strand of black hair from his eyes. "It's okay if I don't believe you on that, right?"

I laughed. "No, I meant that I'm gonna lie even more than usual."

"Oh," he said. "*That* I believe."

7:15pm
NON-APOCALYPTIC EVENTS
AND LOOKING OUT FOR NUMBER ONE

The heater dying on a cold night apparently wasn't bad enough for the God of Shit Luck. Both of our microwaves decided that they'd toiled long enough in the service of hungry addicts and expired within minutes of each other. There was no other way to reheat the food that had been cooked in advance for the weekend. Cold junkies found themselves faced with the prospect of cold food and were understandably upset.

"*Da fuck dis shit?*" was the typically eloquent response.

I gave as non-committal a shrug as I could manage while shivering and pulling a blanket tighter around myself. "I just work here," was said in my best *don't-kill-the-honky* voice. "But if you guys are gonna revolt, I get to be that French chick in the dress with my right tit hangin' out."

Distributing extra blankets just seemed to worsen the prevailing mood. Nobody enjoys being in a cold, dirty building where other addicts wander around wrapped in multiple blankets. It's bad enough to live in a rehab/halfway house, but having it resemble a homeless shelter really does a number on everyone's morale.

I wasn't too happy with the state of affairs, either. Our stash of the one thing we have that didn't require heating, cereal, had dwindled to a few crumbs. I quickly polished them off to save the junkies from reducing themselves to desperate scavenging.

It looked like I would have to go down into the basement and break into the Christers' storage room. My grumbling stomach and sense of self-preservation told me it had to be done. It's bad enough having work as your primary food source. When that dries up, too, you start seeing visions of yourself on the cover of National Geographic, all swollen-bellied in the dirt with vultures lurking in the background.

The storage room downstairs was filled with pile upon pile of old clothes. It contained all the necessary supplies for looking unfashionable in any time period over the last fifty years. I picked a random spot and started rummaging. Tossed aside polyester suits and parachute pants, dug under tweed jackets and tie-dye shirts. Sure enough, stuck in a small freezer hidden under layers of unwanted crap and used footwear, the Methodists had a crapload of frozen sandwiches.

A food truck dropped off about a hundred pounds of donated sandwiches a week to the Methodists. I had always wondered why, when it came time to dole them out to the homelies, they seemed to run out so fast. Looked like the Christers were hoarding the sandwiches, and—from the expiration dates on some of them—had been doing so for some time.

What the hell? I had to wonder. Was this their anti-terrorist stash? Did they start hoarding food back during the Cold War and just couldn't break the habit? I had never known Methodists to be more weirdly apocalyptic than any other Christian sect, but, on the other hand, it's not like they had any greater claim to pragmatic rationality, either.

I grew up around a lot of Mormon kids. Sometimes we would play in their garage shelters, full of the canned goods and other non-perishables that their families kept in preparation for some upcoming apocalyptic event. Not sure what it was supposed to be, exactly. Nuclear war, maybe? They never said, and I lacked the proper security clearance as a nonbeliever. All I ever found out was that after this big-shit event there was expected to be a year of famine and horror, during which time the faithful would get the pleasure of chillin' in their garage shelters, praising the goodness of the Lord while living off creamed corn and Spam.

I can't help but think that there'd also be plenty of chuckling at how emaciated the heretics were getting outside. After all, there's no point in being the Elect of God if no one's around to whom you can feel superior.

If memory serves me well (and it rarely does), said apocalyptic event was supposed to occur sometime in:

1997.

So, like most things in this modern world, I guess it's just a little behind schedule.

I fished out a sandwich whose expiration date didn't scare me too much. Then, I heated it up in an old microwave I found underneath a card table. A stylish leather jacket was also appropriated.

I looked good and felt good.

Properly satiated, my ass toddled back upstairs. Everyone there was still bitching about the lack of edibles. "The fuck we 'sposed to do 'bout eating?"

84

I settled back into my desk and picked at my teeth. Good question!

Scratching myself for the fun of it, I tried to recall the advice my old man always used to give me. What was it? Something about...

Oh yeah!

"If I was y'all," I told them, "I'd start with cannibalizing the small and the weak."

7:19pm
MY GRANDPA COULDN'T GET IT UP IF HE TRIED

The girl, all slender 5'4" of her, turned and gave a fingers-only wave to my co-worker as she stepped out the door. Jack pretended not to notice her exit. I raised an eyebrow at him, hoping the explanation would prove more interesting than the book on theodicies I'd been reading.

Jack grinned like the world's naughtiest schoolboy as he sauntered over to the front desk, beaming that his old black ass could show up a young cracker like myself. He just stood there grinning, so I asked, "Well?"

Like I'd slipped a quarter into his coin slot, Jack came to life. He doubled over and slapped the edge of the desk.

"*Ooooooh-weee!*" he squealed. "In a chapel! That's *nasty*!" My fellow Tech was obviously on the verge of bursting with self-satisfaction.

I had been covering for Jack during the past half-hour while he and the mini-skirted girl absconded to the chapel. '*Covering*,' of course, meant sitting at the desk with my feet propped up, clicking the door-release button whenever someone tugged on the door handle. The usual.

For all I knew, Jack and his girl could've been in there saying their respective rosaries. The last thing I was going to trust was the insinuations of a seventy-something ex-crackhead. Working in a halfway house quickly taught you to not believe anything you were told. And junkies, whether practicing or recovering, told lies like bees made honey. Only faster and in greater quantities. It's just their nature.

One more time with *New Start Rule #1*: Never Trust a Junkie.

But just because I had my personal reservations about whatever bullshit Jack was about to try on me, didn't mean I wouldn't play along. Everyone has their own little persona they try to present to the world. Being skilled with the alternate sex is a common facet of the male facade. So long as it's not annoying and you're in a generous mood, hey, what's the harm in playing along?

Besides, she wasn't the first young girl to come visit Joe.

"Not bad," I said. "She's cute, man. And she was on the clock, too."

"Ya know, you right!" Jack said. "I do believe George just paid me for a bit of fun!" The thought of our miserly CEO coughing up money to get his employees a little play was way too funny for us. We both convulsed with laughter. Jack's high-pitched seesaw of a laugh dueled with my own impression of a rhino having seizures.

Once we finally stopped laughing. I asked, "Was she my age?"

"You twenty-two?" asked Jack.

Dear fucking Christ! "Twenty-three, actually." And here I was, single and miserably celibate. It almost made me wish there was a God, so I could introduce my foot to His crotch.

"Close enough," Jack said. The smile on his face got even bigger as he sat down on the couch across from me. He was the happiest black man I'd seen all month, but it's not like there was a lot of competition in this place.

Worried that Jack's good mood would interfere with everyone else's suffering, I decided to take him down a notch: "Any particular reason why your women always show up here on payday?"

7:22pm
GLASS HOUSES IN A WORLD WITHOUT WINDEX

Jack said he'd cover for me while I '*took care of important business.*' So, thanks to him, I was able to go to the movies on the company's dime. The first 45 minutes of watching *Lost in La Mancha* covered the ticket price, and every minute after that I was getting paid to stare at the screen by the kindly folks who employed me.

My Sunday shift lasted sixteen hours, from four in the afternoon Sunday to eight o'clock Monday morning. That's a while to breathe the hopeless contagion of the rehab, so I figured everyone would understand if I took a two-hour break somewhere in the middle. And if they didn't understand, I knew they could at least be counted on not to care.

My ex showed up to grab me after Sunday check-in. She had finally given in to my requests to '*just hang out and chat.*'

Real kind of her. Especially since I was getting tired of my own pleading. And all the blatant bribery was threatening to turn expensive. Had she not been sending back all my presents unopened, there's no way I could ever have returned them. Not even for in-store credit.

At a bit past seven there was a commotion outside the front door. I knew that somebody had either dropped a two-pound crack-rock on the sidewalk or a female was in the immediate vicinity. A woman's presence is a disruptive element in a building full of hard-up males, many of whom were just beginning to feel their sex drives return after years of drug-induced dormancy. All unescorted women over the age of 11 and under the age of sixty got mobbed upon setting foot on the premises. My ex had the additional bad timing of showing up right as a group of junkies were pouring out the front door.

I called to Jack that my ride was here, and hurried outside to snatch my ex from the mob of swinging dicks. "All right, back off, fuckers." I elbowed my way through the crowd. "She's with me!"

The clients booed and jeered as I walked off with my ex. It was likely that I'd have to listen to them go on about her once I got back.

Crackhead: *Man, Ray, that yo girl?*

Ray: *Ex-girl, actually.*

Junkie: *Cool! Is she single?*

Ray: *Along with being too good for you, yes.*

(general uproar at being slandered by uppity white boy)

Crackhead: *Goddamn, the booty that girl got!*

Ray: *Hey fuckers, see previous response!*

Typically, I wouldn't mind that a couple dozen guys were going to be stroking themselves that night to my ex. Flattering for most of the parties involved, in its own little way. A lot of the clients tended to get excited whenever anyone came to see me, whether it was a girlfriend, my mom, or one of my sisters. I'd even pretended to give numbers out to a few of the more persistent ones (which would invariably connect them with the day care center for St. Jerome's Catholic Church).

Tonight I just wasn't in the mood for their desperation. It reminded me too much of my own.

Staring up at the screen next to my ex, I fought the urge to grab her hand. There's a thing or two to remember when hanging out with an ex. The most important of these to carve into the frontal lobe of your brain is to Maintain Personal Space.

Yes, yes, yes, it's obvious that *'personal space'* has to be the most horrible concept ever conceived by the human mind (next to genocide, lite beer, and regressive tax structures). The idea that we shouldn't come within three feet of each other goes a ways toward making our society the sick place that it is. In such a sterile environment, it's no wonder that so many people turn to drugs in order to just feel *something*.

Keeping this 'personal space' concept in mind, however, should prevent you from making the huge *faux paus* of acting like you did while dating. Basically, it'll keep your stupid ass from being absent-mindedly affectionate towards your ex. Maybe I'm the only fucker on the planet who has this problem, but I doubt it.

Lodged in your body's memory is how to physically respond to the presence of everyone you know. Around some people your body automatically remembers to cringe. Around others it knows to puff itself up. Around those it was used to rubbing all over, well…

At the movie I had to stop myself from trying to hold my ex's hand. Afterwards, I had to consciously keep from slipping my arm around her waist. Tell myself not to touch her hair. Not to kiss her cheek. Not to smash her head in from the sheer frustration of it all.

Having to reassert the concept of personal space after you'd finally overcome it with somebody was probably the lousiest part of a defunct relationship. Like playing *Risk* and only conquering Rhode Island, then having to give that up as well. Back to square one in that *You vs. The World* thing.

It bugs the crap out of me. I'm always like, *'goddamn, weren't you one of the few people in the world with whom I could dispense with that sick, keep-your-distance bullshit?'*

But *whatever*. I had blown it with my ex, just like the junkies had burned their own bridges with their loved ones. They proved time and again that they loved their drugs more than their mates. I was apparently just an asshole. Myself and the junkies both had something else in our lives that we'd cared about more than the people we'd been with.

For some of us it was crack, for others it was our own selfish asses. Kind of understandable that our significant others would get sick of playing second fiddle to it. It looked like we'd all have to live with the consequences of our unsociable actions.

Movie over, my ex took me back to work. On the drive there she chain-smoked like hell. Cigarette after cigarette after cigarette. Sucking carcinogens like mother's milk. She didn't used to smoke. Not when we were together. But, I guess that after dating me lung cancer doesn't seem so bad.

We stopped in front of my work. The facility squatted on the side of the road, oversized cross on the exterior like a particularly pungent mausoleum.

Steeling myself with a deep breath, halfway out of the car, I told my ex that I missed her. I was sorry for what an ass I'd been. Sorry that I hadn't appreciated her like I should have. Sorry that I wasn't a good boyfriend. Sorry that I wasn't even a decent one. Sorry that I sucked the big one and didn't deserve a precious jewel like her.

Sorry that I was sorry that I was sorry that I was sorry.

Silence. She stared straight ahead.

Was I, I prompted, missed in return? Just a little?

My ex kept staring ahead, irritated at what she'd been dreading.

"*Get out,*" she said.

7:26pm
IF SELLING PISS FOR PROFIT IS WRONG, WHO WANTS TO BE RIGHT?

I asked Scott if he wanted me to turn on the faucet to help his urinating.

"*Please,*" he said, straining like his life depended on it.

His life didn't depend on his ability to piss quick and piss clean, but his place of residency sure did.

Scott had shown up for Sunday check-in in a funny mood. '*Funny*' meant that he was slurring his words, rambling incoherently, and generally making a relapsed spectacle out of himself. If Jack hadn't been around, if Scott's stupid ass hadn't been so obvious about his drugged-up state, I'd have let him get away with it.

So he was fucked up? So what? His life to ruin as he saw fit. What business was it of mine?

Right?

Isn't minding your own business part of the American way? Myself, I'm a non-interventionist at heart. M.Y.O.B. and all that. Had I been born Woodrow Wilson or FDR instead of the middle-class cracker that I was, I'd have been like, '*Eh, let the fuckin' Europeans kill each other. What else is new?*'

But I was working the Sunday evening shift with Jack, and Scott was rambling at the other clients about the Knights Templar and the International Jewish Banking Conspiracy and the healthy goodness of Quaker brand oatmeal. So, my hand was forced in the matter. I had to get some Financial Consultant-flavored piss out of the guy. I did that, or risked being too obvious about how little I had grown to care about my job.

Flaunting one's apathy *is* somewhat discouraged in most fields of employment.

Scott looked like a Cabbage Patch Kid grown up bad. He had a soft white face and easily tousled hair that would've rated a maternal hug, if only all the warmth hadn't been snuffed out of me months ago. Snuffed, buried, then dug back up to be raped and killed again.

What can I say, being around human suffering every day in this job did the same thing to your soul that cigarettes do to your lungs.

But...thankfully, I don't believe in the soul.

Standing over the toilet, Scott farted with the strain. He was really putting a lot more effort into this than was required.

"Ease up," I told him. "It's just the urine that I'm after."

He tried to laugh but only farted again. From where I slouched in the far corner of the bathroom, I could tell the guy was shaking. Somebody was going to be pissing a stream of pure narcotics, and we both knew it.

It wouldn't be the first time. Jack had told me about Scott's frequent visits to the facility over the last five years. He'd show up, try to get clean, and fail. Then he'd try again, and fail again. Try and fail, try and fail, *ad nauseum*.

Scott always paid in cash, though, so they always let him back in.

"You...you h-hear about Anderson?"

I didn't look up from cleaning my nails with the facility's key ring. Just stayed squatted in the bathroom's corner, looking at anything but Scott. "Anderson who?"

"Dave," he said. "Dave An-Anderson."

Oh. That guy.

Dave had been a client a few months back. He was an airline pilot and hopeless drunk all rolled into one affable package.

Nice guy.

Real friendly.

I liked him.

"He's dead," said Scott.

Ah well.

"It happens," I replied, and then had to know: "How'd it happen?"

Scott interrupted his grimacing for a second, "How'd what..."

Stupid fucking junkie. I pictured Dave standing next to my desk, telling me his horrible Polack jokes. I took a deep breath. It didn't help. "*Gee Scott*, I was wondering how the Ainu originally got to Japan so many centuries before the Koreans? Did they build primitive floatation devices or just evolve there from snow monkeys or—*How Did Dave Fucking Die?*"

"Oh…" Scott looked like he understood the question for a second, then it was gone like an alcoholic's paycheck.

"Cirrhosis?" I prompted. "Cancer of the kidneys? Liver give up and chuck itself out his ass?"

"*Oh!*" The light went back on in his eyes. "Dave! Yeah…no. No, Dave died in a car wreck. Church bus ran a stop sign. Decapitated him."

"No shit?" I was mildly impressed.

"*MM-hmm.*"

"Wow," I said. "Gimme some of that old time religion, huh?"

Instead of devising an insensitive remark of his own, Scott stopped trying to strain fluids into the plastic cup he was holding. He turned his head to look at me.

"How much do you earn here?" Scott asked.

I knew where this was headed. They'd warned us about it in training. "Starvation wages," I answered.

"Did you have to take a urine test to work here?"

My evaluation of workers' rights in America came packaged in a defeated shrug. "Ya gotta piss in a cup to work anywhere in this fuckin' country."

I had cheated on my own urinary analysis, but that wasn't any of Scott's business. I could smell the scent of filthy lucre, and since Scott had his own financial consulting firm to go with his pill addiction, I knew he was good for a decent amount. Still, I figured I'd play a little coy. "Why ya asking?"

"One hundred dollars," Scott whispered, still holding himself over the toilet.

"For what?" I asked innocently.

"*You know,*" he hissed.

"Do I now?" Just couldn't resist the opportunity to fuck with the guy.

Scott made a noise of exasperation. "Look—"

"Two hundred," I interrupted him. What the fuck, why not?

"All I have is a hundred-sixty," he whined.

Why not put my job on the line? This way, I could actually afford groceries for the month. Or a higher grade of pot. Booze that didn't come in plastic bottles. If my employers wanted me to honestly execute my duties, they should pay me a living wage.

"*Two hundred,*" I repeated, glancing at the bathroom door to make sure it was locked. "You can give me the other forty later tonight."

"Okay," Scott said, looking even more nervous as he zipped himself up.

I took the cup from him and whipped my dick out over the toilet. All that water running from the faucet had me needing to piss like hell.

"Get me that money by the end of the shift," I said, penis in hand, looking at Scott as sternly as I could. "Or you're *fucked.* Breathe a *word* of this to any-fuckin'-body…"

'*Didn't you used to be a nice person?*' asked a little voice in my head.

'*Nope,*' I told it. '*You must be thinking of someone else.*'

"Right," said Scott. He was now far, far away from his white-collar office. His addiction had taken him into a shadowy land distant from those respectable cubicles. A world where he paid young men to urinate for him. A world where he was mesmerized by the shriveled organ I held in my hand.

His staring was interrupting my attempt at pissing.

"*What*?" I asked. "It hypnotic or something?"

Scott turned increasingly bright shades of red and looked away.

The piss then started to flow. I occupied myself with trying to remember all the shit I had done at those Halloween parties the previous night. I vaguely remembered adopting a bottle of Jack Daniels to drag from party to party, and somewhere in there, people kept shoving blunts in my mouth. After the first few of those it got kind of hazy. A fellow partygoer claimed to see me doing a line of coke or two, but damned if I recalled.

Busy pissing for Scott's money, I also wondered if the Percodan I'd munched earlier would show up on the test.

7:54pm
ON THE IMPORTANCE OF ASKING FOR IDENTIFICATION

There was a round-table bullshit session in the lobby while Todd played everyone an acoustic parody of *Beat It* on his guitar. The topic of discussion: prison stints and why.

It was Paul's turn at the imaginary microphone. Thanks to how my horror of my job had developed into a form of car-crash fascination, I appreciated Paul with a connoisseur's eye. Any physical imposition that his height could give was offset by his twitchy movements, all sharp and jerky like he was living claymation. Paul looked like someone had sucked all the color and life out of Gumby and gave him a drooling problem thanks to the painkiller addiction that landed him here.

This time.

Paul's visit last winter was for alcoholism.

Obviously, the treatment didn't take too well. That's pretty common. Anyone making it through their stay here sober still has a pretty good chance of relapsing after they leave. This speaks worlds about the effectiveness of the program.

Paul had spent six months in the LA County Jail. He denied ever being ass-raped while incarcerated, but hey, I'd lie about it, too.

"I got off the plane in LA in full black-out mode, so I remember none of this," he said, adding in the excuse about being on antibiotics at the time. "But I knew I was supposed to meet my girlfriend downstairs, so I apparently dropped my luggage in the middle of the terminal and walked on down to her car."

Drool was wiped off Paul's chin with the back of his hand.

"Me and Cindy get in a big argument about me being sober enough to drive, so I went back to get my bags. When I got back outside I staggered up to the car that was at the curb, stuck my head inside and shouted at the woman:

'*Cindy, get out of the car before I beat yer ass!*' And she did and I hopped in the car and pulled off without her." He paused to wipe the drool off his chin again.

"Bitch call the cops on ya?" someone asked Paul, and there was a general shaking of heads. No matter what horrible shit the junkies put their loved ones through, they always regard the contacting of law enforcement as the ultimate betrayal.

"Got the cops called on me, all right," Paul resumed. "Big problem was: that wasn't my girlfriend's car and that *wasn't my girlfriend!*"

Six months in a cage.

8:25pm
GRAND SLAM JUNKIE

He spoke into the cell phone in a voice dripping with self-pity and rage. "I'm just trying my best to love you!"

Hearing his weak-ass whining, I cackled like a hag.

For somebody who'd spent so much time on the front pages of newspapers, this Local Boy Made Good was one sorry motherfucker.

Bagger (obviously not his real name, but that's par for the course in this book) was a big-time sports star with a big-time drug problem. An MVP for three years running, he had blown it all through repeated drug arrests, relapses and highly publicized jail time. Now he was here, sentenced by the courts as part of his parole (since the rich and famous don't stay long in jail) to spend a month at The Best Little Rehab/Halfway House in Texas.

Having a celebrity here wasn't entirely unusual. I mean, this isn't the Betty Ford Clinic, but I've seen my share of the famous here. Athletes, mostly. My boss, being ex-NFL himself, still had plenty of connections that netted the rehab some big-name clients. It was never anyone I gave a shit about, but it's hard for me to get excited about being around people who make millions from playing a fucking game. After all, we had dumb jocks back in high school. Meeting people who had gone professional with the act didn't exactly blow my little pink socks off.

A lot of the junkies, of course, were in awe of the athletes that ended up here. When Bagger first arrived he was bum-rushed for autographs. Everyone about shit themselves at how someone they had watched on TV was now slumming it in the same facility as them.

"Man, Curtis rushed up to the poor guy and asked him to autograph his fuckin' hacky-sack!"

Me and a few of the junkies were discussing Bagger's presence in their humble home while Bagger yelled into his cell phone further down the hallway. I was shaking my head at the stories about their housemates overreacting to a sports star.

"I didn't know they had professional hacky-sackers," I confessed. For all the attention I paid to pro sports, their existence was something of a possibility.

Hell, ESPN could show 24-hour lawn dart competitions and I'd never know about it.

"They don't," Robert said. "Curtis just an idiot." The other guys nodded in agreement.

"No comment," I said, grimacing at the number of kids to whom the guy had passed on his idiocy genes.

Bagger bellowed into his phone, *"Why won't you let me love you?"* The other clients cringed with sympathetic embarrassment, but I just rolled my eyes in contempt.

Corey had been walking through the lobby past our little group, but hearing that we were busy slandering other people, he decided to join in. "Y'all know that Johnson called his family to let them know Bagger was staying here."

A collective groan went up. So much for the facility's confidentiality clause!

'Stupid motherfucker,' was the term on everyone's lips.

"Surprised to hear you're not hero-worshipping the guy," I said to Corey. He was a pretty religious chap, so I figured the IQ necessary for admiring athletes was similar to the numbers required to have imaginary friends past the age of five.

"There's only one *supa-star* for me," Corey said, his eyes looking upward as he pointed towards the ceiling with reverence. "And that's *Jesus.*"

Another collective groan. I glanced up at the ceiling. When somebody mentioned their god while pointing up, I always expected to see something clinging to the ceiling like Spider-man.

"Fuck y'all," Corey said, and stormed off.

"Is that what Jesus would say?" I called after him.

In the background, Bagger was still whining, "Why do you always have to bring that up, goddamnit? I *said* I was sorry!"

"Look," I said, "So long as *he's* here—" I motioned back at Bagger, "—Dude gets the same treatment as the rest of you scumbags. End of story." There was a general murmur of agreement, with only a single '*hey!*' when someone caught the *scumbag* part.

"*Fuck you*, then!" Bagger yelled into his phone. We went silent, straining to hear the next part of the drama. "*Baby?...Hello?*" No matter how many times you've graced the cover of Sports Illustrated, there's apparently still a limit to the amount of shit people will take from you.

"*Goddamnit!*" Bagger yelled. I could hear him stomp towards the back of the facility, and then up the stairway.

"Yeah," Robert said, " I 'member what it like when I first got here, so everybody just treat him no different. He just like us."

Nods all around. It was unanimous.

A minute later Bagger came back through the lobby with Johnson in tow. I had always thought of Johnson as a muscular guy, but Bagger's bulk and height eclipsed him entirely. "Sign me out," he said to Johnson, who went to the front desk to do just that.

"*C'mon*, damnit," Bagger growled when Johnson took too long. Unable to wait another three seconds, Bagger stormed out the front door. Johnson ran after him.

We all watched the twin spectacles of submission and dominance as they got into the Hummer at the curb and sped off.

"*Wow*," said one of the guys said. "I want one of those."

"Not me," said Robert. "Already had me a puppy dog."

8:59pm
TURNING THE OTHER CHEEK,
IF ONLY TO MOON

Eddy loomed over my desk, big and wide with an excess of prison-honed muscles. He stuck out his hand. I flinched before realizing that he desired a mutual shaking of appendages. I looked at the proffered hand, then up at him. His face shown with self-congratulatory delight. He was proud of what he was doing, that much was clear.

I grasped Eddy's hand, twice the size of my own, and gave it a manly pump or two. His smile got even wider. He said, "You okay, man," as if bestowing a priestly benediction. "You all right."

Had I verbalized any sort of reciprocation it would have been a lie. So I just said, "*Thanks*," and left it at that.

Eddy had only been here a short while. In that time he'd already managed to lose his cool and toss a promise that he was going to '*beat yo white ass*' in the direction of *my* white ass. Eddy was under the impression that I was picking on him, and, *by god*, he wasn't going to take it anymore!

(This from somebody I've talked with only twice: once to ask how his weekend went, and once to remind him to do his assigned chore.)

It'd all gone a little something like this:

"I'm fuckin' sick of it!" Eddy screamed at me. Eyes bugged out. Nostrils flared. Hands clenched into very large fists aimed in my direction. I took a step back. "No more shit from you, motherfucker!"

Why the violent reaction? Beats me. Everybody tries to fill the drug-shaped hole in their life somehow. I guess Eddy thought he could do it through the random assaulting of cracker-ass employees.

He took another step towards me. "Gonna beat yo white ass into the *ground*!" I took another two steps back. Hoped I didn't look as scared as I felt.

His blow-up caught me by surprise. I wasn't expecting to segue from my question of how his weekend went to him screaming in my face. One second I was mentioning that his chore needed to get done, then the next thing I knew he was bathing me in angry spittle. And the *breath* that fucker had...

"Show all you motherfuckers who you're fuckin' with!"

I mean, I've got enough practice at being a dick that I'm *very* aware when I'm doing it. I felt pretty sure that wasn't one of those times. Eddy obviously disagreed. Fortunately, the large hunk of oak attached to our facility's key ring kept homeboy in his place.

I held it up in front of me. "You wanna try something?" I interrupted his screaming with my bluff. "Go right ahead." We were out in the back lot, gnats swarming the light posts over our heads.

He almost raised his fist, but stopped short. "You thinkin' of using that on me?" he asked, pointing at the cudgel. The fucker sounded almost offended, like I was violating the rules of etiquette established by centuries of more compliant weaklings.

An honest question deserved an honest response, so I said, "I know my defensive capabilities."

Grade school was the last time I'd been in a fight, and my skills had never improved much beyond the biting that was so effective back then. Maybe I could have pulled Eddy's hair, if he wasn't shaved clean.

Eddy came closer. Instinct told me to keep backing up. "I pays cash money to be here!" he shouted. "Three thousand a month and I don't gotta put up with nobody's shit!"

My heel bumped against the fence. He'd backed me up a good ten yards. "I could give a hemorrhaging *fuck*," I replied, voice calmer than I felt. "I get paid the same no matter where your stupid ass is."

"This 'cause I black, ain't it?"

Lovely. Of course everything in life has to do with one's melanin levels. Nice to know that if the crack hadn't made you paranoid enough, there was always the Black Persecution Complex.

"Sure it's because you're black," I told him. "All of us crackers have weekly meetings where we get together to watch NASCAR and discuss how to keep the brothers down."

Eddy reared back like he was going to swing at me. I reared back like I didn't want to get hit.

Jack picked that moment to break through the crowd that had formed around us—since there's always a crowd around two guys who might hit each other. Jack steered Eddy away, talking softly to him the whole time. Probably asking the guy to wait till the 4-12 shift was over (and Jack went home) before killing me.

"Don't worry, Ray," a few of the other addicts told me later (once they could no longer be of any help). "We wouldn't let him do shit to ya."

"Thanks," I said, a lot more relieved than I wanted to admit. I didn't know if Eddy would actually have tried to kill me, but I do know that everyone would have found it entertaining. Considering our size differences and my lack of fighting prowess, his pulping me wouldn't have been too difficult. At most, Eddy might've bruised one of his knuckles while giving my face a full-contact massage.

Or maybe the violence that had seemed so imminent wouldn't have happened. Maybe Eddy would have simply kept up the macho posturing till it deteriorated into him beating his chest and tearing up the surrounding foliage. Or, maybe he had been planning on making a few more threats and then walking off. Had he done so, *my* plan was to wait for his back to be turned before taking the cudgel and cracking him across the back of his skull.

I know, *I know.* It's never sporting to hit someone when their back's turned. But notions of fighting fair meant fuck-all to me when it would entail having to watch my own back at work. I'd be damned if I was going to wait for some crackhead to decide that today was the day he would take it no longer from his white oppressors...with Yours Truly as the franchise's local representative.

And besides, I find face-to-face confrontations pretty difficult when I'm stoned.

Despite our brief and acrimonious history, I wasn't too surprised when Eddy later offered me a handshake. I especially wasn't surprised to see how full of self-righteous pleasure he was at doing it. I had walked past the chapel earlier and, glancing in, noticed him kneeling on the floor. His head had been resting on the seat of a chair, hands clasped tightly above it, whining to his god about all the persecutions and tribulations contained in a life that he'd managed to fuck up enough to find himself here.

Apparently, his god told him to forgive those persecuting him (like me, for example) and to be as smug as possible while doing so.

Fucking sklavmoralist, I thought as we squeezed hands. But hey, if both of the delusions born from the lack of crack in his life (my persecutions and the god of the 12-Step) canceled each other out, then no harm done.

Still, as Eddy was walking away, self-satisfied for having turned the other cheek, I had to wonder if I should still give the back of his skull a good whacking.

9:09pm
CHORE TIME AT YOUR FRIENDLY NEIGHBORHOOD REHAB

It was past nine, and that meant it was time for the more industrious of the junkies to get started on their chores. Everyone living here had a chore. "Take Care of Your Community," as the signs posted on the walls read. It's odd to expect any form of civic pride out of people who used to rob and beat their neighbors for drug money, but changing old habits is what this place is supposedly all about.

Mops and brooms were taken from closets. Arms scarred with needle marks pushed them along the floor. Fingers that held red-hot crack pipes without feeling pain gripped the edges of toilet bowls and gave a half-assed scrub. Everyone had a chore to do, myself included.

My chore was to sit on my ass and watch the cleaning going on around me. It's tough, but I manage.

My chair was scooted out of the way to accommodate a mop being pushed by a client. He's a sweet guy, asking questions as he works around me: *How'm I doing? How's school? Did I get that flat fixed on my back tire? How'd my sister's birthday go?* I tended to forget that, like a lot of our guys, he's only been out of prison for the past month or two. He was in there for stabbing a guy to death in Vidor, TX. (*Never* say '*nigger*' around these people.)

Or so he claimed. Junkies tell lies like Starbucks sells coffee. Hence, *New Start Rule #1*: Never Trust A Junkie.

Junkies also have a great propensity for shirking responsibility. I can identify with that, but it also meant that I was supposed to go check to see if each one of these grown men had completed their assigned chore. If this made them like a bunch of over-grown teenagers, then following that simile made me the sorriest excuse for an authority figure imaginable.

There was a chart on my desk that everybody was required to sign after completing their chore. I was supposed to make sure the junkies had actually done their job before letting them sign it, but that's easily avoided with a wave of my hand and a simple declaration. "*Eh*, I trust ya."

I didn't, of course—*New Start Rule #1*—not any further than I could shotput my weight in crack. But, my apathy and desire not to have my reading interrupted outweighed any responsibility that I might've felt. If these guys didn't want to clean up their temporary home, if they felt like living in a garbage dump, more power to them.

I didn't live here, what did I care?

"I used the crack to keep everybody at arm's length," said the client cleaning around my desk. I hadn't even noticed that he was still talking at me. "It was like, my shield 'gainst the world."

I nodded without bothering to look up from my book. "Whatever works, man."

9:13pm
SO LONG, AND THANKS FOR ALL THE SHIT

I wish I could say that I knew Gerry, but he was just another sullen, black face that I used to see wandering the hallways at work, dying for one more bit of whatever used to get him through the day. I'd grace him with the occasional '*hey*!' or '*howdy*!' but that'd be about it. Gerry was pretty quiet and kept to himself. I didn't know his name, didn't know his problem, and most of all, I didn't fucking care.

So it caught me by surprise when he utterly lost it. Like most kids of the past few generations, I liked to pretend that my life could be arranged into something resembling an orderly movie or novel. Maybe a series of slightly amusing anecdotes, at the very least. This made it unsettling when one of the peripheral characters decided to grab the limelight of their own volition, foreshadowing be damned.

It upsets the balance of things. Takes a little while to get adjusted.

I didn't think too much of it when client after client came in from their 8pm 12-step meetings. They walked through the front door, looking over their shoulders with frightened expressions. Frightened, and maybe even a little bit jealous.

I figured the cause of the disturbance was some bum smoking crack on the nearest street corner. This isn't the swankiest part of town, and public drug use occurs around here plenty. I find it amusing, but to the clients it's a temptation that they don't particularly need. It would be like munching on a seafood buffet in front of starving Somalians (or whoever the *en vogue* hungry are these days).

If one of the clients hadn't screamed the bum out of the neighborhood yet—which is what usually happens—then the task would fall to me. Far be it from my ass to interfere with a non-client's attempt to enjoy themselves. I wasn't even keen on getting involved in the clients' business; live and let live had become my policy after only a few months at work. But, if some crackhead bum was riling the herd, then it'd probably be best for me run him off.

Whatever kept my job as trouble-free as possible.

I was about to drag my lazy ass out the front door, but Robert met me half-way.

"I need to talk to—"

Wanting to spare myself the five feet to the door, I asked Robert, "What's goin' on out there?"

"Gerry out there," he said.

"Which one's he?"

"He tall, bald head, huge gut." A *slightly* useful description. It takes a bit of paying attention before you realize that the only time most people don't bother to mention ethnicity as a physical detail is when it matches their own.

Robert was black as they came; *ergo*, so was Gerry.

Another client rushed up while my Apple II processor of a brain was still working on this. "Gerry's outside chuggin' a fifth!" he cried.

Once it became apparent that snitching was now an acceptable option, another five clients came to tell me the same damn thing. Gerry was standing out in front of the building, pulling a non-stop chug-a-thon on a fifth of *something*. Vodka or gin or tequila or paint remover, depending on which hysterical recounting you believed.

I guess Gerry figured that if he was going to relapse, he might as well go public with the act. Fucking drama queen.

I was about to stop relying on second-hand information and actually look out the goddamn door myself when Jack hurried into the lobby. Some of the clients had by-passed me to squeal directly to Jack.

It was annoying to be reminded that a curmudgeon like Jack was Head Tech while I was *just* another grunt. I looked like being almost fifty-years younger than him would have to compensate me for our differences in job seniority. Knowing that I'd still be in the prime of my life while Jack was fertilizing a graveyard lawn made up for a lot of things.

We both moved towards the front door. "You hear?" I asked Jack.

"I hear 'bout it."

I reached for the door. Before I could make contact, it swung outwards to admit a scruffy, bald black guy. He listed strongly to one side. His t-shirt was torn at the shoulder, and blood caked his chin. Someone had probably fallen down a few times getting here.

We can't all smell like concentrated rose powder, but *Jeeezus*, did that guy reek of booze! I took a step back, pushed by his alcoholic shield. My amazing deductive skills told me this was probably Gerry.

Holding the door open with one hand, he still had the bottle of *Night Train* in the other. It swung back and forth in erratic circles like a broken pendulum.

Ewww, I thought. *If you're gonna relapse, why not do it with a little bit of style?*

I also wondered if I should mention that he'd missed the 9pm curfew.

Me and Jack stared at him for a few seconds, and him at us. Or, at least he tried to stare back. The emptiness of the bottle explained why Gerry was having trouble focusing. No doubt it hadn't been his first.

Gerry tossed the bottle out the door behind him. It shattered on the street with the sound of a million broken promises. The noise snapped us into action…or as close to action as lazy bastards like myself and Jack can manage.

"You know I can't let you in here like that," said Jack. I stood next to him, trying to look like an authority figure.

"*Thass* cool," Gerry slurred, almost flooring us with his breath. We stepped back even further to get out of range. "*Ah jus'…wan mah trug…*" A thin sliver of drool crept over his lips and sprinted down his chin to hang like a noose.

"His *what?*" I asked. Ebonics had been tough enough to master, but the drunken variety was one dialect that I still hadn't gotten the hang of.

"Can't let you drive outta here like this," Jack said back to him. "Why don't you give us your keys?"

"C'mon Gerry," I said. Dude was *fuuuuucked* up! "Toss those puppies over this way and we'll go make us some coffee and chill out some, huh?" Actually, I planned to take his keys then push him back out the door to sleep it off on a sewer grate, but he didn't need to know that.

Gerry paused for a second. Maybe considering my offer. Maybe waiting for his brain to cut through the booze that his body wasn't finished processing.

"Fuck y'all," he decided, and pushed past us towards the back of the building.

I looked with dismay at the handprint he'd left on my shift, then exchanged a shrug with Jack. Gerry could go sit in his truck in the back lot all he wanted. No way he was getting far with the back gate being closed.

Still, me and Jack followed Gerry, making sure he stayed out of trouble. He stumbled into the back door, bounced off it, then wasted a few seconds pulling rather than pushing it open. I followed him ahead of Jack, who was having trouble keeping up with the pace. Through the door, into the back lot, was an unexpected sight:

The back gate was wide open.

"*Fuck!*" I shouted. "Jack, go get the fuckin' clicker!"

"The what?" Jack asked.

"The *clicker!* The *fuckin'* remote!" Should I have sprinted back to desk to grab it myself? "The gate's open! Grab the fuckin' clicker!"

Jack could close the gate from the front desk by himself. I stayed shadowing Gerry.

For all the good it did.

He climbed into his truck. Gave me a disgusted look and slurred, "*Fugg off, hongy*," as he slammed the door closed. A group of clients stood behind me, watching the show.

"C'mon, man," I pleaded with Gerry, my used car salesman smile on my face. "Let's talk about this, huh?"

Gerry used his left hand to shoot me the bird and his right hand to fish under his seat. And since there was no accounting for the man's tastes, he came up with a fifth of *Stoli's*. A smile—or maybe a smirk—was flashed in my direction before Gerry twisted off the cap and, head tossed back, proceeded to down the entire goddamn bottle.

The.

Entire.

Goddamn.

Bottle.

I stood transfixed by something I'd only expect at a sideshow or family reunion. "*Jesus*," I managed to mutter, a sentiment echoed by the rest of the crowd.

Robert busted out the back door, distracting from the alcoholic marvel before us. "Jack can't find the clicker!" he yelled.

Fuck! The gate!

Finished with his display of alcohol tolerance, Gerry started up his truck. The engine growled, nearly stalled in an admirable show of foresight, then gave an angry roar before shifting into gear.

"*Dude*!" I shouted at him, out of words and giving as many universal signs for pleading as I could recall. Gerry just flipped me the bird again, using the wrong finger, and with an alarming squeal of his tires skidded out the back gate. He drove straight at the building across from ours, then busted a sharp right at last second. The truck bounced off the curb and tore off in a cloud of garbage scraps and bad choices.

The back gate hummed to life and creaked itself shut.

Surrounded by the other halfway house voyeurs, I stood there staring after Gerry. I could hear his tires shrieking in the distance.

"*Fuck!*" I screamed after him. "*Fuck! Fuck! Fuck! Fuuuuck!*"

Life-saving attempt over and officially failed, I stalked back inside.

The group of clients watched me go. One of them muttered, "That boy got a mouth on him."

9:18pm
THINK OF ENGLAND

Johnson reminded me of a young Arnold Schwarzenegger. Not that Johnson was a political tool of Californian energy conglomerates, it was more his muscles and height. Johnson had the sort of rugged charm that shouted at you from across the room. When he dipped his head slightly in an *'aw, shucks'* display of humility, I realized that I'd be sopping wet if granted the proper equipment.

The only thing off was his eyes. One moved slightly independent of the other. It lagged behind by a half-second when looking about the room, and never seemed to settle on the same point of focus.

I was having a similar problem with my eyes, but mine was more about keeping them open. Of course, the Vicodin I'd munched probably had more to do with this than any natural defect. The best method for preventing myself from nodding off seemed to be concentrating on maintaining eye contact with Johnson. I made a game of it. Picked one of his eyes and tried to follow its gaze.

I found this entrancing. So entrancing that I was having trouble paying attention to the gut-spilling Johnson was doing. He had started off by cornering me in Gim's office and, without warning, gave me the director's cut of his recovery/relapse history.

The junkies had a tendency to do shit like that. If there's one thing that no member of our species can resist, it's talking about themselves. *'How I'm dealing with this drug-shaped hole in my life'* is how this manifests in a rehab.

Way too many of the clients did this to me, the effusive spilling of guts. I was just somebody else for them to blather at and bore with details of their less-than-mediocre existence. I was a giant ear taking the place previously filled by their bartender, priest or dealer.

"I really feel like I'm going to do it this time," he told me, and I nodded, slow and appreciative.

Jack picked that time to stroll past the open door. "And I really feel like you gonna relapse like you always do."

Johnson muttered a *"Fuck you,"* at Jack's receding laughter. He then gave me an expectant look, like it was my responsibility to toss him a verbal lifesaver. Some phrase to keep his ass afloat in the hostile waters of Jack's well-earned doubt. Took me a while to think of anything, but I eventually managed to spit out, "Ya gotta do it…sometime. Why not…now?"

Johnson was a mere quarter-century old, and had already been in rehab and relapsed six times. He was an alcoholic and occasional sampler of crack. He had been sober now for five days, only three more to go and he'd beat his last time. As he rambled on, Johnson was probably dying for a drink.

Fuck, me too.

I wondered if the state of Johnson's eyes was a result of all his drug intake. Then I realized that the cause of other people's misfortunes wasn't half as important as the entertainment value.

Johnson kept talking, and I kept nodding and making the appropriate noises at random intervals, all the while watching his eyes. It's odd, but I was generally known around here as the Tech to whom you could talk. That was why so many of the guys came to me when it was gut-spilling time, though I got the feeling that anyone, even a brick wall or water fountain, would do.

How I ever got a reputation as a good listener was beyond me. Like most of my generation, my attention span was screwed. I couldn't listen attentively if an anecdote was punctuated with free money and topless girls. So I guess it's good that I never cared enough to pay attention in the first place.

When listening, like with most forms of human interaction, all you needed was to display a few simple mechanical responses and no one could tell the difference. Smile, nod on occasion, and try not to let your eyes wander too much. Whether you actually had any interest in what was being spewed at you was irrelevant.

It reminded me of a good friend from high school. She was a short blond girl who—in addition to owning the label of *school slut*—was also gifted with the reputation of being The Greatest Lay on Planet Earth. Some of us just peak young. I asked her once what her secret was (and requested a demonstration, of course). She said, '*I dunno; I just lie there and try to look interested.*'

Indeed.

There may be a lesson here for all of us, but goddamn if I know what it is.

9:31pm
BOX WINE IN A JEWELED CHALICE

"Toilets are all done, sir." His plastic gloves were stripped off and tossed into the wastebasket next to my desk.

I said, "Thanks for taking care of your shit," and didn't bother looking up from my homework. Just one more class and I'd graduate. I'd have a big, bad college degree and could go off and find myself a *real* job. Something that paid better than starvation wages. Something where I didn't have to watch people urinate through units that dwarfed my own.

"Did you want to check it before I signed the chore list, sir?"

I still didn't bother to look up, just waved my hand and said, "*Naw*, I trust ya."

"Thank you," he said, oblivious of my lie.

I considered the matter closed until he asked, "*Umm*…could I please borrow your pen, sir?"

I handed it over. "As long as you stop calling me, *sir*."

I looked up for the first time at the guy I'd been communicating with. He was paunchy and black, with a slight ring of graying hair around the back of his skull. A general vibe of harmlessness wafted off the guy like watered-down cologne. On sight, you'd let him baby-sit your kids.

He smiled at me as I handed my pen up to him. "Thanks…*Ray*." He was reading it off my nametag. This rapid-fire literacy put him a few steps ahead of most clients.

I smiled back. "No prob." Maybe I'd pay attention to my actual job for a while. Anything for a break from neurology homework. "What's your name, man?"

"Davis," he answered, and we shook hands firmly. "Sorry about the '*sir*' convention. It's just best to play it safe in these places and hard to go wrong with such a standardized form of address."

"I dig."

Davis motioned at my book. "I take it you're in school. There aren't too many people who read textbooks for fun."

I said, "Yep, studyin' psychology up at UH. This is my last semester." My last semester, and I hadn't learned a goddamn thing. Seriously. My tuition money would've been better spent on twenty-grand worth of coke and hookers.

Davis gave a little smile. "Going to get your masters then, are you?"

"Yeah, eventually." I said. "Turns out there's not too goddamn much you can do with a bachelors in Psych. Wish I'd known that about three years ago."

He laughed politely. "I know, I know. Realizing that I was going to have to get my Ph.D. was something of a shock."

"Whatcha got a Ph.D. in?" An educated crackhead. Rare specimen. *Weird...*

He shrugged with what I could tell was false humility. "Oh, just aerospace engineering."

"*Goddamn...*" I tried to whistle to show how impressed I was, but whistling's never been a skill of mine. "So, whatcha do?"

Davis was unable to contain his smile. "I worked for NASA. Shuttle design."

That had to be one fat paycheck the guy used to drag in. And his job was probably what Davis used to assure himself that he was better than the other wrecks here. All the clients have some sort of ego-defense like that. It's human nature to try to defend ourselves from uncomfortable truths (such as: '*I've fucked up my life and am currently living with a bunch of other failures*') in any way we can.

The junkies used everything possible to distance themselves from the other failures around them. Everything and anything along the lines of: '*At least I only drank instead of shooting up, at least I ain't a nigger, at least I ain't poor white trash, at least I've got a job, at least I've never been to jail, at least I never sucked dick for my habit,*' etc., etc., etc.

I know this because they never fail to tell me, usually as a sort of disclaimer at the end of a story about ripping off their mom's jewelry or killing the guy who stiffed them on a rock. '*Yeah, I did some lousy shit, but at least I ain't as bad as some of these other scumbags*'

It's right there on the bottom rung of Maslow's Hierarchy of Needs: food, clothing, shelter, and someone to whom you can feel superior. I wondered if everyone here was aware of the low regard in which everybody else held them.

Of course, a college boy like myself doesn't bother with such delusions.

I smiled up at Davis. He smiled back before giving a disgusted look around the lobby at the rest of his fellow addicts. He was probably telling himself how his multiple degrees from Yale and MIT (he made sure to name-drop those later), and the high-paying job he once held, made him not only better than his fellow addicts, but also higher and mightier than the lowly cracker from a state college earning eight bucks an hour to baby-sit him.

Davis was welcome to feel that way. I knew which sides of the desk we were on.

9:40pm
...IN ALL THE WRONG PLACES

Jack rolled his eyes as the phone kept squeaking. "Yeah. Yep. *Uh-huh.*" He was a man of few words and even fewer worth remembering. I watched from the corner of my eye as I lounged on the lobby's couch. The slacker sees all and acknowledges nothing.

"Yeah," Jack said into the phone, "I see yo Daddy earlier. Yeah, he right here about noon or so. Lookin' kinda bad."

We're not supposed to give any information about the clients over the phone, so I listened as attentively as possible while pretending to be engrossed in my book. *"...the EPR paradox does suggest that distant parts of the universe are connected in some peculiar way not yet understood..."*

"Yeah, I tell ya if I see him. *Uh-huh.*" He rolled his eyes again. "Yeah. Yeah. Sweet dreams to you, too."

He hung up the phone. "The hell was I thinkin'?"

"Homicidal ex, again?" I asked.

Jack gave a mischievous grin. "I don't want you thinkin' less of me, Ray, but..."

Yeah, like he gave a shit, or like it was possible for me to think less of an elderly ex-crackhead. Someone was obviously preparing to brag about something.

"That was Cassandra."

I looked at Jack's smile and understood everything. *Oh god.* The undercooked chicken we'd had for dinner begged to see the light again. *Oh...dear...fuck.*

Not her and Jack. I almost fell to my knees to plead with a god in whom I didn't believe.

Not Jack. Anyone but Jack.

He nodded at me: *Yeah, I done hit that.*

"Is it your goddamn fault that my crotch has been itching in three-week intervals?"

Jack smiled even wider at my joke and gave a little shrug. I couldn't believe that I might have stuck my dick in the same zip code as Jack's. Had we been sleeping with Cassandra around the same time? I felt like breaking into the nearest pharmacy and bathing myself in penicillin. Either that or I needed to rush home and scrub with a wire brush.

"Just tell me when," I requested.

His face beamed with the pride of senior virility. "Oh, you too?"

"We'll vote on who gets to be club president at the next meeting," I assured him. "But right now I just need a time frame." There was no way I had humped the same person with whom Jack had played human sewing machine. What sort of horrid, super-resilient crap can you get from a seventy-something ex-crackhead? Anything Jack had could've been picked up in the Korean War, brought back to the States and then incubated for several decades, strengthening itself on crack and the carcasses of weaker STDs.

"Time frame?" Jack asked. "I figure I lasted 'bout twenty, twenty-five minutes." I laughed, 'cause he had me beat, and then remembered that my genital health was at stake here. "Bless that *Cialis*," Jack said, giving his pocket a pat. I heard the rattle of pills. They were apparently something he never left home without.

"Not what I meant." I've never been one of those hypocrites who advocated promiscuity for themselves and monogamy for the rest of the world. I just wanted some warning if my dick was in danger of rotting off soon.

I seriously considered adding welfare mothers to my list of people to never trust. Did Jack's probably-diseased cock pull Cassandra's AM shift while I worked the PM? How long had the two of them been shagging?

"Oh, I get ya" Jack said. "Happened about a week or two ago. It okay for once, but nothin' I'd pay to ride twice." Then he laughed at his own little joke.

Thank fuck…

It had been months since my Corporal Work of Shagging with Cassandra. Damn good to know that I was in a no danger of having sampled Jack's sloppy seconds. My immune system breathed a huge sigh of relief.

I did kind of admire Jack for fucking someone a half-century younger than him. How could I not? But sharing in the viral downside of decades worth of questionable lays wasn't too appealing an option. Of course, I'd been tested since being balls-deep in Cassandra (*can't be too careful!*), so I guess the momentary panic was for nothing. This honky needs to switch to decaf.

Still smiling, Jack asked, "Gotcha some of that, huh?"

At this point in the conversation I realized that not once had we referred to Cassandra with anything resembling an acknowledgement of her humanity. Jack talked about her like an amusement-park ride, and I had thought of Cassandra as a potentially dangerous petri dish.

Charming.

"Long time ago," I answered. It never would have occurred to me that the two of us would share the same notch on our bedposts. I wondered if I should be insulted or impressed that someone who found me attractive also had space in their sense of sexual aesthetics for Jack's decrepit old ass. "Who the hell goes cruisin' for guys at a fuckin' rehab?"

Jack shrugged. "The desperate kind," he said. "The only kind of person you gonna meet around here."

THE CRASH OF THE HINDENBURG CONSIDERED AS A MATTER OF *'PRINCIPAL'*
or
THE MEANEST NIGGER I KNOW

"You wanna fight? *C'mon*! I know you wanna fight! *Somebody* wants to fight!"

Something was wrong with Johnson's medication level. Or maybe something hadn't mixed with his anti-psychotics too well. I hear crack doesn't go well with much else besides more crack. He was in the middle of a full-on violent rage, and looking for someone—anyone—to take it out on.

Portrait of the Junkie as a Young Psychopath: Johnson was one of those people for whom the phrase, *'like a brick shithouse,'* was invented. He was wide enough to be almost a perfect square in shape, except for the muscles that erupted from his body like an anabolic nightmare. I swear the guy's cheeks were buff.

He was also out of his head with self-righteous belligerence. This was worse than the time he tried to hang a Confederate flag in his room.

"Fight me, you fuckers!"

Johnson was slamming holes into the walls of the stairwell, each furious punch leaving a fist-sized crater. I was trying to calm Johnson down, using soothing tones and phrases that were as effective as trying to piss out the sun.

"It's a matter of fucking principle!" Johnson screamed. Then he threw himself into the wall. *BOOM!* He seemed to enjoy the experience, repeating it immediately. *BOOM!* And again. *BOOM!*

There was a hollow reverberation as the wall dented around Johnson's massive bulk. The *'matter of fucking principle'* referenced was his earlier refusal to take a piss test. That's grounds for instant dismissal from the rehab.

Johnson had shown up from a weekend pass in a state of complete disorientation. He didn't know what day it was; couldn't string together a coherent sentence; became increasingly hostile when questioned about his behavior. That's what we call *begging* for a U.A.

He had gone upstairs to grab his stuff and *'clear the fuck outta this fucking shit-hole with you fucking homos always wanting to look at my dick.'* Jack followed after him. I followed too, wanting to ensure Johnson didn't let his instability loose in the direction of other clients. With everybody housed upstairs, there were plenty of targets for his chemical rage.

I was halfway up the stairs when it occurred to me just how much Johnson's size dwarfed my own. I ran back downstairs and grabbed the cudgel. Better safe than sorry, especially with the mentally unstable.

I made it back upstairs, grabbed Jack, and sent him back down. I had a feeling Johnson would be less likely to attack me. There were plenty of non-deranged clients who'd beat Jack into the ground, given half an excuse.

Not that I blamed them.

"You *wanna* fucking fight?"

I was trying to herd Johnson back down the stairs (in much the same way I'd herd a bus down the street) when we ran into another client on the way up. It was Sam, our resident ex-skater and probably the least likely combatant at the rehab. Johnson instantly locked onto this scrawny cracker as a potential release valve. He puffed himself up, bared his teeth, clenched his fists, and waved them about. Typical aggressive primate behavior. "I know you wanna fuckin' fight me!"

"We're all friends here," I said as I tried to move myself between the two (breaking a cardinal rule of dealing with the unstable by turning my back on Johnson). "We're all friends. Let's keep moving." I made '*get-the-fuck-outta-here*' motions at Sam, who was now frozen up against the wall.

He wasn't moving. Sam seemed scared enough to piss his acid-washed jeans, so I pushed him ahead of us—always staying between him and Johnson, who never stopped shouting threats. We made it out of the stairwell into the back hallway. Walking in front of Johnson was like riding a freight of nitro-glycerin down a Nigerian highway. You knew at any second your rough ride could get rougher, and then *BOOM!*

Some of the clients followed at a distance. Johnson was a mad gorilla on display, and when he wheeled around and screamed "*C'mon!*" everyone jumped back ten feet. Then resumed following.

There was conflict in the air, and no one wanted to miss it. Violence is one thing; it's quick and frightening. The *anticipation* of violence is something else entirely. It has an allure all its own.

I shoved Sam off at the nearest cross-hall and hoped Johnson didn't follow him. "This way, Johnson." I motioned towards the lobby.

He followed, cursing and shouting. "It's about principle, you fucks! About princ—not *p-r-c-i-p-a-l*, but *p-r-i-n-goddamnit*!" Johnson kept waving his arms and shouting more examples of his lack of spelling skills.

We made it to the lobby. Jack was busy at the front desk, dialing the phone. I knew he was calling the cops. It's what we're supposed to do when one client becomes a threat to the others, but I don't like the cops. Not just because they're government-issued thugs charged with repressing the rest of the lower classes, but due to their lousy history of dealing with the deranged. They tend to kill them. Call in the pigs to handle somebody unstable, and you're basically signing their death warrant.

I motioned for Jack to hang up the phone as I walked Johnson to the door. Thankfully, he did. Johnson caught me motioning to Jack and started screaming even louder; angry, incoherent shit about the government, Mormons, and how Jack always picked on him.

I managed to get Johnson outside where he changed tunes and started screaming about how he needed his breathing machine. He had to have it. He'd '*fucking die*' without it. Apparently this great white beast of a man had asthma.

I ran upstairs to grab the machine, then raced back down to the lobby. Jack was no longer at the front desk. I looked about, and what I saw through the front door registered as a worst-case scenario. Jack was outside arguing with Johnson.

"*Jesus!*" I expected Jack get a hole punched through his sternum. This was why I had originally sent Jack downstairs. It's why I had wanted my coworker away from Johnson. Jack was guaranteed to set him off even more.

Johnson was screaming louder and louder. Arms swinging more and more wild. I swung open our front door to bring it between the two of them, then grabbed Jack by the arm.

I growled, "*C'mere*, goddamnit!" yanked him inside, and waved goodbye to Johnson.

The door locked behind us. I started to vent the stress of the last ten minutes at Jack. "The *hemorrhaging fuck* did I tell you about staying away from—"only to be distracted by Johnson tugging on the front door. A second yank and he ripped it open, locks and all.

Then other clients in the lobby all stepped back. Me and Jack were rooted to the spot. Within striking distance.

"I just wanna say…" he started, before lapsing into more incomprehensibility. Angry blather and nonsense showered us. Johnson took a step closer. Then another. I waited for him to take a swing. Waited for the violence. Johnson kept screaming before finishing with, "…and *fuck you*, Jack." He pointed at my coworker, seething with righteous fury so intense there were tears in his eyes. "You're the meanest nigger I know!"

With that—having broken the ultimate taboo at the rehab—Johnson stormed out the door.

We said nothing.

No one moved.

We all just stood and stared at each other. Shaking slightly. Myself, Jack, and all the guys who had watched the spectacle still held our breaths.

No one was dead. It was like seeing the A-bomb fall to the streets of Hiroshima and lay dented on the pavement, a total dud. No one was dead. We were all in shock.

"*Gah*-damn," Jack said finally, his legs giving out and depositing him in the closest seat. More silence. Despite Jack having given the *all-clear* signal, no one else moved. No one else spoke.

Finally, I said, "Don't sweat it, Jack," loud enough for everyone to hear. "I know *plenty* of niggers meaner than you."

It wasn't funny, but we all started laughing and couldn't stop.

10:01pm
YOU GET MY VOTE FOR JESUS IN THE NEXT ELECTION

"I'm a good person!" Corey asserted as loud as possible.

His wife had finally agreed to talk with him over the phone, only to use the opportunity to tell him all the several kinds of bastard he was.

Corey was now apparently in need of the sort of reassurance that only he could provide for himself at top volume. He wandered around the lobby, repeating this affirmation.

Some people have trouble reading silently. Corey couldn't even *think* to himself. I was beginning to suspect that anyone who believed in egalitarianism had never set foot outside a college campus.

"I'm a good person!"

"Sure ya are," said Jack. "We all good people here. We just got real shitty decision-making skills."

"I *know* I'm a good person," Corey repeated with even more conviction.

It didn't seem worth it to bother replying. We're all Good People. Each and every one of us. It's always the rest of the fucking world that has a problem. We're all just a bunch of well-meaning shmoes who have the misfortune to be continually abused and confounded by the other paragons of evil that surround us.

So we occasionally do stuff not condoned by our society's moral code...*hey*, these things happen! Nobody's perfect. So I ripped off my parents, so I cheated on my girlfriend, so I sold some bad crack, so I killed someone, so I continually act in a selfish, shitty manner...*hey*, I'm only human!

I am a Good Person, *goddamnit*! Ignore all the evidence to the contrary!

As for myself, I had always thought of myself as a Good Person, too. Why not?

I always thought of myself as a Good Person until I started working here and heard junkies, rapists, and murderers referring to themselves in a similar manner.

I'm a good person!

I know I'm a good person!

I be a damn good person!

I'm still a good person inside!

Fuck them! I'm a good person and I don't have to hear that shit from them assholes!

Hearing this, day after day, from people considered the scum of society gave me insight into the amazing powers of self-delusion. If the junkies and crackheads could have convinced themselves that they were only a half-step from canonization, then what kind of crap could I have been feeding myself? What sort of preposterous bullshit did I tell myself in order to avoid having to face some sort of horrible self-awareness?

Was I a Good Person?

Was I? In spite of how I steal food and clothing meant for the homeless? Even though I'll throw old men out onto the freezing streets in the middle of the night? Despite how the junkies come to me looking for sympathy and I respond with sarcasm and mockery? And what about my leaving porn on Gim's computer and making sure other employees caught the blame?

Was I still a Good Person?

Was I ever?

The answer came bubbling up from my forebrain. From the newest, most recently developed part of my goopy think-box came the instant reply: *Who fuckin' cares?*

It had a decent point.

Be concerned about shit like that and I risked becoming another 12-Step weakling like the junkies. It was a slippery slope from worrying about how well you're following some arbitrary moral code to spending your Sunday mornings kissing the ass of some middle-eastern slave god.

Boo-hoo-hoo, I'm powerless over my addictions and myself. *Boo-hoo-hoo*, help me god, help me somebody, help me *anybody*, because I'm too fucking weak to do it myself.

Piss on that.

I resolved to never waste my time wondering about shit like that again.

Thanks, I said to my forebrain.

No problem, it replied. *Now let's wait for Jack to leave and then go scope out some porn on Gim's computer. You can always blame one of your coworkers for it!*

I smiled to myself. Sounded like a plan.

10:31pm
'TIS BETTER TO HAVE LOVED AND STALKED

A lot of the clients destroyed their families through their addictions. As we all know, misery loves company, and most addicts are like giant toilets, sucking everyone down into the shit with them. That's the price we all pay for being social animals, I guess.

Some of the smarter spouses had restraining orders taken out on their addict husbands to prevent their families from being dragged down with them. I doubt it's an easy thing to do, filing a court order to ensure that a loved one stays the hell away.

Not an easy thing to do, and not much easier to have done to you.

Corey had just come back from his house—well, what *was* his house—where his wife not only refused to let him inside, but also reminded him through the screen door that he wasn't allowed within 500 yards of his family.

Corey screamed and banged on the door, then ran like hell when the police showed up. It took him a while to ditch the cops, but he eventually made his way back to the facility, and was now crying on his roommate's shoulder about it all.

"She-she say I can't come 'round no more," he sobbed, apparently surprised that people might get tired of you selling their possessions for crack after the third time. "She call the cops on me. She *really* called the cops on me!"

He was the saddest black man I'd seen all day, and considering my job, that's saying quite a bit.

Love that was once returned but no longer is? That can be a *real* bitch. Especially if you had once earned someone's love but then lost it.

Unless you're the one whose love has done the disappearing act, you just can't imagine how a person could just *stop loving* somebody. It's such a mystery. But, just like most ways of hurting people, it makes perfect sense from the other side. After all, it's *your* prerogative to get sick of people. Always comes as a bit of a shock when someone does it to you first.

Some variation of *requited-then-unrequited* love has happened to everybody at some point. It had graced *my* life recently when my girlfriend told me to take a fucking flying leap. Thus was I reminded me of the eternal lesson: suffering is only funny when it happens to other people.

You love, they love, and then one of you—but not the other—has a change of heart. Sometimes there's a reason, like you destroying the family through your selfish addiction, and sometimes that love just dies all on its own.

It happens.

The rejection of a previously mutual love is simply another example of the old adage that Nothing Lasts Forever and Everything Changes. Few things teach this like a deflated relationship. The Buddha wasn't enlightened, just heartbroken. It's tragic that love tends to die in one person before the other, rather than occurring simultaneously in both parties, but *C'est la vie*, right?

If you want a perfect world, go live at Disneyland.

I considered telling Corey all this, but one look at him and I decided to keep the insight to myself.

10:34pm
NO MOVIE SCRIPT ENDING

Frankie set his pill bottles on the med room desk. "I takin' one each of these," he said. "And then two of this one." He held up his Trazodone bottle for me. A lot of the junkies do something along those lines: the pill bottle charades. It's simpler than trying to pronounce those big words on the label.

"Gotcha," I said. Before logging the information in the med book I went and changed all the mathematical mistakes my coworker, Reginald, had made earlier during the complex and tricky process of subtracting one or two pills from the previous amounts.

"No IQ test to work at this fuckin' place," I said to Frankie.

Bent over the med book, I watched out of the corner of my eye as he dumped more than the stated amount of pills into his hand. Tried to act sneaky about it. Frankie was probably desperate for a high, but all he'd get off Trazodone was the joy of sleeping for the next day or two. Or hell, maybe oblivion was exactly what he was after.

"Don't take no genius to end up here, neither," Frankie said. The man was living proof of his own theory, so I had to agree.

Frankie stood and watched me fudge a few numbers on another med sheet to hide how I had *borrowed* a few Adderol from the stash of a younger client. I could cover my tracks in clear view of most of the guys, confident that they didn't know what the hell was going on.

"That ain't my med sheet," Frankie pointed out. Apparently, his literacy extended to recognizing his own name. Good for him. "Whose med sheet that?"

"I'm correcting Reginald's mistakes," I said. "I have to do this every day." Half-truths are said to be whole lies, but they're good enough for most social situations.

"He a dumb motherfucker," Frankie said. A couple other guys popped their heads in the door while me and Frankie wasted oxygen. They asked for linens and towels and other supplies stashed in the med room. I motioned for them to grab the stuff themselves. My back being turned to all the supplies, medical and otherwise, could make it pretty easy for someone to raid the medicine cabinet without me noticing.

More power to them, if that's what they wanted.

"Can't believe Davis relapsed," Frankie said. I had personally given the boot to Davis' rocket scientist, Ivy League ass, and taken no small amount of pleasure in doing so. "He's just not one of the people I expected to do that."

"I expect all of you to," I said. Frankie looked offended. "Hey, I'm right more often than not!"

"You ain't got no faith in us," he accused me. "That's harsh, man. Even from a white guy. Ya gotta have faith."

"Got something better than faith," I said. "It's called *observation*."

If Frankie was more observant, himself, he could have pointed out that I spent most of my time ignoring the clients rather than observing them. Instead, he just said a hurt, "*Whatever*," and walked out, forgetting his pills on the desktop. I decided to let them sit there a while before I claimed scavenging rights.

10:42pm
BEGGARS, CHOOSERS AND THOSE STRUNG-OUT IN-BETWEEN

I hadn't seen JDZ for a few months and had figured him for dead. No one lives on the street, shooting heroin, to increase their life expectancy. So, it was surprising when I came downstairs from rooting through the med-room to find him sitting in the lobby.

"Hey, remember me?" he asked. I did, but it took me a little while to decide if I had been wrong about that death supposition.

JDZ looked like he'd just scaled the fence at Auschwitz. He was a tall guy, over six-feet, but it seemed like his clothes weighed more than the rest of him. His short, curly hair looked ready to abandon ship and drop right off his head. His face was so sunken that it wouldn't have been the least bit surprising to learn that somebody had just painted flesh tones on his skull.

Luckily for him it was a Saturday night, and most of the clients were off at some miserable AA dance. Had more of the guys been home, it wouldn't have been too long before he was recognized and chased off. It was popular opinion that JDZ was a thief, degenerate, and should probably be put down for the good of society.

We can't all be Nobel Prize winners.

"Can we talk?" JDZ motioned towards the door.

He's gonna ask for money, I thought. *Unless he's about to try to sell me something he boosted.* Someone asking if they can speak with you never bodes well. It's normally assumed that we all have an inherent right to communicate with each other. Anyone who actually takes the time to prepare me for it sets off my alarms. Nobody has ever asked permission for a conversation and then given me a wad of hundreds or a free handjob.

JDZ opened the door and we both stepped out into the cold. "Don't worry," he said, "I'm not going to rob you." I hadn't expected him to, but, on the other hand, it wouldn't have surprised me. You don't survive four junk-sick months on the street simply through the generosity of others. Not with our species, you don't.

What JDZ wanted, of course, was money. No surprise there, but I didn't have any that I'd give to him. JDZ would just blow it on drugs, and that was already my plan.

Switching tactics, he tried small talk. "How's school?" he asked. I told JDZ that I had graduated in May.

"Then what're you still doing here?"

"What are *you* still doing on the streets?" I countered.

"It's *sooo* fucked up out here," JDZ said, telling me about eating out of dumpsters (*Subway* has the best). He talked about boosting stuff to trade for money, food, or drugs. He rambled about the people he thought were trying to kill him, the people he was *sure* were trying to kill him, and a whole bunch of other paranoid babblings in the classic junkie style I'd grown to know and love.

Looking down—avoiding his sore-ridden face—I noticed he was wearing sandals. It had been cold as shit this autumn, and here was JDZ on the streets in *sandals*. No coat, either. He had owned shoes the last time I'd seen him, but they'd probably been traded for a fix or some food or *something* a long time ago.

I also wondered whatever happened to his old girlfriend. My last encounter with JDZ ended with him cold-cocking her. Hopefully she had grown some brains and hooked up with somebody whose life wasn't an express train to Hell.

"Can you help me out?" he asked. The best response at that point would've been to whip out my sawed-off twelve-gauge and blow away the top of his head. But, unfortunately for JDZ, I'd left all the high-caliber firearms in my other pants. *Still...*

Though the facility's glass front wall, I pointed at the shelves full of do-nated books. "You oughtta be able to get a few bucks for 'em at *Half-Price Books.*" His eyes lit up, and I'm sure he was already dreaming of fixes to come.

It took less than three minutes to load JDZ with two shopping bags full of paperbacks and encyclopedias. I helped him pile in the books, wondering if it would be kosher to ask how many times he had whored himself for dope. JDZ hadn't been too bad looking in his less strung-out days. One glance at the desperation that soaked his body told that he wasn't above gagging if it meant scoring his fix.

I didn't get the chance to ask him about it; he babbled endlessly about his need and inability to get clean. "I gotta do something soon," he said. "Before I either kill myself or somebody else again."

I pretended like I hadn't heard that last word.

The door was propped open for JDZ, and he waddled out like a penguin. Then, overwhelmed with either gratitude or the need to spread contagion, he set down a bag to shake my hand. '*Fuck,*' I grimaced. '*Wasn't he just telling me about dumpster diving? When was the last time this fucker washed up?*'

I waved good riddance as JDZ headed down the street, fast as possible. He was smart enough to not want to be in this part of town at night with an excess of material goods. His sandals slapped against the concrete as he shuffled through the cold and past the other bums huddled in their doorways. Quick clouds of breath puffed over his head as he continued his locomotion down the street. JDZ was the little junkie who could.

Sloth was waiting for me as I came back inside. He asked, "Whatchu give 'im all our books fo'?"

"Shut the fuck up," I explained.

Then I went into the bathroom and scrubbed my hands with scalding water. When I was done with that, I scrubbed them again.

10:50pm
OLD SPICE AND REGRET

Todd sat across the lobby from me on the couch. Occasionally he would try to play a song on his guitar. Occasionally he'd try to make conversation.

Neither attempt was very successful.

Todd's playing was fine. The lack of connection was my fault. Recently, everything felt like my fault.

I kept going over, in Technicolor detail, the last conversation I'd had with my girlfriend. I was deep in the process of revising everything in my memory so that I had a perfect answer for everything she said at the moment she had said it. Snappy comebacks and merciless putdowns were delivered with skill and just the right touch of disinterested malice for maximum emotional effect.

It didn't make me feel any better, but I couldn't stop myself from doing it. This was much more funny when it happened to the junkies.

Readjusting the Rastafarian beanie he always wore, Todd said, "I bet you meet some pretty interesting people, working here."

Usually, I didn't mind talking with Todd. He was close to my age, and we shared some similar interests. Of course, sharing interests just meant that the same marketing strategies had suckered us both. It gave us something to talk about, at least. Todd mentioned music, movies, and toys we played with as kids. I made an affirmative grunt whenever I recognized a brand name. Since he was a similar age to myself and Todd, I had the same conversations with Sam the skater-boy.

What commercials you enjoyed were the American equivalent of personality tests. And liking the same things as another person was just as good as liking them, since in a materialist society like ours, you are what you consume.

Or, in the junkies' cases, what you couldn't stop consuming. What you thought you were consuming, but was actually consuming you.

There was a thought, addiction as nothing more than the typical consumer impulse taken to its gruesome and inevitable conclusion. It's what will eventually happen to all of us TV-watching, SUV-driving, latte-guzzling losers. We'll all be eaten alive by our need for the shiny new shit we see on TV, and then our possessions will take over our lives and inherit the earth.

I'd like to think of my job as proof that such a thing was possible. Sure, the pleasure the junkies derived from their drugs was incredibly short-lived, but it's not like that 42-inch digital television you've been saving up for will have you shitting rainbows for the rest of *your* life.

Todd plucked a few more strings. He sang, *"You can meet any freak you want, at A New Start Halfway House..."* It didn't rhyme, but so what?

"You'd think so," I said. "But it's a more dull than exotic job. I got a college degree to do shit that I could've done in grade school. Ninety-percent of the time here's spent sitting on my ass. And if ya seen one junkie, you've seen them all."

There is an old maxim about how it's good for your mental health to have a job that you feel makes a difference in the world. My job doesn't. I'm just part of a janitorial crew monitoring human wastes. And these guys weren't even the big-time losers. They were strictly bottom-rung mediocrities. The junkies had only ruined a couple lives. Maybe killed a few people. Some theft. A rape or two. They hadn't started wars for oil or poisoned anyone's water supply to make a few bucks.

They were bad news, but nothing worth a Made for TV movie.

"I had a girlfriend who loved meth," Todd said while he strummed. "And when she'd do it she'd just start freaking and shaking, and the only thing I could do would be put a dust rag in her hand. Give her somewhere to focus all that energy. I had a meth-head for a girlfriend and the world's cleanest apartment."

Todd had killed his girlfriend and her little brother while driving fucked up. Right into a concrete culvert at fifty miles an hour.

Todd, of course, was fine. The seriously drugged always are. The coroner's report said that everybody else had survived the initial impact, too. Maybe they'd have lived if Todd had gone for help instead of running away from their drug-filled car to save his own intoxicated ass.

Maybe not.

It's amazing, the shit people will tell you. They'll do it because they're convinced that all the horrible things they've done is the fault of their *'disease.'* Like they were just riding shotgun in their lives while the drugs swerved from lane to lane. Like you can admit to anything once you're given a ready-made excuse to grant your ass some absolution.

I decided that I would hate everyone in here if it were worth the effort.

Of course, it wasn't.

The lobby was empty except for the two of us. He kept picking at strings while I stared into space.

"Could you tell what that was?" Todd asked. He strummed a few chords again. I shook my head, admitting defeat. "*Floyd*, man! It's the start of *Wish You Were Here!*"

He played it again. "*Now* can you tell?"

"Kind of…"

I leaned back in my seat. "You know, ya never get a full view of the people you meet. Just little snippets of 'em as they paddle around in and *sometimes* try to climb out of their own self-created hells. We never get to know each other, and I don't think we really want to."

Todd gave me a funny look. "You're talking about here?"

I shrugged. "Sure."

"You got a girlfriend?" he asked.

"Did," I said. "Used to. Now I guess they can smell the failure on me."

Todd laughed. "So *that's* what failure smells like!"

"Yup," I said, "Like a mixture of Old Spice and regret."

He bent over his guitar. "*This'll* cheer your ass up." Todd strummed away for a few rapid minutes. "You know what *that* was?"

I shook my head. "No."

11:11pm
DARWIN WAS A HOPELESS OPTIMIST

Someone came and got me when Swanky wouldn't stop vomiting. Since I was working a double shift and doing the second half by myself, I'd let Jack leave early. Of course, everything had waited till then to happen.

Swanky was hunched over the toilet. He concentrated on spewing his stomach contents with as much effort and volume as possible. His entire body shook with the force of the regurgitations. In the small space between the fits of retching, Swanky found time to cry. His body shook with the sobs, then his body would shake with the vomiting. He almost had something of a rhythm going.

"You okay?" I asked. A rhetorical question, obviously, which was fine since I inquired more out of social protocol than compassion. After having a few of them die over the past year, there wasn't much the junkies could do to faze me. Hell, I'll admit that this entire place could burn up with everyone trapped inside, and all I would do is light a joint off the smoldering ruins and shrug, '*Eh, no big loss…*'

Used to feel the same way about my high school.

"I—I took my meds," Swanky said, echoing into the toilet bowl. He might have been about to say more, but—right on schedule—violent retching interrupted his attempts at communicating anything other than a general lack of well-being.

I leaned back against the far wall of the bathroom, watching as his tiny body changed tempo and returned to shaking with sobs. Swanky was the kind of guy who gave crackheads a bad name. A frighteningly skinny wreck of a human being. He was small, bald, illiterate, and possessed of a manic nature that caused him to rocket around the building like he had trained his brain to manufacture its own crack so that being in a rehab wouldn't kill his buzz.

Swanky was...well, to give you a decent idea of the guy, it'd be like if you took Corky from *Life Goes On* (remember that show?), made him short, black, and started off each of his days by replacing his Rice Krispies with a bowl of sugar-coated crack rocks.

And then stuck him in a building with me for eight to sixteen hours.

Swanky had been caught the other day fucking some fat old homeless woman behind a dumpster. *Sans* protection, of course. He had apparently bribed her with a plate of the pasta the junkies had for lunch. It was just another example of the weak taking advantage of the even weaker.

"I don't recall giving you any meds," I commented, already bored with Swanky and his suffering. The junkies were required to turn in all their medication to me. I gave them back in the specified doses at pre-arranged times.

Yeah, for some reason they didn't trust the addicts in here with their own medications. Still scratching my head over that one.

"Dentist—" pause to retch, "Dentist give 'em to me today."

It would've been pointless to stand there lecturing Swanky about facility rules while he did his damnedest to turn himself inside out. Instead, I counted Swanky's pills, handed to me by his roommate. They were some kind of antibiotic. The directions on them read: '*take with food...one pill two times daily.*'

Seven pills were missing.

"Did you take all these at once?" I asked him. Swanky tried to answer. It took me a while to discern his nodding from the usual convulsions. "Well, there's your problem," I said to his quivering form, still hunched over the toilet bowl. "Turns out you're a fuckin' idiot."

Diagnosis complete, I stuffed the rest of his meds in my pocket and headed back downstairs. Technically, Swanky's medicinal misadventure would be classified as an overdose. I was going to have to document this. Fill out the appropriate paperwork. And thoroughly. *Goddamnit.*

The sound of Swanky gagging followed me through the hallway. I called back over my shoulder, "Someone let me know if homeboy starts bringing up blood."

11:31pm
THAT'S JUST GOD WHEN HE'S DRUNK

Corey was bawling in the chapel again. Same low keening and barely decipherable pleading. Whining and crying to his god to deliver him from a life he had fucked up beyond all recognition. Some times it sounded like he was talking in tongues and I'd get excited by the possibility of having my very own Pentecostal Crackhead. Then I would catch a recognizable word or two and realized a simple truth: Ebonics is even tougher to understand through sobbing.

Corey had shown up at the rehab/halfway house just a few days previously. He mostly kept to himself. Didn't mix much, didn't mingle with the other clients. Knowing how tough it can be to adjust to life here, I made the mistake of initiating a conversation with the guy. Simply caught his attention when he walked past my desk. Asked how he was doing. How his day had been.

It was like somebody yanked the Little Dutch Boy's finger out of the dike. "Oh, *blessed*," he spewed, his face suddenly rapturous as his eyes zeroed in on mine. "Just *blessed*!"

(Explanatory note: the term "blessed" *<bless-ed>* is commonly used by recovering addicts possessing sufficient levels of melanin and newfound religiosity; the word is used to indicate a state of extreme well-being—the kind experienced when one is no longer pawning stolen goods for drug money—that the user attributes to the deity of their choice, typically Jesus.)

"The devil tried to trip me up today," Corey said, arms waving and voice rising like I was playing congregation to his televangelist. "Oh, *yes he did*! He tried to trip me up *real good*!"

I nodded in response. Somebody was doing horrible things to my impression of their IQ.

"But I didn't let 'im; *oh no*! I fought back against that devil. I got him behind me! With the help of—"

"That's great," I interrupted.

Theatrical motherfucker. Unbelievably so. I did a quick look around the room to make sure I wasn't on Candid Camera.

At first it sounded to me like Corey was being a little over-exuberant in telling me about how he resisted smoking rock. Figured the guy just liked his metaphors. Drugs equaling The Devil wasn't the most creative allegory possible, but it wasn't like I was in Senior English discussing Puritanical myth and metaphor in *Pilgrim's Progress*.

Corey could be forgiven for the low-level clichés.

The truth, unfortunately, turned out to be way more amusing than that. More pathetic, too. Nothing was meant as metaphor. Nothing was allegory. The guy really did think he was going toe-to-toe with The Dark One *<cue scary organ music>*.

Turned out that Corey had been trying to get ahold of his wife for a few days. They had just gotten separated (a common state of marital affairs here), so she was understandably trying to avoid him. He, also understandably, was having none of that. If it's a reflex with our species to want to avoid the person

118

you've just demoted, it's also a reflex to desperately seek out the one who gave you the demoting.

I don't know why we're sick like that, but we are.

Corey told me about tracking his wife to a Women's Meeting at the church they both attended. Corey's woman was pissed when she saw him there. She ran off to hide. The church service going on at the time was disrupted, but Corey refused to leave until she spoke with him.

(This is the account that I translated from his rambling story about being holy and righteous, yet unfairly put-upon for some reason—some reason like *The Devil* tormenting him! Corey's version of the story made him sound like a cross between Martin Luther King Jr. and Sir Galahad.)

After the commotion he caused, another member of the church drove him straight back here. "Good thing they did," he said. "The *devil* was tryin' to get me. The devil was tellin' me to go back home, go back to my house. Break down the law that woman made to keep me out."

When he said '*home*,' I figured Corey was referring to a place of residence other than our hallowed halls. No one wants to think of this place as being anything but a highly temporary residence. Like a motel, but with steep rates and real shitty room service.

"That *is* my house," he asserted. "I just lettin' her and the kids stay there while I busy with my recovery."

"Gotcha," I said, trying to figure out the best way to shut up him up.

"And the devil wanted me to—"

Time to interrupt: "Why do you keep blaming the devil for everything?"

His eyes got huge like I'd just asked the world's most rhetorical question-like where the sun was going to rise now that it had set in the west.

"That 'cause the devil in here," he pointed at his temple. "And he tryin' to-"

"Ever think that maybe *you're* the only thing up there?" Although I was beginning to suspect that maybe even Corey wasn't all there. It reminded me of that part of the Big Book that Jack always quoted in his own vernacular: '*an addict by his self be in some bad company.*'

"Why would the devil give a shit about what you do? Is it a '*Convert 50 Christians, get a free toaster-oven!*' kinda deal?"

He stared at me, aghast.

"If you were the devil, wouldn't you have more important crap to worry about than some fuckin' crackhead in Pasadena?"

We went on like this for a little while. Him asserting that I obviously didn't know about the spiritual war going on; myself countering that I most certainly *did* know contemporary Christian mythology—especially the IQ-lite versions so popular here in the Deep South.

(No, I'm not supposed to fuck with the new clients, but in my defense...hell, I confess; there is no excuse. I just felt like passing the time that way.)

Finally, grown tired of the conversation, I conceded defeat. "All right, man. You win. There is a devil." Corey's face lit up. Doubt he'd ever won an argument before in his life. "And he told me to test your faith like that."

"*That right*!" Corey said, about to launch on another self-righteous tirade. "That right! I said—" He stopped short. "You just say the *devil* told you?"

I nodded. "Well, *asked* me, actually. We do favors for each other."

"You playin'?"

I shook my head. "No playin'." This had started out funny, but was now rapidly moving towards pathetic. "He just wanted me to let you know that it was a close call, and that he'll try harder next time."

There probably wasn't too much difference between what I was doing and pushing a polio victim down a stairwell. Both are easy beyond belief, and neither makes for an anecdote that you'd share at a cocktail party. But, I guess only one will get the cops called on you.

Corey's attachment to Iron Age superstitions got the best of him at that point, and in the words of the popular Texas colloquialism, he lit out of there like his ass was on fire.

I chuckled for another few seconds then went back to reading.

And now, for the third night in a row, he was lying face down in the chapel (I peeked in after hearing the noise). Sobbing loudly and piteously to his god like a little kid who just dropped his ice cream on the sidewalk. Corey was doing a great job of reminding me why I'd always thought Christianity was such a pussy religion.

(Although it's actually very *anti*-pussy.)

Bigot, I teased myself, and then headed back to the desk to crank up the radio. An old Tom Waits song flooded the lobby.

I turned the volume up again. Corey's wailing still cut through the music.

11:44pm
GRACIAS ESPIRITU SANTO, POR MI SALVADOR

Warren leaned over my desk. His hair looked like it had been viciously raped by a blow dryer, and the red circles around his bloodshot eyes meant something other than drugs. If I didn't know what a sin it was for men to show vulnerability, I'd almost think he'd been crying.

I had been amusing myself with my new bottle of pepper spray, wishing there was someone to try it on. Warren, unfortunately, was too harmless to be a serious candidate. I gave him a lazy smile. "What's up?"

"I need…" his voice came out fragile and dry. "I need to check into a mental hospital."

I gave Warren a quick once-over. He did indeed look like several kinds of refried shit. "Isn't this place bad enough?"

Warren didn't laugh. Didn't smile. He just pulled up the sleeves of his shirt. Fresh red fissures ran east to west on both his wrists. Done bleeding, thankfully.

A quiet "*Goodness*," was all I could think to say. How disappointing it must have been when it finally dawned on the guy that he hadn't cut deep enough. Slicing both wrists had probably shot his courage wad. No way could he bring himself to do it again. Not right away. The amount of despairing valor required to slash your wrists couldn't be too easy to come by, or we all would've done it by now.

I was about to suggest slapping a bandage on his cuts—before they got infected—when the phone rang. And rang. I looked at Warren. I looked at the phone. I finally gave in and picked it up.

Poor Warren, his big moment had ended with him being upstaged by an appliance.

Staring at Warren's wrists, I forgot the professional phone greeting and just said, "*Yeah*?"

Gim's friendly bass sounded over the phone. Before my boss could get to past his initial greeting, I interrupted with, "There's somebody here you might wanna talk to," and handed the receiver to Warren. "*It's Gim*," I said to Warren, like he was a mixture of retarded child and frightened rabbit. "Why don't you be a dear and tell him what you just showed me."

He took the phone. The waterworks started almost immediately. "I've got—" a huge sob wracked his body, "I've got nothing to live for."

Warren's ability to jump right to the heart of the matter impressed me immensely. None of that *beating-around-the-bush* crap for him. Unfortunately, the lack of introductions probably left Gim wondering whom the fuck had ambushed him with their suicidal longings.

"Warren told Gim that he had been drinkin' bleach," I reported later to Robert. Keeping secrets never was a strong point of mine. "Kinda makes me wonder what it tastes like."

"We got us some in the kitchen," Robert suggested. I shook my head.

"Not that curious, thanks." After Warren had talked to Gim he'd basically crumbled into a little ball against my desk. I had half-walked, half-dragged him into the chapel where he'd be out of the way, then went to find someone to drive Warren to the nearest funny farm. Hopefully they had thought to drop him off with a note about keeping the guy away from industrial-strength cleansers, especially if he looked thirsty.

"Why bleach?" I posed the eternal question. "Why not *Drano*? Probably be the most horrifically painful three minutes of your life, but at least it'd be pretty final."

Robert nodded. "I thought about endin' myself when I learn about my cancer, but I never woulda drank no bleach."

I had heard Warren do a decent amount of gut-spilling to Gim. "Your typical hard luck story," I said. "He's got a couple varieties of Hepatitis, basic death sentence right there, wife left him, unemployed, disowned by offspring, cognizant of his own vast failings in life, *blah blah blah...*"

Robert, who had survived 'terminal' throat cancer, four divorces, six years in jail and two years on the street, just shook his head. "Pussy," he said.

Yeah, we're all heart. But, I really had to wonder how some people ended up with one misfortune after another in their lives. We've all known folks who had nothing but tragedy followed by tragedy followed by more tragedy with an economy-sized helping of tragedy bringing up the caboose. Their job moves to

Mexico, they got hooked on crack, their kids are wiped out in freak tornado, bad investments destroy them financially, they come home to find their house burglarized, their dog hanging from the ceiling fan...all the typical Job-like trials.

How does shit like that happen? Do some people just get on a roll with suffering? Does misery just attract more misery, like attracting like? Do we send our shit-luck vibes into the ether that in turn attract more shit-luck, or would that just be blaming the victim? Was there some big roulette wheel up in the sky with all of our names on it that God liked to spin, asking Himself as He watched it: '*Hmmm, now whom am I going to hate this week?*'

Or, was life just as capricious as it seemed, and if shit happened for no reason, then did shit also happened *repeatedly* for no reason, as well?

Maybe. Doubt too many of us talking monkeys were important enough to rate any sort of celestial enmity. Not that we needed the extra help fucking things up. Most of us handled that just fine on our own.

"You realize that was our third suicide attempt this month?" I asked Robert.

He nodded, causing the lobby lights to dance along the bumps of his skull. "None of us here much good at *anything*."

This place wasn't funny anymore. Everyone's suffering wasn't funny anymore.

I wanted out.

NIGHT SHIFT
(12-8am)

12:30pm
GREEN SCREEN LIFE

I bumped into the doorframe on my way into the building. My attempts at hiding how drunk I was were gonna have to be a wee bit more strenuous. Yep, just a *wee* bit.

"*Wuzzup?*" I said to Reginald. He gave me a nod in return as he packed his things to leave.

"You're late."

I *thought* it was Reginald, at least. It tended to be that fucker that I relieved on these evening shifts. My vision was a smidgen too blurry to be sure. Could've been some other skinny little black guy stuck behind the desk. Some other skinny little black guy with a reedy voice like his balls were waiting till his late 50s to drop.

Closing one eye to cut down on the double vision seemed like a good idea. Then I realized that sort of shit was exactly what those crafty motherfuckers would be looking for. That, and the swaying, and the slurred speech, and whatever else it was that they tried to tell us about in our training classes.

But not from me, they wouldn't. Not from a Tech. Nobody thinks to check a Tech for overt signs of intoxication, nobody watches the watchmen, and that's why I got away with it every time.

"*Howz it goin'?*" I kept myself to short, easily pronounced sentences as I marched my bike past Reginald to the side hallway.

"Paul got kicked out today," Reginald said. "Said he'll come back and shoot everyone here. If he really do show up, don't let him in."

"*Gotcha.*"

I'd gotten it down to something of an art form over the past few months. Go out and drink like it was the cure to all of life's little problems until about 10:45. Rush home. Shower. Douse myself with near-toxic levels of cologne. Arrive at work around midnight, still buzzing like hell and ready to pass the fuck out for five or six hours.

And get paid for it.

God bless my job, and *God Bless America!*

I started to tip to the side, bike and all. Caught myself right before the tilt of no return.

Maintain, motherfucker. Maintain! I steadied myself as I pushed my bike down the hallway. It was taking all my concentration not to fall over the thing as I steered it.

I had belly-flopped twice on my way to work. Was probably bleeding under my jeans. Haven't wiped out on a bike since grade school. Now here I was fifteen years later, a college grad trying not to trip over a bicycle as he showed up at work tanked enough to be flammable.

My mother would be so proud.

Arriving at your place of employment in a state of extreme intoxication probably ain't the smartest thing to do in any profession. Not only is your func-

124

tioning impaired (only a problem if you have a job that requires functioning), but there's a damn good chance that if they catch you, your ass is good and fired. Obviously.

You'd think that more employers would understand. That they'd be keyed into the bleakness of working class life. Living paycheck to paycheck. The dull routine that required chemical coping. The economy that went belly-up just in time for you to graduate. The useless degree wasted at the dead-end McJob…

But they're not. Fuckers just don't understand. Management's got no pity for the workers. Top dogs never care about the ones on the bottom. So it's best that they don't catch you.

Too bad that drunk people are a lot more obvious than they think. Alcohol, from the smell to the effect, runs counter to the very notion of subtlety. Damn good chance that someone is either going to notice that you're obnoxious or that your speech is slurred or your motor-functions are impaired or that you have a strong bouquet of booze seeping from your pores.

And that's just in normal jobs. Imagine if everyone in your place of employment was qualified, either by profession or lifestyle, to sniff out your symptoms. My fellow Techs are trained to look for any and all signs of altered functioning, and most of the clients—especially the alkies—can smell a drop of beer from fifty paces. Being here drunk, being here under the influence of *anything*, is pretty risky. Pretty stupid.

Pretty common on my part.

Screw it, though. If I got fired, what would I have to lose aside from a shit job with shit wages earned by watching shit people?

Right?

Distracted by the act of thinking, my motor skills abandoned me in the side hallway. Myself and the bike were in a heap. Being horizontal and in pain told me I must've fallen at some point. Wish I could've recalled when. Walking with bike, then laying on bike. Gravity's tricky like that. I could guess what occurred in between, but damned if I noticed it happen.

"*Ouchie*," I said, and giggled before I could stop myself.

Took me a few seconds to realized that Reginald might get curious about a loud crash coming from the back hall. It could blow my cover. Get me caught. Kill my buzz.

I struggled to right the bike, and myself, as quickly as possible. It took a few tries. Damn tough to pull something upright when you're off-balance, too. Eventually I stumbled on the method of bracing myself against the wall with one hand while tugging on my handlebars with the other. The bike was pulled upright, and for a second I rejoiced.

It fell back over.

"*Oh*, the kickstand!" I drunkenly clapped my hand over my mouth. Had Reginald heard that? *Christ*, my voice sounded like I was gargling marbles! He'd know!

I pulled the bike upright a second time. Put down the kickstand. Psyched myself out to act normal. Reached into my pocket and popped another mint. Gave myself a reminder to be cool.

I strolled back into the lobby, prepared to sit on the couch and not speak until spoken to. Not give away the game. Fake my way through yet another drunken night of work.

The worrying was unnecessary. The lobby was empty. Reginald was gone. *Thank Christ.*

I started to shout after him, "That's what your mom says when we... *fukkit.*" The hell with our little routine. Considering how the job market had up and shat itself, I'd probably be shouting immature crap at Reginald till I was twice as old as he is now.

How utterly fucking depressing.

The dangerous part of the shift over, I flopped down behind the desk and concentrated to keep the room from spinning.

12:38am
LAST MAN STANDING

The showers hadn't let up all night. I sat outside the rehab with a book and a cup of the second-rate kool-aid the junkies drank and watched Pasadena get washed for the fifth day in a row. It's always raining in my memories of work. The water level's always rising on the street and everyone walks through the door wet and miserable.

Paul was standing next to me on the front porch. He had recently relapsed for the third time this year. The current record is five times in the same month, but I'm still sick of seeing the guy.

He showed me his hands. There were large red blisters on both his palms.

"Ooh, *stigmata*!" I said. "Truly you are the Junkie Messiah!"

Paul just stared at me, so I asked for a cigarette to break the silence. He complied. Two puffs on the thing and I was reminded why I don't smoke. Paul was blathering about some sitcom he liked watching. Not giving a shit about the socially approved ways that he rotted his brain, I asked if he fucked up his hands while high.

"I was playin' with my kid!" Paul said, a little angry.

I reiterated the question.

"Yeah..." he said. "Yeah I was fucked up...but I *was* playing with my kid."
And that makes everything better!

My skepticism wasn't hidden enough, so Paul stalked off to the second floor rooms where we stack our junkies like cordwood. Back to the dormitory sleeping arrangements for him, and back to solitude for me. I was left alone.

Any and all urges to be sociable never really hit until all the junkies go to bed. Then I get sloughed down in an overwhelming need for human interaction. Preferably with someone not fucked up or pathetic. By the time I'm halfway through my double shift, that's the only sort of person I've been interacting with for the past eight hours.

No luck, though. Everybody here crashed out early. Everyone I knew in the real world had to get up early the next day. I still had eight hours to go. After

126

all those months of employment here, I really should've been used to the solitude.

It was just me, my CDs, a computer and a medication room that only I had the keys to. So it wasn't all bad. Could've been worse. After keeping this place running smoothly for eight hours, there was nobody I was responsible for beside myself (and those fifty-plus guys upstairs, I guess). I put a collection of Beethoven's late string quartets on the player and reclined on the couch.

Three different crackheads had asked me today about my ex-girlfriend. They wanted to know, "What happen to that fine little girl usedta come bring ya food and y'all be all kissin' out in front and all?"

"She went the way of all flesh," I'd respond.

From two of them this earned blank looks, but the third asked in horror, "Shit, she dead?"

I'd shrugged. "Far as I'm concerned..."

For a while it was a pretty frequent question: whatever happened to my ex. Or, as they liked to put it, '*dat girl wit dat vicious booty.*' I'm not sure about how 'vicious' it was (or why this was any of their goddamn business), but she did used to have this utter ghetto-booty of an ass that jutted out like a shelf from her lower back. Surprisingly firm and high riding, too. Never seen anything like it on any Hispanic girl besides her. I dubbed it the Ninth Wonder of the World (King Kong being the Eighth).

I couldn't say why my tastes in women had been running more and more along the same lines as the 'thick' type that the crackheads always picked up at their 12-step meetings. Didn't think that was what I dug. Us dumb white boys, after all, are supposed to be well trained by years of *Playboy* and Hollywood to only lust after the *twig-with-tits* variety of the female form. My ex plus Cassandra's *pregnant-minus-the-baby* figure this past year would seem to suggest that my brainwashing was a bit faulty. Made me wonder if I should report for reprogramming.

Still, out of all the habits I could pick up from these guys, an appreciation for full-figured women was about as harmless as it got. If I ever found myself blowing my neighbors for some rock money, *then* I'd know it was past time to find another job.

12:48pm
TIME FOR US TO GIVE A LITTLE LOVE BACK TO GOD

Even at night in December the weather was warm enough for shorts, so that's what I wore. If this kept up, it'd be another Lawn Chair Xmas here in Pasadena.

It was probably due to the temperate weather (and neurological damage from Pasadena's petrochemical pollution) that my new coworker was wearing a Hawaiian shirt. It was covered with all the Warner Bros. cartoon characters dancing in hula skirts. Occasionally, you'll see someone for the first time and you instantly go: '*Oh. That's all I could ever possibly want to know about you.*'

I saw Chris in his shirt created by a merchandising committee and instantly lost faith in the notion of human progress. Knowing that I belonged to a species committed to creating—and spending money on—soul-crushing banalities, I felt despair. There was an overwhelming temptation to go hang myself in the bathroom using a roll of double-ply, but suicide attempts weren't covered by Workman's Comp in Texas.

"Amazing," I said as we shook hands. "Your wardrobe manages to represent everything I loathe about our culture."

If I die alone and unloved, at least I'll have only myself to blame. Well, myself and the alcohol.

"*What?*" he said. Chris turned out to be a little hard of hearing. He also had a few other quirks that would blow his chance for a seat on the last shuttle to safety if the earth ever fell into the sun. Nice guy, but nobody would ever consider using him for breeding stock to restart the human race.

Chris looked to be in his mid thirties. His tiny, near-set eyes gave him a sort of Clueless and Inbred vibe. He had a lumpy body, and representing it to the world was one hellaciously puffy face, like Chris dipped his head in a beehive every morning before work. There was a resemblance to the Pillsbury Dough Boy, if Mr. Dough giggled when you poked him in the ass instead of his belly.

It was the first day at work for Chris, and Yours Truly was to show him the proverbial ropes.

No problem.

For his first lesson, I led Chris over to the front desk. Our rotting chair was pointed at. Making sure not to breathe margarita on the guy, I ordered, "Sit."

He looked at me and grinned a little, unsure.

"*Sit!*" I repeated. He did.

"Feet up," I said, pointing at the desktop. Chris got this on the first try. He was improving quickly.

"Just do that for eight hours," I told him. "That, and try to kill your sense of compassion before your next shift when you'll have to be around the homeless."

I didn't mention how much he'd grow to hate the clients, too. I was sure pissed at the bastards. One of them had told Gim that I'd left my post last week to hit a fraternity party. Actually, I don't attend *frat* parties. I'm graduated, and they always have such crap beer at those things. Besides, I totally had Sam covering the front desk for the hour I'd been gone to a friend's birthday celebration.

Lying sacks of shit. I couldn't believe my boss had even considered believing them. It seemed like Gim had yet to learn *New Start Rule #1.*

"Is this all there is to it?" Chris asked me.

"*Basically.*"

."Do I have to be able to speak Spanish?"

I shook my head. "Nope. Just Ebonics, White Trash, and Self-Pity…"

"Oh." Chris just stared at me. I could tell he was going to be loads of fun. I wondered what made a harmless chap like him sign up to work with the burn-outs and degenerates that comprised the rest of my coworkers. And me.

"...a few local dialects of Uneducated and maybe a bit of Crazy-Talk. If you can't understand what somebody's saying, it's a good bet they're talkin' shit to ya."

"How long have you worked here?" Chris asked.

"Just about a year."

"Do you *like* your job?"

"Love it," I lied. "But careful; it destroys the weak and gives an ice-cold moral enema to the rest of us." Instruction over, I flopped down on the lobby's couch and commenced earning an hourly wage for searching through the Help Wanted section of the paper.

"You'll get the ass calluses in a month or so," I assured Chris. "Things'll get easier from there."

1:11am
ASK MASTER P

Rap music tended to fall flat with me. It always sounded like the singer was either bragging or threatening me, two things I get enough of from insecure black guys in real life. And hell, the last time I cared about a rhyme scheme was when reading Dr. Seuss.

I was listening to *Master P* on the stereo (left my own CDs at home) and reading obituaries with some of the clients who couldn't sleep. Some months I was guaranteed enough company to keep me up all night. Other months I could get four to five hours of solitude.

One of the junkies, six days fresh off kicking the habit, was making a morbid experience even cheerier. "Lucky fuckers," he said at each obit read aloud. Sobriety was apparently not agreeing with the guy.

Everybody signs an agreement to refrain from self-harm while staying here, but I was keeping an eye on him just in case. *New Start Rule #1*, and all that jazz. Dead junkies mean plenty of paperwork for yours truly, so it was something I wouldn't mind avoiding. Learning his name could be a waste of time if he ended up relapsed or dead, but he told me it's Jamie.

Jamie was a scuzzy little bastard, his hair matted in clumps like he'd sworn off shampoo as a useless luxury years ago. I looked over his arms and noticed a nice, jagged scar on both wrists. They went well with the tattoos that circled his biceps, twin snakes that stopped just short of swallowing their own tails. Noticing the direction of my gaze, Jamie just shrugged. "I was young and stupid."

There's no standard social protocol for responding to something like that, so I said, "Yeah?"

"*Yeah*," he said. "Next time I'm cutting down, not across."

"This fella seems to have led a pretty full life," Curtis said. He read aloud the obit of some guy who'd worked on a refinery team for Exxon. He held up the picture of the deceased for everyone else to see. It seemed like Curtis was trying to score substitute Parenting Points by reading obituaries to junkies in lieu of bedtime stories to his own distant children.

I shook my head. "So he did his part to help destroy the environment? That's a *great* legacy."

"What killed him?" It was the same question Jamie asked every time. He'd be real fun at parties.

"Doesn't say," Curtis shrugged. It never does, but the junkie always asked. I guess hope paradoxically springs eternal for the chronically morbid. Then Curtis' head jerked up to look at the stereo. "*What'd* he just say? *What* was that? The hell's wrong with music today? He just said he killed a nig—uh, *fella* for no damn reason."

Curtis wasn't going get a Rhodes scholarship anytime soon, but he had eventually caught on that there are words you don't say around here without sufficient melanin levels.

"There ya go," I suggested to Jamie (it's his CD). "Maybe Master P killed that guy."

"He's killin' my ears." Curtis was set on sounding as old as possible. "And the dead guy was white. *Feller* on the stereo's only talking about killing black people."

"Master P's a *playah*," I told Curtis, "Not a bigot. I'm sure he'd kill the honky, too."

Honky and *cracker* were the only racial slurs allowed in the rehab. This was likely due to my own inability to stop using them. They're just fun. Some of the crackheads (not all of whom are black, but it's a 90-percent thing), when they were doing chores, would refer to each other as '*house nigger*' or '*field nigger*.' I found this hilarious, but they were eventually told that such terminology was Old Behavior (the sort of stuff that landed them in rehab in the first place), and that put an end to that.

"Who else we got?" Jamie asked, impatient for Curtis to keep reading.

"Umm, thirty-eight-year-old mother of...three," Curtis said, and the death-list rolled on.

1:23am
EURO-WHORES and *BARELY 18*

I listened to Eddy talk about his romantic strategies. About how he wooed the shattered women he encountered at 12-step meetings. Once he'd decided against his initial plan of killing me, Eddy had leapt to the other side of the social spectrum and decided we were pals. I was his token white friend. He now came down to talk at me every damn night. Sometimes I was drunk enough to ramble back at him; sometimes I just pretended to listen.

It'd be a lie to claim that I cared about anything Eddy had to say. But, considering our past interactions, so long as he stayed non-violent I was an attentive audience.

"…and I put the sparkling apple juice next to the bath tub," he said. "That goes at the head of the tub. And then there's the tape player at the foot. Close enough to make sure she don't miss a sound, but far enough to where can do your own sweet talkin'."

I scratched my head. "People really fuck without booze?" Man, just when I thought this place couldn't get any weirder.

Eddie assured me that such marvels really occurred, and promised to lay a few tips on me the next day. "I'll show ya how spot the *vulnerable* ones," he said. Then we knocked knuckles (causing me to flinch), and he headed upstairs for the night.

I was now alone to entertain myself.

A nice thing about working night shift was the opportunity it provided to snoop through the offices of the day workers. Sometimes I turned up interesting stuff. For example, my boss has a HUGE pornography collection. Nudie mag after nudie mag, just stuffed in the bottom filing cabinet in that man's office. No videos, unfortunately, just paper-based porn.

Don't know why, but finding the stuff in his drawers is so much cooler than just using his computer to snag it on the net.

I guessed that the administrative hassles, on top of having to deal with the junkies and crackheads, got way too stressful sometimes, and this is what Gim used in lieu of going back to the bottle. Still...couldn't help but wonder if—when it's time for a little *stress relief*—if the guy sneaks off to the bathroom with them, or if he just locks his door.

Hopefully the former, since his office door has a small window in it, and there'd be something funny about another employee walking past his door just in time to catch his orgasm face. And since he's about Seven Fucking Feet Tall, if I ever caught sight of his dick I'd be forced to kill myself before the inferiority complex could fully set in.

But on an odd note: some of the magazines with the younger girls had the titles cut off the front page. As far as typical shame-motivated behavior goes, this was a new one. I realize that lots of people would be embarrassed to be caught with a magazine full of stuff designed to <gasp> sexually arouse them, but why get rid of the titles?

What was Gim hoping for? That, if somebody saw a magazine cover featuring buxom teens squatting on mag-lites—but with no title—hopefully they'd figure he was into extreme performance art? How lurid can a title be to where you don't mind being caught jacking off to something, you just don't want to be caught jacking off to something called *that*?

I picked out two or three of my favorites, poked my head into the hallway to make sure the coast was clear, then fast-walked to the bathroom.

1:34am
WRONG PLACE, WRONG TIME, WRONG SPECIES

I was talking with one of the junkies about the latest U.S. military action. Curtis couldn't sleep, and I was trying to read the newspaper, so the guy just happened to be in the wrong place at the wrong time. We discussed and argued our personal feelings about it all.

Curtis was more patriotic and gung-ho than myself. He'd been a veteran for about a decade or so. Knowing that Curtis had fallen for the Army recruitment commercials on TV, my already-low opinion of his IQ sank to new depths.

I made my usual case about what a crock of shit the newest invasion was. While the U.S. Ruling Elite used the usual terms like 'liberation,' 'freedom,' and 'democracy,' I argued to Curtis, it all came down to killing shitloads of people who had as little say in their country's politics as I did in ours.

"Yeah," he concurred. "*Ah* was stationed in the Persian Gulf back in the nineties. That's basically what we did." I decided to pay attention for a change. Maybe this would be more interesting than the usual client-babble. "They told us, *kill everybody you find*, and we did…"

I nodded. A good nod can make up for a lot of things.

"We'd just walk into a building and shoot everybody in there," Curtis said. "Mostly women and kids. *Ah* dunno where all the men were."

Well, it wasn't like the guy was the first murderer I'd met in here. Although, since he killed foreigners on command, I guess the proper term would be 'Hero.' I'd read a study once that showed how Americans rarely won battles unless they outnumbered the enemy by at least two-to-one. Little surprise then that they tended to slaughter people in impoverished third world countries. Bullies always prefer easy targets.

"What part of Iraq were you in?" I asked. It was a bland follow-up to a hell of a revelation, but I decided to wait a little while before asking him what sound babies made when gut-shot.

Curtis shook his head. "We weren't in Iraq," he said. "*Ah* was stationed in Kuwait. Never made it to Iraq."

New Start Rule #1 was dancing in the back of my head, but I just asked, "No shit?" It was all I could think to say.

"No shit," Curtis replied. It was all he could think to say, too.

We sat in silence for a minute. Me wondering what it took to slaughter a family with machine-gun fire. Him remembering what it took to slaughter a family with machine-gun fire.

Curtis finally spoke. "It really chops them up." Typically, my memory is such shit that I would've already forgotten what we'd been discussing. But not this time. "Bullets do. They really do a number on the little ones. The kids and the babies. It's like an eraser on them cartoon characters. One second they got a hand, next second it's gone."

I nodded again. It's part of being an attentive listener. "Fuckin' Arabs," Curtis said, as if it was *their* fault. He pronounced the word, *Ay-rabs*, like a good patriot should. "Fuckin' Arabs."

Then he started to cry. Quiet little mewlings that retained his country twang. Tears ran down the side of his nose to collect in his moustache.

I went back to the paper. People crying had ceased to interest me. I used Curtis's distraction to pop another Valium.

"*Yeah…*" I said to Curtis. "And just think how they felt about it."

1:57am
INEVITABLE LANDSCAPES

A heavy fog had settled over downtown Pasadena. I couldn't see more than forty yards up the street in either direction. There was a palpable thickness to the air, like always during an East Texas summer. Streetlights and security lamps gave off an eerie, pinkish glow, causing this section of town to resemble a post-industrial version of Hell. Bums walked out of the fog, stumbled past our building and disappeared further down the street. I half-expected to hear screams coming from that direction, some indication that the night felt weird and shitty for any reason other than because I did, but there was only the occasional and distant sound of car engines. Besides that, the entire world could have disappeared except for my own private, addict-filled island.

"FREE CRACK!" I screamed out the front door, desiring more signs of life. "Get your FREE CRACK right here!"

I waited a while before closing the door and heading back to my boss' office. I felt lonely. Maybe I should've tossed a toaster oven into the deal as well.

2:03 am
WHAT I HATE ABOUT MY JOB
AND WHAT MY JOB HATES ABOUT ME

I heard the door to the chapel close and soft footfalls padding their way to the bathroom.

'*If he comes outta the chapel,*' Jack had told me, '*You send his ass along.*'

When the bathroom door opened up, I was waiting for him, shoulders straight and chest puffed out in my best *Pretend Authority* stance. Somebody had relapsed before my shift started, and Jack had left it for me to deal with. I molded a stern scowl on my face. You have to look hardened if you're going to throw someone out onto the freezing streets in the middle of the night.

He stepped out, and I finally saw whom it was that had shown up drunk tonight: Old Herman. About 65-years old, stooped with age, and wrinkled like he was twice what the calendar insisted. Addiction ages no one well.

I deflated. *Shit.* Now I knew why Jack hadn't been able to toss the guy out like we're supposed to. Now I understood why he had made Herman a pallet in the chapel and told him to sleep it off. Now it made sense why Jack had passed the buck to me. Who would want to throw an old man to the gutter?

Give it to the honky, he'll toss anyone.

Fucker.

"*Hey*, Ray!" Herman smiled wide at the sight of me. Damn, the guy could've been my grandpa...if, like, my grandpa was shorter, blacker, and more of a hopeless alcoholic.

"Time to get going," I said, maintaining distance between us so he couldn't smell my own booze reek, hoping he wouldn't fight me on this.

Herman did, of course. *Fuck you too, God.*

"But...*but...but...*" he started protesting. Herman insisted that he had been told that he could stay until morning. Insisted that it was way too cold outside. Insisted that we were in a horrible part of town. Insisted that there were still too many hours left in the night.

He looked so pathetic and helpless with his hunched frame and slow, arthritic movements. I imagined my own grandpa having to humiliate himself by begging some uppity white boy to not throw him out in the cold.

Very easily, I reached up inside my own head and shut off that little part that makes me human. It's a little trick I've picked up here. Nothing too difficult about it. It reckon cops and soldiers do it all the time. It helps with the job 'cause I'm just following orders, the same as I would if I were on a firing squad or manning a guard tower at Belsen.

My eyes got heavy-lidded and my face went slack like it always does when Nobody's Home. "Don't need to repeat myself, do I?"

It wasn't a question.

Herman left, gathering his things and whining the entire way. I didn't watch him walking out the door then down the street, easy prey for all the desperate types that wander this area. I just went back to my desk, tossed on another CD, and propped up my feet.

I couldn't believe his eviction had been left up to me. I couldn't believe that my coworkers had stuck me with the unpleasant job. And, worst of all, I couldn't believe how easy it had been.

2:12am
COMMON AFFLICTIONS

Chris stared at me in horror. "That's...that's one of my addiction triggers."

I met my coworker's eyes from across the room. Chris was learning the nuances of the night shift from me. This meant the lobby's lights had to stay on, but it wasn't all bad.

"You're addicted..." I couldn't believe I'd heard him right, "To *masturbating*?" And then, God help my insensitive ass, I laughed. And laughed. And laughed until my stomach cramped around all the beer I'd drank earlier.

Tears were wiped from my eyes. "I know what you mean," I assured Chris. "And I understand where you're coming from, brother. With me, it started out as just a weekend thing. Seemed harmless enough. Everyone was doing it. Then the next thing I knew I was doing it twice a week. And then three times. Then it was every day."

I sank my head into my hands. "And then there was the wank before work, and then the wank *instead* of work, and I'll never forget the dark, shameful day they had to resuscitate me after my heart stopped from protein loss."

Too amused for my own good, I looked up at Chris. I was the only one smiling.

"You're serious," I said. My coworker gave a solemn nod. *Jesus Christ...* "You're addicted to masturbating?" He nodded again.

"Me, too," I assured him.

"Really?"

"Really."

His eyes lit up with the joy of comradery. "Do you go to the meeting down by—"

"No!" I shouted. "It's called I'm a *fucking human being* and so are you!"

I had met a couple people who claimed to be sexual addicts of one kind or another, and they all struck me as having healthy sex drives with an unhealthy amount of Judeo-Christian guilt. Figures they'd make some kind of 12-Step bullshit out of it.

"But I have to do it to Internet pornography," he said, as if that was supposed to shock me. I had half an urge to jump on the guy and flail away at him, screaming, '*You monster!*' in a voice of high patrician outrage.

Instead, I nodded in understanding. "Yeah, growing up with Fantasia and MTV killed my imagination, too."

Chris seemed really disappointed, so an assurance was in order. "Look," I said, "I'm not trying to rob you of your pathology. Be as sick as you want. I'm just having a hard time agreeing that there's something wrong with listening to what your body's telling ya. You eat if you're hungry, don't you?"

Of course, that was a viewpoint that could be fatal in a place like this. Most bodies here were telling their owners to smoke crack and keep smoking it until their hearts exploded.

Maybe Chris was going for pity points, or maybe he was just trying to depress me, but the guy gave a sad little shrug and said, "I haven't had sex in over four years."

Ooooohhh...

That was officially The Worst Thing I'd Heard All Night. My own current bout of celibacy paled in comparison.

Chris wasn't the most attractive of guys (never seen a face so damn *puffy*), but nobody deserved something like that.

I suppressed a chuckle at his expense.

Stretching for something consoling, something to help me fight down the giggles, I went on to say, "*Ummm*...well, it's been a damn long time since I...*uhhh*...I dunno...made love?"

Chris shook his head. "That doesn't help at all."

2:23am
CLUB COMBO, HOLD THE GRADITUDE

I'd started turning the lights off in the lobby when I worked the night shift. This had a three-fold purpose:

1) It's easier to sleep with the lights off.

2) The clients were discouraged from bothering me with whatever little need they may have at 4am.

3) The homeless were less likely to try to get in the building in the middle of the night.

Reason 1 was the main focus of *Operation: In the Dark*, but when the clients asked, I always shared Reason 3 with them. None of their damn business, anyways.

There's a large cross on the front of our building. The homeless who wandered the streets of midtown had a tendency to identify cross-marked buildings with charities and shelters and the like. Equating Christianity with selfless kindness was just one of the many places where the bums and I differed.

I had an average of three after-hours visitors a night. Seven if I left the lobby lights on. Sometimes I just ignored their repeated knocking or ringing of the doorbell. Sometimes I stood in front of the door and mouthed—and gave the hand-signs for—'*We're Closed*' through the glass. Sometimes I opened the door and chatted with them. They usually wanted to sleep in the building, get free food, get my pocket change, or use the phone.

My self-centered ass filed the homeless under the heading: *Not My Fucking Problem*.

Maybe if all those state hospitals hadn't gotten their budgets slashed over the past twenty years, with so many of their inhabitants tossed to the curb. Maybe if social programs weren't so horribly under-funded in this country. Maybe if all our tax dollars didn't go the military or other forms of corporate welfare.

Let's just say that the homeless problem was something that a few free sandwiches weren't going to fix.

And speaking of free sandwiches:

There was a desperate ringing of the doorbell, one quick ring after another. Worried that a client was being dismembered on the front porch while I wasted time tucking my erection back into my pants in the women's bathroom, I hurried out to the lobby. Latex gloves were stripped from hands and tossed into the trash before I glanced at the door. A tall, scraggly black man sought entrance. I almost flipped the switch to unlock the door and let him in, then gave a second look. He was maybe a shade *too* scraggly to be a client. Just a bit much on the seedy side.

We stared at each other in the dark, separated by a locked door and wall of glass. I peered at him with curiosity. He returned the look with frustration and annoyance. Then the guy tugged hard on the door: *Open up, motherfucker!*

Grabbing the cudgel for insurance, I stuck my head out the door.

"Yeah?"

"Gotta let me in," he said.

"No, I don't." His face turned angry. Sweat dripped down it. Cold as it was outside, this guy was perspiring like a hippo in a sauna. Had to be crack or some other stimulant.

Apparently a fan of rhetorical questions, the bum asked, "Why not?"

We played the '*if-you-have-to-ask-you'll-never-know*' game for a while before he demanded to use the phone. Angry bums were the last people I wanted to spend time with. Especially when the rest of the building was asleep. I imagined the junkies coming down in the morning to find my bludgeoned corpse behind the front desk.

'Ray make any coffee fo' he die?' they'd ask.

The bum continued to insist on his need for the phone. "I wan' call my momma," he said.

I was in the middle of informing the guy that the lobby phone opened for public use at nine (like the sign said on the door), when it hit me: *I knew this guy!*

Well, I *kind of* knew him. He had promised to kill me once, but besides that we weren't too close. It had been a few months since we'd seen each other. Mr. Switchblade wasn't looking too well.

It was dark, thanks to the lobby lights being off, so I doubted that he recognized me. Hell, maybe I was mistaken in thinking that I had recognized him. The homelies weren't much more than one-dimensional caricatures to me. That might be vapid on my part, but it's hard to appreciate someone's deeper qualities when all they do is beg for change or threaten bloody death.

I was in the process of closing the door on the guy when he asked for some food. Well, more like *demanded* it:

"*Jus' some food, goddamnit! Jus' a sammich! Jus' a gah-damn sammich!*"

His panhandling technique still needed some work.

Perhaps moved by how much skinnier he was than the last time I'd seen him, maybe wanting to surprise myself, I told the guy to wait while I went to fix him something. A minute later I was back with a ham sandwich and potato chips. Not the healthiest meal in the world, but it beat starving. Maybe.

I opened the door up just enough to hand the plate on through. Even though he hadn't recognized me as being on his *To Kill* list, I still felt like being careful in case something jogged his memory. And in case he still had that knife. The guy looked down at the plate, his face screwed up in confusion.

"Mustard, lettuce, onions and mayonnaise," I told him. "We're outta pickles."

He looked even angrier. "What, no salad?"

I slammed the door.

Fucker spent the next few minutes banging on the front walls. The sandwich was smeared against the glass, leaving a yellow and white slug-trail of ingratitude. I wondered if he would write messages on the glass with the rejected condiments. Maybe some empowering slogan like '*Fight the Real Enemy!*' next to a crude mustard caricature of the pope. But, life being the endless disappointment it is, he only smeared abstractions while the rest of his body shook in the universal language of impotence.

"I'll fucking *kill you!*" he screamed after I'd flicked him off through the glass. "Fuckin' kill you!"

Yeah, I'd heard *that* enough times with this job.

He kicked and punched at the glass. "Fuckin' kill yo white fuckin' ass!" It was like watching a rampage at the monkey house, except that I was the one inside the glass cage.

"*Kill you!*"

Charmingly repetitive bastard. Intensely quotable, too.

I flicked him off once more and then went to the kitchen to grab the biggest knife I could find. For protection. Just in case it occurred to him to scale the back fence.

2:30am
AT LEAST IT'S NOT *THE HARDY BOYS*

Todd ran down the back hallway, shouting my name. This gave me time to stop rifling through Gim's desk and saunter back out to the lobby. Todd's lanky form was followed closely by Sam, who had just celebrated his 26th birthday in the confines of The Best Little Rehab in Texas. "If my dad was still alive," Sam had told me, "He'd shit himself with pride."

Everyone else was long since asleep, but these two young'uns were bursting with energy. They slapped at the light fixtures and *literally* bounced off the walls as they ran down the hallway. It was impressive. I would've given them both piss tests if I'd been in more of a mood to watch other men urinate.

Todd called my name for the fifth and loudest time before asking, "Will you read me Sweet Valley High books while I touch myself?"

It was an odd request, but not the weirdest one I've ever gotten. Definitely, however, the most unusual that didn't involve an offer of money.

Sam playfully slammed his shorter body into Todd's, sending them both into the lobby wall. "Fucking shut up, man!"

I shook my head at them. "I can't believe you kids are talking about filth like that? Sweet Valley High? *Jesus!*"

"How's about the Baby Sitter's Club?" Todd asked. "Or that sexy Nancy Drew bitch?" He dodged another slam-attempt from Sam. Seeing two young guys beating each other while discussing erotic stimulation to pre-teen literature might win a few points for novelty alone, but I wasn't really in the mood for. My wholesome self wanted them to bugger off so I could watch Muslim decapitation videos on my boss's computer.

"Samuel," I asked in my best Freudian voice, "Do you have somezing zhat you'd like to discuss with ze class?"

Todd laughed. "Tell 'im, you pedophile!"

My male intuition told me that someone had spilled their guts during a bullshitting session. Apparently, the recipient of that info hadn't been too open-minded about it. As usual. Our tolerance for deviation tends to stop with our own perversions.

Sam blushed a stoplight shade of red. "Fuck you both," he said, ducking behind his hair. "I was sixteen years old!"

I asked, "Weren't the Sweet Valley Twins only fourteen?"

(Not like I really know; the only childhood lit that sticks in my mind are the Choose Your Own Adventure books...and damned if those things didn't always make me die in a volcano).

This started Todd jumping up and down again, pointing a condemning finger at Sam, "I knew it!" he said. "Fucking pedophile!"

I shouldn't let people know that I was aware of the distinction between such things, but…"Actually, when the target of your lust is post-adolescent, it makes ya an *ephebophile*."

But they weren't listening. Sam was chasing Todd again. They made a few circuits of the lobby, trying to slam into each other or place a kick in the other's backside. I was tempted to suggest that they strip on down and oil up for some genuine junkie-on-junkie action. If you're going to sublimate sexual frustration, you might as well make it interesting.

The grab-ass continued till Todd darted out the lobby, past the chapel, and down the back hallway. Sam followed him, shouting back over his shoulder at me, "At least I'm not a *pederast*, right?"

No, I suppose he wasn't.

Not that I would've cast down fire-and-brimstone on the guy if he were. The only useful thing I'd ever learned in my psych classes was that sexual orientation was nothing more than the result of accidental imprinting mixed with some genetics and a little conditioning. In other words: a bunch of shit that's beyond your control.

Being the simple machines we are, can we do anything but follow our original programming? And why does knowing this not stop me from loathing everyone around here?

"*Homo*!" I heard Todd yell. There was the sound of something heavy hitting a wall.

I know that it's our duty as good Americans to hate, fear and generally abhor those whose sexuality differs from our own. Keeping focused on people who find different uses for their genitals is a great diversion. It makes sure our attention is elsewhere than on all the powerful people and interests who are *really* fucking us.

Like, if you're too concerned about why those guys over there are holding hands, you're nicely distracted from the important shit. You have a safe outlet for your proletarian rage and don't need to vent at things like the ever-widening income gap, your disappearing pension fund or all those vanishing civil liberties that you weren't using anyways.

Few things play better in American politics than homophobia. Killing foreigners, maybe.

(And no, I'm not some bloody leftist. I've just got a real sensitive sphincter and can always tell whose dick is up my ass.)

Laughing, grunting and squealing, Sam and Todd's voices drifted back to me long after they had disappeared into the rear of the building. It must have been hard to live in a building filled only with males (for the hetero-types, at least). *Especially* when that building not only had a strict 'no booze or drugs' policy, but also shared space with a flock of self-righteous Methodists.

Denied every pleasure of the flesh while getting a daily dose of Jesus. As much as I've grown hardened to it all, I can't help but pity the clients sometimes.

2:37am
CELESTIALLY NUMB

In my own special, American way, I *liberated* some liquid codeine from the med room (although not being a true-blooded patriot, I didn't kill anyone to do it). It helped with my strep throat. A tablespoon of the stuff every hour—when nobody's around—and I could start consuming relatively solid foods again. Two tablespoons of the stuff and I could chew brambles and gargle razor blades.

The codeine blankness was enough to make me eat in front of a mirror to ensure that I didn't bite off my tongue while chewing. A mental note was made to conserve the stuff so I'd have plenty left to chug for fun once my case of strep throat was over.

The codeine belonged to Robert, who'd had throat cancer once upon a time. Things had been getting worse and worse until one night his dead mom showed up in his dreams and declared him cured. At his next doctor's appointment, sure enough, not a trace of cancer in his body.

A similar thing supposedly happened to Magic Johnson and his HIV infection. Of course, being a rich basketball player, Magic got his healing message delivered by Jesus *His-Own-Bad-Self*, instead of some dead black lady. Apparently, even the celestial realms work on an economic hierarchy.

And on a personal note, I used to know a girl who claimed a similar experience. She was dating a good friend of mine and, after a pregnancy scare, she turned Catholic. *Hysterically* Catholic. As in: no more sex and she started planning on being a nun. This went on for a few months until, once at a party (after making sure that I'd left the room), she confided to everyone—tears in her eyes at the beauty of the experience—that she had been visited the previous night by an angel who restored unto the dear girl her long-lost virginity.

I was listening in on this touching story from outside, and my first thought was, *did she get her hymen back?*

So I strolled back into the room, unable to keep the grin off my face, and announced to everyone that I had been, for some time now, regretting my childhood circumcision, and did anyone know of a cost-effective method of reversing the process?

Having the greatest religious experience of your life mocked is something that few of us would take well. Realizing that's exactly what I was doing, the girl responded with a quick and savage kick to my genitals. I made a noise like a broken chew-toy and crumpled to the ground.

That night, no celestial beings had appeared in my dreams to heal my aching crotch, and I don't think I've ever really forgiven them for the neglect.

2:42am
APOPTOSIS

It was raining and I couldn't sleep. I read a book. Worked on a cover letter for a new job I wanted. Felt my pre-work buzz subsiding. And when the junkies were all finally asleep, I turned off the downstairs lights and sat in the dark. Just me and that goddamn sewage stench.

The soft illumination of streetlights shone through the front glass. The overwhelming applause of the rain on the streets was accompanied by a string quartet on the radio. Groups of the homeless huddled under the roof of the covered bus stop down the street. I sat on my desk in the semi-darkness and watched the *Good Load* piss on the just on the unjust alike.

The air quality in Pasadena had to be the cleanest in months. The days and nights of rain piled upon more rain had finally washed some of the industrial pollutants from their normal place in the sky. I marveled at how, for the first time, I might actually not have been killing myself with every breath I took.

Amazing.

If I had any cigarettes, I'd chain-smoke the pack.

The long day, plus the empty time, alone got me thinking about how stupid and pointless life could be. The endless failures, the boredom, the fact that radiation gives you cancer instead of superpowers, and how we spend our existence being herded from one cage to another. School during our youth, mind-numbing jobs throughout adulthood, and by the time that's all over there's not much else we're capable of besides soiling ourselves in some state-run nursing home. Having served our purpose to the machine, we're put out to pasture where everybody waits for us to die.

But, I have to say; the sponge baths you get in nursing homes strike me as the only positive aspect of aging. I'd soil myself every hour, on the hour, for those. Yeah, *that'd* make it worth waking up every day to pain.

"Dude," I said to myself. "Shut the hell up."

Existential whining was just the sort of mental habit I thought I'd kicked a long time ago. But in my teens there had been more despair behind the thoughts, rather than the current sense of resigned acceptance.

I scratched myself a few times, decided that I missed my ex-girlfriend, then decided that she could go fuck herself, then decided that I missed her, then decided that—

Screw it.

Being depressed is juvenile. By the time you're out of high school, you should have figured out an emotional strategy for dealing with life's little letdowns. We're all stupid and going to die, but that's no reason to mope. If all you saw around yourself was pain and suffering, wouldn't it be pretty maladaptive to be bothered by those kinds of things?

I decided that if life really was as Stupid and Pointless as my mind was telling me, then it had to be even more Stupid and Pointless to do something as lame as sitting around thinking about *how* Stupid and Pointless it all was.

Right?

Relieved at how my idiocy had cancelled itself out, I decided to make myself a sandwich and then go catch some porn on Gim's computer. Nothing was better, nothing had been solved, but at least I no longer cared.

3:04am
SO LONG AS IT'S UNFAIR IN MY FAVOR

"Seriously, Michael Jackson does not *deserve* to own that man's skeleton!"

I never thought I'd hear the ownership of anyone's corpse discussed with such conviction, let alone the remains of that great Victorian grotesque, the Elephant Man.

The inanity of it all forced a laugh out of me.

"I didn't think you could buy people's remains," I said to the young junkie sitting across the lobby from me. "Did he bribe a cemetery owner, or what?"

Todd shook his head. "It was probably at a university. Some folks they just don't bury."

I nodded. The last assertion carried the weight of truth that only self-evident things can at three in the morning.

"Remember that part in the movie where he's in front of the mirror?" Todd asked. "Trying to make himself look all good for that girl he's got a date with?" I shook my head, but Todd didn't care. "God, it was horrible! That scene made me want to go hug my mom."

I laughed again. "Guess there could be worse deformities..."

"There could also be better ones than having your head so big that laying down makes you suffocate," he pointed out. "Like, I saw this kung-fu movie once that had this bad-ass guy with hands but no arms who could twirl a bostick like a fucking champ!"

Todd withdrew his long and skinny arms most of the way into his shirt and proceeded to pantomime this particular brand of crippled karate.

"Holy shit!" I cried, sitting upright in my chair. "They have Thalidomide Babies in kung-fu movies?"

Todd wrinkled his forehead for a second before lighting up with comprehension. "Oh! *That's* what those are called! We've got one of those in my Narcotics Anonymous group."

"I'll bet y'all do," I said. "And I bet he's the only one of y'all with a decent excuse to be there."

Addicts hate nothing worse than to be robbed of the excuse that they've ruined their lives due to some disease that they can't control, instead of their own

142

personal weakness (a popular Victorian Age theory). So Todd ignored my remark.

I'd caught the guy relapsed the other night. Stumbled into the women's bathroom downstairs and there was Todd: nodded out on the toilet seat, pants around his ankles, slumped half off the seat and against the wall. I would've busted him, but was myself a bit too drunk at the time to bother. My motor functions too impaired for any finger-pointing.

Instead, I had just closed the door and staggered down the hall to throw up in the men's room.

Todd: "But this guy...this guy's got like...his arms stop about halfway down his forearms and just form these flipper things. Like, he's only got three fingers, like they're fused together with a huge finger nail on each one."

"Like the Penguin in the second Batman," I offered.

"Yeah!" said Todd. "And I was sitting next to him the other week and he starts sharing about his problems with lust, and I'm like: *oh God, I don't wanna hear about how much money he spends on prostitutes*."

I could imagine. The suffering of others is only amusing at a certain level before it descends into pathos or accelerates into farce.

"Imagine," I said, determined to follow this train of thought no matter where it led, "Not only does he have to pay for sex, but the best he can hope for is that the girl doesn't cringe when he touches her."

Todd's face dropped. "*Jesus*," he said.

Todd got up to wander out of the lobby in a semi-daze. I watched him go, dragging with him the horrible knowledge that life could be even worse than you had imagined. "I need some fresh air," Todd announced as he headed out back for a smoke.

The lobby was quiet after he left, so I gave a quick shrug at the basic unfairness of life and went back to scanning the newspaper's Help Wanted section.

"Hey!" Todd poked his head back around the corner. "I gotta wonder...how the hell, with hands way up by his shoulders, how the hell does the guy masturbate?"

It was time for my own face to fall. "*Jesus*," I muttered, before Todd stuffed his arms back up his sleeves and bent over, pretending to make desperate grabs for his own genitals. We both burst out laughing.

Why do bad things happen to people who did nothing to deserve it? Why is there such horribly unfair shit in the world?

Well, sometimes I almost believed Joe Orton's classic response: '...because it's *funnier* that way.'

3:10am
DENYING THAT YOU PLAY WITH YOUR FOOD
(and other homophobic bits of fun)

Tennil's hair was in geometrically precise cornrows. Looking closely, I could see the beads of sweat starting on the top of his skull and zig-zagging down from row to row, gathering mass and moisture as they sped towards abrupt slope of his forehead. Tennil didn't wipe them from his forehead so much as he intercepted each bead with a mighty slap like he was being assaulted by imaginary mosquitoes.

Maybe that would come later in the night. An assault by fantasized insects wouldn't be too surprising, seeing how he was speeding harder than a Ferrari on nitrous.

I decided to leave word to bust him with the morning shift. For now, though, Tennil's company was worth granting him a short reprieve. My own state of mind played an important role in the clemency, since I was more tolerant of the presence of others when I had a decent drunk going.

Tennil twitched and nervously twisted his football jersey between his fingers. He was in full-blown confession mode. It's easy to achieve that state with stimulants, but while the average cokehead can ramble on at Mach 5 about nothing at all, Tennil was kind enough to actually hold my interest. This was good for him, since it meant that when he came down he'd have somewhere to sleep before my coworkers threw him out.

I detest the empty verbosity of cokeheads enough that, were he less entertaining, I would piss-test the guy just to get rid of him.

Tennil's rambling was amusing enough to distract me from the interracial porn I'd been watching online, so I let him sit across Gim's desk from me. He blathered on about his secret predilection for teenage boys.

"Don't nobody know," he told me, and I suspected that your average homophobe wouldn't identify Tennil in a police line-up of sodomites (if they held police line-ups for that, which I don't think they do anymore, except maybe in Wyoming). He didn't possess any of the stereotypical characteristics that TV and movies have told us to expect in those frequently given to homoerotic acts. No earring in the right ear, no lisp, no 'screaming queen' behaviors, no impeccable fashion sense.

It was weird to meet someone here who didn't act like a bad stereotype.

Tennil looked slightly more attractive (strong chin and lean, muscular build) than most of the black youths seen on the average episode of *Cops*. He claimed to have been on the show a few years back, and when I voiced my doubts, promised to get the tape from his mom's house.

Tennil was also quite insistent that, despite his predilection for the backsides of Korean boys, he was *Not Gay*. Or, as he so eloquently—almost pleadingly—put it time and time again (in case I had missed the first fifteen assertions), "...*ain't no fuckin' faggot.*"

At those moments, he sounded remarkably like the hicks I'd attended high school with back in the tiny town of Bullfuck, TX. If Tennil could restrain them from assaulting his regrettably darker-hued body, they'd probably all get along great.

And to support his '*Not Gay*' thesis, Tennil whipped out his wallet and showed me photos of his kids. All four of them. Some of the pictures were a bit old, but he hadn't seen a few of the kids in a while, since he only got along with two of the three mothers.

144

Apparently, nothing says 'die-hard heterosexual' like being a deadbeat dad. The kids were pretty cute, though.

When Tennil managed to pause for breath after spilling his guts for over fifty minutes, I filled him in on the notion of sexuality as a verb, rather than a noun. That there are no such things are 'homosexual' or 'heterosexual' people, just people who sometimes perform 'homosexual' or 'heterosexual' acts.

By the same logic, there'd be no 'druggies,' just people who sometimes did drugs (in which case I'd be out of a job).

That's a decent theory of sexuality, as far as those things go. It's consistent with post-Fullerian psychology, and it's what I told my little cousin when she became interested in girls around the same time she was inundated with the typical *God Hates Fags* propaganda at her Catholic school.

Tennil was more interested in the man behind the notion than the notion itself. "Where'd ya hear that?" he asked.

"Umm…book of essays," I said, slurring a bit. "One of Gore Vidal's."

"He a fag?" Tennil asked. Somebody had entirely missed the point.

"*Sure*," I sighed. "Totally."

Tennil sank his head into his hands, like he'd just lost his last friend in the world.

"*Shiiiiiiiiit*," he said.

3:18am
YOU GOT TO HAVE FEAR IN YOUR HEART

Someone was howling outside the rehab. One long wail followed by a minute of silence, then another drawn-out howl. It was eerie. The wailing permeated the walls and oozed a sonic slime-trail across the lobby to the couch I was lying on. It seeped into my ears. I listened to it for a while, and was able to make out words. Whoever felt the need to be extra loud at three in the morning was delivering an important message to the sleeping world.

They were saying: *MoooooOOOOOoooootheeerFuuuUUUUUckeeeeers!*

Male voice. Long and loud and slurred just enough to give the proper tone of resigned despair.

MoooooOOOOOoooootheeerFuuuUUUUUckeeeeers!

Got kind of eerie after awhile. There was no change in tone or pitch or speed or tempo. Just the same gutter-wail of profane sentiment over and again.

MoooooOOOOOoooootheeerFuuuUUUUUckeeeeers!

Probably a drunk. Some street bum coping with street bum existence thanks to a few bottles of Night Train. Maybe a 40oz of Olde English. Whatever gets you through the night.

MoooooOOOOOoooootheeerFuuuUUUUUckeeeeers!

It was really screwing with my ability to sleep on the job.

MoooooOOOOOoooootheeerFuuuUUUUUckeeeeers!

I poked my head out the front door. Looked up the street one way and the other. No sign of the elusive Urban Howler Monkey. Still, just because I couldn't see the bastard, didn't mean that I couldn't hear him.

MoooooOOOOOooootheeeerFuuuUUUUUckeeeeers!

It seemed to echo off the surrounding buildings and drip its despair in stereo. Like having the landscape moan at you. This made sense. I mean, if there was a sentiment that this part of town, with its bums and slums and trash-strewn streets, would be trying to impart, it'd have to be:

MoooooOOOOOooootheeeerFuuuUUUUUckeeeeers!

Running through my head as I scanned for the source of the howling were all the lessons I'd learned as a kid about aiding people in need. About how when somebody was hurting you should comfort them. Be a Good Samaritan. Lend assistance. Help out.

"SHUT the FUCK UP!" I screamed into the night. It was a nice idea, but did no good.

MoooooOOOOOooootheeeerFuuuUUUUUckeeeeers!

We've all got something to bitch about, but unless you're being creative or amusing in the expressing of discomfort, keep it to yourself.

MoooooOOO—"SHUT UP Before I *FUCKING KILL YOU*!"

That did the trick. The howling ceased and I stumbled back to the lobby couch. My own physical tiredness was now tinged with the extra weight of disappointment. Twenty-four years of life had led to my participating in screaming contests with winos. I sighed and tried to fall back asleep.

3:24am
SELLING YOURSELF AN EGYPTIAN RIVER

Few things suck worse than waking up in the middle of the night with a hangover. One of those is waking up in the middle of the night with a hangover at work, especially when it felt like your body was about to find somewhere new for the contents of your stomach.

And that's why I was hovering over the toilet in the women's bathroom. No way in hell I'd touch the thing. Not after homeless ass had been on it all day.

Bent over at the waist, my arms propped me against the wall as I retched and heaved, aiming at the water a few feet below. My mouth burned from the acidic wash of upchuck, and I shuddered to feel tiny drops splashing my legs. I'd puke, flush so I didn't have to endure the sight or smell, and then puke some more.

It'd been a mad dash to the bathroom from the lobby couch. Didn't think I'd make it.

Forgive me, Father, for if I knew not what I did, it'd show a real poor grasp of cause and effect. My initial guess centered on blaming the cheap margaritas from earlier in the night. Or maybe all the beer. The bong hits probably figured in there somewhere, as well.

And yeah, showing up for work in a state of intoxication is typically one of those signs that you've got 'a problem.' But, with myself, I was certain it was a sign that I had a useful job. It didn't interfere with me going out for the night— even if going out for the night occurred right before work.

That's what I was thinking about when I regained consciousness, and it put me in a bit of a funk. It almost ruined my mood as much as vomiting gallons into the downstairs toilet. It doesn't take a degree in psychology—even though I've got one—to recognize a classic case of denial. Was I denying that I had a tendency to overindulge these days? Denying that my overindulgence occurred with increasing frequency? Was my willingness to show up for work in delightfully altered states less of a good thing then I usually took it for? Did I need to start cutting back on my chemical in-take?

Maybe, but just a little bit. Total abstinence is for the overreactive. I'd just switch to having fun every other night of the week. Cut my habits in half. Maybe drink less, toke more.

After Happy Hour tomorrow.

3:27am
JESUS LOVES YOU
BUT I'M ACTUALLY HIS FAVORITE

I figured the baggie of coke under the table in the dining room to be that God chap's last attempt at making things right between the two of us. It sat there, partly hidden behind a table leg, alone and sad like the discarded nutsack from a midget albino. I found it while locking up the dining room for the night, scoping out all the crap on the floor that should've been swept at chore time.

"Worthless, lazy motherfuckers," I had been mumbling to myself. Then that vision of CIA-funding, Columbian joy caught my eye. I thought, *'Is that...?'* and leaned down for a closer look at the heavenly gift.

Tiny twenty-sack. Stuffed to the brim.

'Here you go, Ray,' I could hear The Non-Existent One say. *'Hope this makes up for you being stuck in a dead-end job and having no relief for the past few months but humping your own fist.'*

'We cool, right?'

Quick look to the left, quick look to the right. All clear. I picked up the baggie and stuffed it in my pocket. "It's definitely a start."

The original plan was to save the stuff for the next time I went out clubbing. Do bumps off my apartment key in the bathroom. Being coked and drunk always makes for a better night than being merely drunk. Makes me feels powerfully stupid and beautiful. Like five-feet, ten-inches of pure erectile tissue. Like I could fuck the world and make it beg for seconds. Like all the shit techno, strobe lights, and desperate women in the club were actually appealing.

It makes for a great twenty minutes till I need to head back to the bathroom for another bump.

That had been the original plan. But, my brain switched to autopilot, and when the manual controls came back online I was in the bathroom, chopping up a line with a kitchen knife. Just a short line. Something to help with the nagging remains of my hangover from all those tequila shots before work.

And, what the hell, it would help with the tedium of the night shift.

The last dollar bill in my wallet was rolled into a cylinder. Maneuvered up my right nostril like a cannon of pure happiness aimed at my brain. Facing away from the counter and its frosted goodness, I exhaled thoroughly, then dove back in on the coke, sweeping the line from left to right. Grain after grain of coke, and whatever the fuck it was cut with, lacerated my sinuses on their way to do more damage further up the canals.

I tilted my head back, dollar still jutting from my nose, and gave the makeshift straw a thump or two with a spare finger. Snorted each time I did. Finished off any coca survivors of the nostril holocaust.

And then waited.

Five seconds…four seconds…three...tw—

There was a familiar burst of light in my frontal lobes. Like someone hooked electrical wires to an ice pick then shoved it through my forehead. Like John C. Holmes ejaculated pure uranium in my morning coffee and offered me a drink.

We're talking total *dirty* goodness.

There was a sudden driving sense of energy and purpose and I wanted to dance I wanted to fuck I wanted to twirl around the bathroom to the beat of water dripping from the faucet this was some good stuff dear *christ* the average coke on the street's so adulterated that the only way to get the blast you're wanting is to mix the high with something else 'cause on it's own it's cool but not quite enough being coked and drunk is what you need or being coked and stoned or mix the stuff with heroin which I've never tried doing or *BAMBAM-BAM!*

"*Yo*, Ray!"

Jesus! I almost pissed myself. It sounded like the Big Black Voice of Death. My heart and colon fought over whom had the right to explode first.

BAM!

"You in there, Ray?"

Some asshole was banging on the bathroom door.

It's not the cops. Deep breath. It's not the cops.

BAM! "Who you talkin' to in there?" *BAM!*

Frankie. It was Frankie. Big fucking 'fro-boy Frankie. The guy who couldn't spell past a third grade level but could eyeball a rock to the nearest eighth of a gram. Motherfuckin' Frankie.

BAM! "Hey man!"

I finally responded. "WHAT?"

Outside the door I heard him chuckle. "Thought you was in there."

Yeah, me and a heart that was on the verge of erupting from my chest.

"Fuck do you want?" Goddamn needy fuckin' crackheads can't do shit for themselves always needing somebody else to take care of them like addicts are

148

the ultimate in arrested development like they never matured past the age of four always selfish shit and immediate personal fulfillment like they—

"The kitchen locked, man. You gonna let me in?"

"*The fuck*?!" I screamed at Frankie, and it occurred to me that I'd always been screaming at him. "Of course it's fuckin' locked! It's always locked at night. It was locked yesterday! It'll be locked tomorrow! Why the fuck would tonight be any different; the hell were you expecting?"

There was a slight pause of silence, another slight pause, and for me it stretched out into a silence that went on and on as Frankie tried to starve me out on the other side of the bathroom door and I valiantly resisted his efforts and my veins pulsed in time with my heroic resolve to resist the evil crackhead resist his entreaties to leave the safety of the bathroom where he'd laid a trap that had to just had to consist of fifteen huge black men all hung like polar bears waiting quietly waiting for me to leave the bathroom so they could punish me for years of black oppression and how my middle class upbringing depended on centuries on black enslavement and how it was my fault that the ERA had failed in the eighties and how all the shows on BET were crap and my cousin called it Niggervision and that they knew how my—

"I need to get in there, Ray!"

Right! Frankie! Shit!

What to do what to do what to do what to do what to what to what to do?

"Fuck off!" I settled on shouting through the door. "The fuck do you think I'm doing in here?!"

Please don't say coke please don't say coke please don't say don't say don't say coke don't say coke *please* don't say coke.

Frankie adopted a more conciliatory tone. "I...I just need to get me somethin' when you done in there."

Aha!

Something like a little lost baggie of coke, perhaps?

"Whatcha need?" I asked with a certain relish in my voice. Ray was no longer on the defensive. The world's sexiest Tech now had the upper hand and was using it to punch other people in the ball sack. "Gotta grab something?"

It took Frankie a long time to answer. 'Course, it always took Frankie a while to answer. Somebody stole his brain as a baby and replaced it with an Etch-a-Sketch.

He babbled something about a drink of water, as if there weren't water fountains upstairs, while I held a staring contest with my reflection on the faucet handles. I kept losing, but so did my image. Me versus the crazy man. Yours truly on one side, and some distorted, scruffy bastard on the other. He needed to shave. He needed a haircut. He looked like a Hitler Youth grown up apathetic. Blond-haired, blue-eyed decadence. His eyes blinked again and again like he was attempting flight with his lashes. Pupils huge enough to host a dinner party in—provided, as Hemmingway would've said, that it was a small dinner party and you wanted to host it there.

"Ray?"

"Ray!"

"FUCK OFF!" I screamed. "Fuck off before I reach in the toilet and smack you with the first thing I find!"

There was quiet on the other side of the door. Then, "What you say?"

"*Jesus Christ*!" I put my hand over my heart. It's a bad thing to do on stimulants, and that's why I can never resist. My ticker was two seconds away from exploding through my ribcage and showering the bathroom with blood and bone shards. I was going to die. I was going have a heart attack at the age of 24. The paramedics would bust me out of the bathroom and the body bag's zipper would get stuck on this throbbing erection I'd popped out of nowhere.

"Ray? C'mon and let me in the—"

I threw myself against the door. Kicked it twice. "Leave me the fuck alone!" My voice was cracking. "Go to fuckin' bed or I'm gonna give myself a piss test and sign your fuckin' name to it!"

I was about to freak out. I *was* freaking out. I sat down in the sink. Calm down. Calm down. Deep breath. Deep breath. Calm down. Inhale, count to four. Exhale, count to four.

"Ray?"

Deep breath.

"Ray?"

Calm down.

"*C'mon* Ray."

I sat in the sink. Tried to calm the hell down. Tasted the coke dregs in the back of my throat. My butt was getting wet.

"Ray?"

I was trapped.

"I need in the kitchen, Ray!"

And worst of all, that fucker was totally killing my buzz.

3:33am
SUCH A LACK OF ACHIEVEMENT
THAT IT'S AN ACHIEVEMENT IN ITSELF

After hanging around the rehab long enough, I'd come to the grim conclusion that it was far more likely for people to fail in life than succeed (or why would success be such a big deal?). I'd also come to the conclusion that life needed to come with some sort of consolation prize.

We needed an award for all those poor fuckers that try *so* hard but fall flat on their goddamn faces every time. Give them something to say, '*thanks for playing and better luck next time.*' We could enlist Ed McMahon to fly out with a camera crew to present the award to each hapless participant.

There would be awards for the starving Honduran farmers, whose crops and children get doused by U.S.-sponsored herbicides. We could give posthumous prizes to depressives and suicides the world over, who gave life their best shot but just couldn't take it anymore. One for single-parent households who fell short of making rent each month, and another for my sorry little addicts relapsing over and over again. Awards to everyone who's tried to quit smoking more than once. Awards to all the blank, brutalized people who start each day with smiles and always go home at night in tears.

The award itself could be a little statuette showing God, in his bearded-old-man guise, with His holy foot on the neck of some unidentified individual, who would represent the broken spirit in All of Us. It'd be kind of like a glorified version of those participation ribbons they'd to give to all the slow and fat kids on Field Day. We could call the awards *Hitlers*, after the biggest 20th century example of a sad bastard who tried his damnedest but still failed miserably.

And if there were going to be awards for Trying-but-Failing, then in all fairness we needed awards for people who knew better than to even try in the first place. We could give out a little plaque with a stick figure on it, shrugging deeply. Not sure what we could call those, though I'm kind of tempted to name them after myself.

3:38am
THROB FROM THROB, POUND FROM POUND, LIGHT FROM LIGHT

There's a nifty little technique for dealing with headaches that I got out of Robert Anton Wilson's book, *The Earth Will Shake*. Just visualize and concentrate on a mental image of your brain and then a bright, white light surrounding and enveloping your brain. If you can concentrate well enough, your headache will fade from your consciousness while you're doing this.

POUNDPOUNDPOUNDPOUNDPOUNDPOUNDPOUNDPOUNDPOUND-POUND

It's basically just a distraction, but especially handy for when you're hung over and waiting for the aspirin to kick in.

POUNDPOUNDPOUNDPOUNDPOUNDPOUNDPOUNDPOUNDPOUND-POUND

And dear *fucking* Christ, if only I could find some of the stuff! But of course, aspirin wasn't allowed in the building. Couldn't have the junkies munching entire bottles of the stuff in sobriety-fueled fits of despair. Thanks to those fucking weaklings I was stuck with the pain. *God*, if only my head would just explode and get things over with.

POUNDPOUNDPOUNDPOUNDPOUNDPOUNDPOUNDPOUNDPOUND-POUND

The lobby's lights were out and only a small glow was coming from the hallway. I was sitting hunched over on the couch. It was a filthy fucking thing. Cracked leather and discolored stains. I was probably absorbing countless little germs from the countless asses of the countless bums who sat on it during the day. God knows nothing in the building ever got cleaned except the floor and an occasional toilet. And hell, before it was donated to *Christ in the Gutter* the couch had previous owners. Those fuckers probably took turns sneezing on the thing.

*POUNDPOUNDPOUNDPOUNDPOUNDPOUNDPOUNDPOUNDPOUND-
POUND*

Any relief would do. I sat upright, straight-backed, and took a deep, relaxing breath. The tension drained from my body in degrees. First my neck, then shoulders, back, arms, hands, legs, toes. It was meditation time.

*POUNDPOUNDPOUNDPOUNDPOUNDPOUNDPOUNDPOUNDPOUND-
POUND*

I formed an image of my brain in my mind's eye. The picture-maker pictured itself. Focusing that electro-colloidal mess in my skull was difficult even under normal circumstances. Living in the modern world assured that my attention span that had been raped, killed, and then raped again by cheap entertainment and flashy images that blurred into one meaningless tableau after another. Flicker to one thing. Flicker to something else equally meaningless. Flickering back again. It becomes such a habit for the mind that it can't imagine needing an attention span exceeding three seconds. It's addicted to the flash and flash and flash and flash so much that its basic structure comes to mimic the empty quickness. Just like a junkie's metabolism restructures itself for heroin.

*POUNDPOUNDPOUNDPOUNDPOUNDPOUNDPOUNDPOUNDPOUND-
POUND*

But still, I strained to hold an image of my aching brain in my mind's eye. Just a bit of focus and a bit of relief. I pictured the lobes, the brain stem, the hemispheres. Hold the image. Hold the image.

Don't think about—

*POUNDPOUNDPOUNDPOUNDPOUNDPOUNDPOUNDPOUNDPOUND-
POUND*

Shit.

*POUNDPOUNDPOUNDPOUNDPOUNDPOUNDPOUNDPOUNDPOUND-
POUND*

Hold the image.

And then I imagined the hemispheres being—*shit*—hold the image. And then I imagined my brain being consumed in a blissful holocaust of white light. It was a million suns, a nuclear explosion of healing energy in my head, and as long as I stayed focused on the image—*shit*—as long as I focused on my brain being filled with and overpowered by—

Shit!

*POUNDPOUNDPOUNDPOUNDPOUNDPOUNDPOUNDPOUNDPOUND-
POUND*

As long as I stayed focused on my brain being consumed by this white light all the pain faded away. All the hurt in my head went somewhere else.

*POUNDPOUNDPOUNDPOUNDPOUNDPOUNDPOUNDPOUNDPOUND-
POUND*

Focus.

Focus.

Focus.

That's *better*—I mean, Focus....

Focus.

152

Focus.

The door to the stairwell banged open and footsteps headed in my direction. *Fuck!*

The pounding in my head picked up right where it let off.

POUNDPOUNDPOUNDPOUNDPOUNDPOUNDPOUNDPOUNDPOUND-POUND

I made plans to kill and dismember whoever this turned out to be. Somebody had *better* be having a heart attack or gushing blood from a stump wound. If this was the usual bullshit junkie desire to chew my ear off or get some ice from the kitchen I was going to take the nearest copy of the Big Book and fucking *bludgeon* them with it.

POUNDPOUNDPOUNDPOUNDPOUNDPOUNDPOUNDPOUNDPOUND-POUND

The footsteps got louder and closer, my head went back into my hands, and a little black head poked itself around the corner in my peripheral vision.

POUNDPOUNDPOUNDPOUNDPOUNDPOUNDPOUNDPOUNDPOUND-POUND

"That you there, Ray?" Swanky asked.

POUNDPOUNDPOUNDPOUNDPOUNDPOUNDPOUNDPOUNDPOUND-POUND

I sighed. "What's up, man?" *And it had better be real fuckin' good...*

POUNDPOUNDPOUNDPOUNDPOUNDPOUNDPOUNDPOUNDPOUND-POUND

"Not much," he said, stepping around the corner to take a seat next to me on the couch. Swanky looked like the long-lost eighth dwarf. The black one that Disney would have to insert into the story for a multi-cultural remake. He was short, muscular, and had lupus scars on his face.

POUNDPOUNDPOUNDPOUNDPOUNDPOUNDPOUNDPOUNDPOUND-POUND

"*Not much*," I echoed in despair. My path was now clear. Before the night was over, I would have the blood of a midget crackhead on my hands.

POUNDPOUNDPOUNDPOUNDPOUNDPOUNDPOUNDPOUNDPOUND-POUND

We sat a while in silence, me rubbing at my temples.

POUNDPOUNDPOUNDPOUNDPOUNDPOUNDPOUNDPOUNDPOUND-POUND

"Did...you *need*...something?" I asked.

POUNDPOUNDPOUNDPOUNDPOUNDPOUNDPOUNDPOUNDPOUND-POUND

"Couldn't sleep."

POUNDPOUNDPOUNDPOUNDPOUNDPOUNDPOUNDPOUNDPOUND-POUND

"You...couldn't sleep." That was it. The camel's back was broken. Swanky was a dead man. Or midget...however they classified these guys. I lifted my head from my hands to scan the darkened lobby for the key ring and its attached cudgel. Just a few good whacks and I could go back to meditating. A few good hits and it would be quiet again. Just claim it was self-defense.

POUNDPOUNDPOUNDPOUNDPOUNDPOUNDPOUNDPOUNDPOUND-POUND

They'd believe me. I'm a college graduate. White boy. Swanky's a black ex-con. I know how the system works in this country.

POUNDPOUNDPOUNDPOUNDPOUNDPOUNDPOUNDPOUNDPOUND-POUND

"Woke up and thought I was back in jail," Swanky said. "That been happening a lot recently."

POUNDPOUNDPOUNDPOUNDPOUNDPOUNDPOUNDPOUNDPOUND-POUND

I rubbed at my temples. Looked around. Still no sign of the cudgel. "Think it might have something to do with sleepin' in a room with five other guys?" I'd get Swanky off-guard, make him feel safe, and then—*Crack!* "All that extra breathing and snoring in the room with ya could be doin' the trick. Maybe your subconscious is picking up on it while you're sleeping, so it's the first thing that crosses your mind when ya wake up."

POUNDPOUNDPOUNDPOUNDPOUNDPOUNDPOUNDPOUNDPOUND-POUND

"Could be dat." Swanky nodded in the half-light. "Could be."

POUNDPOUNDPOUNDPOUNDPOUNDPOUNDPOUNDPOUNDPOUND-POUND

More silence. More dead air. More of my head trying to collapse in on itself.

POUNDPOUNDPOUNDPOUNDPOUNDPOUNDPOUNDPOUNDPOUND-POUND

"It sure rainin' hard," Swanky said finally. I looked out the glass front of the building. The world had turned to pounding water. Rain was coming down in wave after wave. Half a world away, American munitions were doing the same in foreign cities.

POUNDPOUNDPOUNDPOUNDPOUNDPOUNDPOUNDPOUNDPOUND-POUND

This stupid fucking planet.

POUNDPOUNDPOUNDPOUNDPOUNDPOUNDPOUNDPOUNDPOUND-POUND

I hadn't even noticed the rain. Too busy concentrating on my headache. Too wrapped up in my own misery. "So it is," I said.

POUNDPOUNDPOUNDPOUNDPOUNDPOUNDPOUNDPOUNDPOUND-POUND

"Couldn't tell what the weather was like in prison," Swanky said. "It just always cold. I was in there four years, and only one or two times I know it was raining."

POUNDPOUNDPOUNDPOUNDPOUNDPOUNDPOUNDPOUNDPOUND-POUND

"That sucks," I said, for a lack of anything better to say. *My poor fucking head!* I had come into work utterly plastered. Had a few martinis at a vegan-feminist lecture (I was there to pick up chicks), and then a good bong rip or two. Showered before work to take care of the smell. A heavy dose of crap cologne and I was ready to earn my daily bread.

POUNDPOUNDPOUNDPOUNDPOUNDPOUNDPOUNDPOUNDPOUND-POUND

"In prison, we'd lay in bed and bullshit," Swanky said. "Tell halfway stories."

POUNDPOUNDPOUNDPOUNDPOUNDPOUNDPOUNDPOUNDPOUND-POUND

"Hell, I'd probably just be getting ass-raped," I managed to joke.

POUNDPOUNDPOUNDPOUNDPOUNDPOUNDPOUNDPOUNDPOUND-POUND

Swanky looked me up and down like he was appraising a particularly disappointing bull. "Yeah," he said. "You would."

POUNDPOUNDPOUNDPOUNDPOUNDPOUNDPOUNDPOUNDPOUND-POUND

I needed to change the subject before Swanky decided a demonstration was in order. Felt so horrible that only being raped by a midget crackhead could possibly make things worse, and I didn't want to give life the chance to test that theory. Where the hemorrhaging *fuck* was that cudgel? Would I actually have to haul myself off the couch to go look for it? "What's a halfway story?"

POUNDPOUNDPOUNDPOUNDPOUNDPOUNDPOUNDPOUNDPOUND-POUND

Swanky thought about this for a while. "It quick," he said. "Real short. Just something that happen that don't take long to tell. The sorta shit you tell your friends about when somethin' cool happen. Like if you gettin' some pussy and somethin' funny happen like her momma walk in and complain that it a school night. Quick story."

POUNDPOUNDPOUNDPOUNDPOUNDPOUNDPOUNDPOUNDPOUND-POUND

Oh. "Like an anecdote," I said. "Or vignette."

POUNDPOUNDPOUNDPOUNDPOUNDPOUNDPOUNDPOUNDPOUND-POUND

Swanky shook his head. "Don't know 'bout that," he said.

POUNDPOUNDPOUNDPOUNDPOUNDPOUNDPOUNDPOUNDPOUND-POUND

"Same thing," I assured him. "Vignette's kind of like a written version of an anecdote or…what was the term?"

POUNDPOUNDPOUNDPOUNDPOUNDPOUNDPOUNDPOUNDPOUND-POUND

"Halfway story," he said. "That the same thing?"

POUNDPOUNDPOUNDPOUNDPOUNDPOUNDPOUNDPOUNDPOUND-POUND

I went to nod, but it just made me feel worse. "Same thing," I repeated. It was time for an explanation using phrases understandable to someone whose mother not only dropped him as a child, but also probably dribbled him up and down the court a few times. Maybe tried a lay-up shot or two. "It's like, you never get the full story or complete picture from an anecdote. What came before, the long-term shit that led up to it all, and all sorts of background details get left out. That sound like what you were talkin' about?"

POUNDPOUNDPOUNDPOUNDPOUNDPOUNDPOUNDPOUNDPOUND-POUND

He nodded. "Spiffy," I said. If there was one thing I had become something of an expert on while working here, it was anecdotes and vignettes. Heard shit-loads of 'em from the junkies—everything from funny drug stories to not-so funny drug stories. From confessions of mugging their own grandmothers to the time someone's piss test turned up positive for pregnancy. Eventually, I could figure out what made a good anecdote or vignette or halfway story differ from one that I couldn't even bother pretending to listen to. They usually tell instead of show. Anecdotes and vignettes don't need a point, just a punch line. They lack a sense of completeness. They're like the drive-by version of story-telling. Just little Polaroid glimpses into people's lives, usually blurry, red-eyed, and underdeveloped. But hey, so long as the thing's amusing, who gives a fuck?

POUNDPOUNDPOUNDPOUNDPOUNDPOUNDPOUNDPOUNDPOUND-POUND

"*Whassamatter?*" Swanky asked me. "Got a headache?"

POUNDPOUNDPOUNDPOUNDPOUNDPOUNDPOUNDPOUNDPOUND-POUND

I almost nodded again but caught myself. "Yeah," I said, remembering my earlier desire to bash his head in. If he didn't leave soon…

POUNDPOUNDPOUNDPOUNDPOUNDPOUNDPOUNDPOUNDPOUND-POUND

"Got some ibuprofen upstairs," he said. "You want some?"

POUNDPOUNDPOUNDPOUNDPOUNDPOUNDPOUNDPOUNDPOUND-POUND

Possession of that stuff was against the rules, but I found myself willing to overlook it this time. "*Pretty please!*" I moaned, and he jumped up to fetch it.

POUNDPOUNDPOUNDPOUNDPOUNDPOUNDPOUNDPOUNDPOUND-POUND

Sitting alone in the dark again, I found myself somewhat glad that I'd let him live.

3:41am
ALL SUFFERING COMES FROM ATTACHMENT
EXCEPT FOR WHEN YOU STUB YOUR TOE

I'd never had a parent plead with me for their child's life before tonight. It's just something new here every day. Almost makes me glad to be alive.

Another bright young member of the Pasadena addict community sat across my boss' desk from me. Zack fidgeted in his seat, shifting his weight, scratching his head, tugging his ponytail, and covering his face with his hands.

And whining.

And whining some more.

By his own admission, he had smoked cracked around two-and-a-half hours ago. Judging by his current state, it was a move he rather regretted.

In his late twenties with strong Italian features, Zack oozed repentance from every pore. The past hour or so of my time had been spent listening to Zack beat himself up over his relapse. The fun was had, and now he was deep in the Magical Land of Comedown.

The psychic territory of Comedown Land was like driving through West Texas. It was bleak, harsh, there was nothing to do but wait for it to be over, and the end never came soon enough.

Shit, this entire place was one big comedown.

I had been in the process of breaking into the chef's office (paranoid bastard had chained the door shut again) when Zack showed up hours past curfew.

"Just wanted you to know I was back," he said. I hadn't even noticed Zack was gone, didn't have a clue how he'd made it back into the building, but now his late return had triggered my Amazing Psychic Tech Sense. Or maybe it wasn't my latent psychic powers so much as seeing Zack twitch like he'd just finished humping an electrical outlet.

I watched his muscles spasm for a while. "Any reason why you're geekin'?"

Well...first he told me a story about being real tired (this when he seemed energized enough to telekinetically cause both our heads to explode), and then it became the fault of all the coffee he drank, and then slowly it came out that he had been around some people who had started smoking crack.

"And you smoked it, too." Not a question. Zack shook his head so violently it seemed he'd give himself whiplash.

"*Bullshit*, man." If only Zack hadn't been so damn obvious about it. I could've sent him off to bed and let somebody else deal with it tomorrow. "You're geekin' so hard your heart's probably about to explode."

(For the record, that's a *horrible* thing to say to someone on any type of stimulant.)

"*No no no I didn't no I swear no I didn't man I...I smoked it.*" It was then that the remorse started flowing out of his mouth like somebody busted a hole in the dam that held back the mighty waters of Lake Regret.

He said:

"*GodI-*
can'tbelieveIdidthatI'msuchafuckupIcan'tstaysoberformorethantwodayswhydid

157

*IdothatafterItookthatshitIwassosorryohgodwhydidIdothatI-
can'thelpbutfuckupwhydoIalwaysfuckuptheguyjustlitupinfrontofmeandIhadabs
olutelynodesiretosmokebutthenthenext—" etc. etc. etc. etc.*

I'd be lying if I claimed it made any sense.

Company policy was to throw homeboy out on his ass. In the street. In the middle of the night. I've done it before. Done it to people almost three times his age in the middle of winter.

*Buuuuuuuuuuut...*I just couldn't bring myself to do it to Zack. Don't know why. Pity isn't a strong suit of mine. Shit, I agree with the Greek and Nietzschean analysis that pity's a spiritual poison. It's unhealthy. Makes you weak. Corrodes that *soul* thingy that I don't believe in.

Doubt it had anything to do with the fact that Zack's had one failure after another in his short life. So have most of the other guys here. They wouldn't be here if that wasn't the case. And it probably wasn't because Zack committed suicide back in February. He hanged himself from one of the rafters in his parents' garage.

Amusingly enough, he succeeded at it, too. Suicide was probably the only thing in his life that he didn't fuck up. Other people ruined it for him. Zack was dead for over five minutes while his dad did CPR on him until the paramedics arrived. It wasn't knowing this that kept me from tossing his ass to the street. Hell, in my slightly unChrist-like opinion suicide would be an improvement for the guy.

But, for some reason I just couldn't give Zack the boot. Go figure. It's nice to be able to still surprise yourself every now and then.

I told Zack he could stay with me till the sun came up. Our section of Pasadena wasn't the sort of area to be out in at this late hour.

"But you're not leaving my fuckin' sight," I told him, along with the caveat that he had to be out of the building before everyone else woke up. And that's how I came to enjoy the cheery company of a young crackhead as he woefully came down from the drug that had already ruined his life several times, was currently running his life, and would probably continue to ruin his life...for ever and ever and ever, self-degradation without end, amen.

Most addicts are nothing if not consistent.

Finally he asked, "C-c-can I call my dad?" And while I may not have wanted to hear him whine to his old man about how he had fucked up yet again, I shrugged out a *'sure, why not?'*

I set Zack up on the phone in the lobby, while I went back to scoping out the usual porn sites in my boss' office. More than anything, I wanted to be able to close the door, to shut out Zack's half of what was probably the most pathetic conversation occurring within a fifty-mile radius. Voyeurism is all well and good, but the pathos of a boy doomed by his love for crack and a father doomed by his love for a fuck-up son wasn't anything I was interested in hearing that night.

Sure, it would be amusing up to a point, but you can only hear the same record so many times before a song's familiarity starts to grate on you. If my job was a jukebox, it wouldn't play too many other tunes.

158

"He's going to throw me out on the street, dad!" I heard Zack say. "You know what this part of town's like. He's just gonna...no, he says he has to. *Dad*! He says he has to throw me out!"

The fuck? I thought. How'd I end up the goddamn bad guy here? Sneaky fuckin' crackhead trying to switch the focus from his relapse to my heartless villainy! *Goddamnit!*

I found myself wishing that the little bastard had learned to tie better knots in Boy Scouts.

"My dad wants to talk to you," Zack called to me, a new note of smugness in his voice now that his high-priced lawyer of a daddy (*mucho* important, *mucho* wealthy, and head of the city council in their small Texas town) was going to make everything okay.

"*Fucker*," I muttered before picking up my boss' phone. My eyes did a spectacular rolling tour of their sockets as I answered with my customary, "*Yello?*"

Zack's dad had a deep and commanding voice. Soaked in authority. I expected him to *order* my peasant ass to absolve his son of all wrongdoing. Then he'd force me to apologize for even considering the removal of such a fine young lad from this establishment, and before the end of the call I'd be agreeing to pay alimony to my ex-girlfriends (or something like that).

Instead, he immediately began to beg.

He asked me if I knew about Zack's suicide attempt (*I did*, I said nonchalantly), and then went on to say that he was afraid—so very, *very* afraid—that Zack would try it again if I threw him out in the middle of the night. That, or the 'niggers in that part of town' (his phrase) might do horrible things to Zack.

I didn't bother informing him of my plan to let Zack stay till sun-up. What would be the point? Daddy wasn't listening to me, anyway, being too busy begging in what he doubtless thought to be the defense of his son's life.

The most important case I ever argued, I'm sure he'll call it in his memoirs.

I half-listened as he pleaded on and on that I not callously kick his boy out on the streets. I scoped out leather bondage sites online while Zack's dad whined into my left ear. He could be there in three hours, he begged; couldn't I *please* just let Zack stay till then?

"Look..." I tried to cut in, to no avail.

"Just give him his meds and send him to bed," his dad implored. "I can be there by six-thirty! *Please!*"

Six-thirty *was* around the time that I'd been planning on giving Zack the boot, anyway. What a waste of breath this had been for the guy!

"*Well...*" I said, as if I were carefully considering the matter. Zack's dad was finally quiet. I could almost hear someone's heart beating like a drum machine on overdrive. "*Okay*. But let me patch you on through to my boss' voicemail. You can explain things to him."

"Oh, *thank you*," he said. "Thank you thank you thank y—" I put him on hold as I tried to figure out how to transfer him to the voicemail of the phone I was already using.

Zack blathered happy words at me as I walked him upstairs to the med room, but I wasn't listening. My mind kept going over the tone of desperation in his dad's voice. For all his success, he was powerless before the love that bonded him to a crackhead son. And, for all his riches, everything he held dear in the world had been at the mercy of some jerk-off slacker earning eight bucks an hour.

I managed to keep myself under control until Zack was safely medicated and in bed. Then I went back downstairs, put on a Bach concerto, sat in the dark and laughed myself sick.

3:54am
WEIGHING SUICIDE VERSUS KILLING THE REST OF THE WORLD

I clicked the window closed on the geriatric porn site and tucked myself back into my pants. A hook shot missed my boss's trashcan, and the used tissue lay soiled on his carpet. I use Gim's computer solely for porn 'cause checking my email means seeing rejection letters from jobs I'd applied to. Rejection after rejection for the sort of jobs that I sweated through college for. The sort that don't involve fighting bums or handling other people's piss.

They're not available. The economy was crap. I was shit out of luck. There were no decent jobs. The only growth sectors were the military and prisons. The American Dream had left to build sweatshops overseas.

I was about to look up another porn site, make a marathon of it, before I was struck by my own lack of interest. Watching other poor people do unpleasant things for money no longer struck me as amusing.

This meant jerking off on the job had *Officially* ceased to be entertaining (usually takes around 5 minutes, so I figure I earned about 67-cents per climax). My most reliable method of diversion had just failed me. Not a fucking clue how I was going to pass the time now.

All the counselors' offices had been searched from top to bottom months ago. No clients were around for me to torment. The Christers had taken to locking up their storage bins. I was in serious danger of becoming bored.

Somebody stop me before I go looking for new ways to amuse myself.

4:11am
PSEUDOSPECIATION

I was tossing on the lobby's couch, pissed that I was at work and unable to sleep. A painful burning sensation in my mouth kept me awake. '*Strep throat*,' the clinic physician had said, but to me the little white bumps all over the inside of my mouth had looked a hell of a lot like herpes.

Dear fuck, I had worried a few days back as I'd shifted my gaze—mouth open with tongue hanging out—back and forth from the mirror to the pictures on the computer monitor. *It's herpes, all right! That's what I get for licking welfare vagina. The WASP-ish God of Propriety is punishing me for shagging outside of my social class!*

The doctor's assurances at the community clinic later on were soothing on the paranoia. However, they did nothing to change how the little white bumps inside my mouth seemed to exist for no purpose other than throbbing with fiery pain. Not only did this fuck with my sleeping ability, but it also made eating solid foods downright impossible. That's why I'd subsisted on milk and Nyquil for three days. The Nyquil was finally cut out when I started excreting a runny shade of pink.

Still, I suppose it beat having herpes.

So I had wandered out to our back lot at work, half-crazed after three days of constant pain. The air was still, muggy and unbelievably hot for the middle of the night. It smelled like microwaved armpits. Pasadena's a hazardous environment, unfit for human occupancy, even without all the airborne pollution.

A shape moving along the fence's perimeter caught my eye. It was a bum, of course. Long, ragged hair whose dreadlocking probably owed more to hygiene neglect than Rastafarian devotion. He had two army-surplus jackets that came to his knees, a bushy beard, and an erratic gait that told he was passing the night with a foreign substance or two in his veins.

Right near the gate he stopped and bent over. It looked like he was fiddling with the chain. "Keep moving," I said, not feeling like his variety of company.

He jumped back at the sound of my voice, his hands balled into fists.

"*Whatchu* say?" he yelled.

"Said *keep moving.*" I hated to repeat myself. Even talking was painful, thanks to those charming bumps on my tongue. Here I was, hurting myself for the sake of some fucking bum. "Nothin' for ya here, man."

His eyes got huge. "The *fuck?*" he shrieked. "The *FUCK?* Think you tell me what to do? *Fuck You!*"

The rest of us often forget that street people have their own sense of dignity. Or maybe we just don't care.

"Ya heard me," I said. "Now get outta here."

The bum was livid. His eyes bugged big and saucer-shaped like he'd escaped from an anime asylum. "I tie my shoes on the street if I wanna! Don't need yo fuckin' permission, *honky!*"

Was that all he had been doing? Maybe I had been mistaken. The strep and its attendant misery making me edgy.

"Oh…well, in that case, my mist—"

"Fuck *YOU!*" he shrieked, slamming himself up against the chain-link fence like a rabid dog. "Come out here and I fuckin' kill ya! Come on! Fuckin' honky! Come on out!"

I watched him throw his entire body into the fence again and again, screaming and practically foaming at the mouth. Now *this* was entertainment. "*Fuck you fuckin' honky fuckin' goddamn kill you…*" And so on…

Not much to brag about in the vocabulary department, but he knew how to get his point across. "*Fuckin' muthafuckin' fuckin' honky-ass fuckin' honky*

161

goddamn fucker..." Unfortunately, he was doing it loud enough to make me worry that he'd wake the clients.

"Wait here," I told him. "I'll be right back. Don't go anywhere."

Back inside, I reached behind the Xmas tree set up in the lobby and grabbed the pepper-spray from my backpack. I had a simple plan that seemed utterly rational. I was going to go back outside, hose the bum down with the spray, and then bring something heavy with me to accept his invitation for a (admittedly unfair at that point) fight.

You'd expect that spending lots of time amongst the Down and Out would make one more compassionate towards them. Not really. What it will do is make you treat them like you would any other human being. Whether that means poorly or not is up to you.

No special treatment. Nor do you ignore them or act like they're invisible. Just treat them normal. Like anybody else.

If I was walking down the street and a random person became violently belligerent towards me, most likely macing then beating them is exactly what I'd do. I'm all about quick and easy solutions, these days.

(This job killed the pacifist in me.)

When I returned to the back lot my new pal had calmed down. He still clung to the fence, but all the fight was gone. The outburst had drained off his hate and anger. He was calm. Subdued.

The bum looked up like he was seeing me for the first time. Probably didn't even remember what had happened only a half-minute before. "Hey," he said. "Hey buddy. Hey…you got some food in there? Got something to eat?"

I smiled and sprayed him in the face.

Screaming, he fell off the fence and writhed on the ground, clawing at his eyes. Pepper spray hurts like a motherfucker. Burns the eyes and closes off the throat. My particular brand also leaves blue paint on your face. The bum shrieked his lungs empty before fighting for the breath to start screaming again. His legs kicked at the gravel. I stood behind the fence and watched my new-found diversion. *Kick, kick, shriek. Kick, kick, shriek.*

Kick, shriek, kick. Like the world's most painful dance routine. Fascinating. I watched him claw at his eyes. He convulsed in the gravel and screamed himself hoarse. *Fascinating.* Even louder than before, but still fascinating.

Unfortunately, it wasn't long before my own eyes started watering from the backdraft. I sprayed him once more for good luck before hurrying back inside.

4:39am
MY DAD, MY DEALER

Robert was giving me his Unified Theory of Everything: what the world's like, why it's like that and why anybody who sees it differently is full of shit. He also discussed his plans to attend chef school. "Got me a second chance," Robert said. "And I'm gonna use it."

He's a likeable guy, so I lounged on the couch and pretended to listen.

162

The lobby was dark, lit only by the filtered glow of the streetlights. Watching the lights reflect on Robert's head made me wish I had somebody to snuggle with, cliché as that emotion may be. All I wanted was another warm body to crawl up on this ratty leather couch with me. Someone to hide under a blanket with me and watch the lightshow on Robert's head for hours. Just one person to snuggle with for the simple, and long missed, sake of human contact.

I would've asked Robert, but I didn't know how close up I wanted to experience his spare-toothed grin. So I just sat and nodded on occasion and appreciated the fact that, after working at the rehab for several months, I had finally found the light switch for the lobby.

"Yeah," Robert said, "I wouldn't mind havin' me a son." He had five daughters, all grown, with four different women.

"Haven't you bred enough?" I mumbled, thinking, *let the non-crackheads have a shot at it, now.*

"Just a son," he repeated. "I'm a good daddy. Just a son."

"Weren't you just telling me what a deadbeat dad you were?" I asked, having caught a few bits of his rambling. "And you want *more* kids?" Not that it's any of *my* business, but I had a definite desire not to be car-jacked by any of his offspring once they were grown up and I was too old to fight back.

"Was in jail some," Robert conceded, "But that don't count. I takes care of my business. I'd be out there at the Crack Corner, doin' my sellin', and somebody be like, '*Ain't that yo kid?*'"

I nodded, wondering what Take Your Daughter to Work Day was like for his children.

"...and my kid be all '*Daddy, I need twenty-bucks,*' and I whip out one for 'em right there on the spot!" Robert smiled at the memory with a close approximation of paternal pride.

I was torn between honesty about how under whelmed I was by this, or just telling Robert that the black community thanked him for providing such an endearing role model for his offspring. Since neither sounded like much of an option, I turned back to watching the lights dance on his scalp. "Now *that's* parenting," I sighed.

It's always easier to criticize than to try something yourself. Don't know about everybody else, but that's why I do it so often.

5:29am
BURNS SO QUICK AND IT MUST BE AMERICA

The anti-carcinogens in coffee transform into carcinogens in just fifteen minutes. I learned this at school, so it must be true.

Occasionally I drank a cup out of the batch meant for the junkies. Mixed it about a third coffee and two-thirds milk. Just enough to get a little boost without having to taste the shit. I always hated the flavor and distrusted the hell out of anything that society shoved down our throats in mass quantities. Especially something that's an addictive stimulant.

Besides, screw that pansy stuff! Why does the American workforce run on such a weak-ass stimulant? No wonder the economy was in the shitter. They should give everyone a bump of meth on the way to the office. Bet your ass we'd see some work getting done then! Chronic nosebleeds and weight loss would become acceptable side effects of earning your daily bread; just like caffeine headaches and nervous tension are now.

If they gave it to office workers, I bet we'd get a classier level of client here. More junior executives and high-priced lawyers rather than all these truck drivers and the unemployed. It made me wonder if those other folks would have as much trouble switching from their favorite stimulants to America's legal ones.

And, if our rulers legalized stuff like meth for productivity's sake, would it fuck us up as badly as the currently legal stimulants had?

Or, as Grant Morrison once put it: "*...like almost everyone else in western culture you're hopelessly addicted to refined sugar and caffeine. Both these drugs are high-level stimulants and here are some of the clinical symptoms of speed psychoses: '...user feels depressed, extremely anxious, irritable, hostile, alienated, fearful, confused, and paranoid.*'"

Yeah, that sounds familiar.

5:37am
JUST LIKE ALL THE DIFFERENT PEOPLE

The doorbell chimed and I clicked the lock release under the desk. Still didn't bother looking up to see who it might be. One of these days my negligence was going to result in some axe-murderer gaining entrance to the building. Not that we'd be able to tell them apart from the regular clientele.

"Hey *Sloopy*!" came the cry. Fidal looked like a black Amish man, or what would happen if ZZ Top had racial quotas to meet. Huge beard, deep eyes, and a brain that couldn't help but misfire. I quickly acted like there was nothing more interesting than the newspaper in front of me. "Hey Sloopy! How ya doin', Sloopy! What's happenin', Sloopy! How's it hangin', Sloopy!"

These weren't questions; Fidal just suffered from a clinical inability to shut the hell up. His speech pattern was a mix between a morning DJ and Hitler at Nuremberg. Cheap enthusiasm and repetition, *repetition, repetition.* "Sloopy been here all night! You crazy, Sloopy! Man, that one crazy Sloopy! Sloopy, why you so crazy! How can a Sloopy be so crazy!"

"Hey," I said, eyes never leaving the newspaper clutched in my hands. The headlines claimed that a couple thousand people died in some Bangladeshi mudslide. Thank fuck they were in such plentiful supply over there, since this sort of thing seemed to happen on a bimonthly basis.

I gave a silent '*Fuck you*' to that useless God fucker for not positioning Fidal a few thousand miles to the east.

"Whatcha readin', Sloopy! That the paper, Sloopy! Man, look at Sloopy over there! Sloopy be Cadillacin'! Hang on, Sloopy!"

164

After being at work all night, the last thing I felt like dealing with was some hyper-verbal homeless motherfucker. Fidal was one of the volunteer/slaves for *Christ in the Gutter*. Day after day Fidal and a bunch of other bums showed up here and did the grunt work involved in keeping a religious charity functioning. They moved stuff, handled equipment, showed up at five-thirty in the morning, kept the other homeless in line: all the shit work. I imagine their presence went quite a ways towards keeping the operating costs down.

"Sloopy learnin' 'bout the world! Look at Sloopy readin' that paper! *Mmm-mmm*, Sloopy love his paper! He sho' love to read! Sloopy always got his paper! Whatcha readin' Sloopy? What happenin' Sloopy? What goin' on in the world?"

I knew it would only encourage him, but I answered anyways. "Buncha dead people." *And why aren't you one of them?*

"*OOOOO-EEEEE!*" Fidal said. "Listen to that Sloopy! Sloopy talkin' 'bout dead people! All them dead people that Sloopy talkin' about! Keep on Cadillacin', Sloopy!"

I took a deep breath and tried to think about something other than killing Fidal. It didn't work. I'm usually pretty irritable by the end of a shift, especially one that I didn't sleep through. Having Fidal around was just kerosene on the fire.

"Sloopy sittin' there in that chair! Look at Sloopy sittin'! Sloopy just love to do that sittin'!"

"Don't you have something to do?" I asked.

Why he called me *Sloopy* was something I never figured out. Maybe it had something to do with him being crazy. Maybe not. Like most of the people I've met, there was no point to Fidal. No overriding purpose or rhyme or reason. He was just annoying.

The doorbell chimed a second time, and I flicked the lock release without checking again. In strolled Coolio.

"*Guten Morgen!*" I called out to him.

"Whazzup, *Mister* Ray?" Coolio gave me a charming smile. There was no subservience or politeness in Coolio's use of the term, *Mister*. It was just something he slapped in front of everybody's name. A generic title and referent, like how the Mormons call each other *Brother* and *Sister* or the Puritans' use of *Goodman* and *Goodwyfe*.

Of course, it sounded a lot more slick when Coolio said it. That the ineffable quality of *coolness* could be possessed by someone who lived in homeless shelters was just another of life's little mysteries.

Coolio had it, though, an air of relaxed acceptance. The guy definitely went with the flow of things, and if the flow had led him to a life on the streets, hey, he seemed pretty all right with that. Or, as all right as anyone could be with sleeping in gutters and doorways. Didn't complain, at least. Kept his discomfort to himself, and that's all the rest of us really ask.

Not to glorify the guy. He still stank like a B.O. bomb had exploded in his pants. Still wore ragged flannel coats in the middle of summer. Coolio wasn't as bad as some of the other homelies, but he still wasn't anyone you'd want to grow up to be.

He tossed an easy acknowledgement to his fellow volunteer. "*Howzzit* goin' Mister Fidal?"

Fidal squealed in response. "You see that Sloopy over there! Man, look at that Sloopy! Sloopy be all readin' and stuff! Sloopy loves that paper! *Woo-ee*, look at Sloopy go! Hang on, Sloopy!"

Coolio raised a single eyebrow at me and we exchanged one of those *brutha* handshakes that I'm so adept at now. "I'm guessin' you be *Sloopy*...for today, at least."

I shrugged. "Such is my cross to bear in life."

Fidal never stopped running his mouth the entire time; *Sloopy 'dis* and *Sloopy 'dat* like he chugged meth-laced cappuccinos to start off his day.

Coolio gave a sideways glance at Fidal and then looked back at me. "What's it worth to you that homeboy here has an accident on the stairs today?"

I laughed. "My undying gratitude?"

He pretended to consider this for a moment. "Toss in a pack of smokes and you got yo'self a deal."

Fidal was doing a little dance around my desk. Shadow-boxing with the furniture. "Whatchu be talkin' about Sloopy! You crazy, Sloopy! Look at dat Sloopy! What makes a Sloopy so crazy! Sloopy just read and be crazy all day! That's what a Sloopy do!"

"Menthol okay?" I asked.

Coolio gave me a sly look and a nod.

"What 'chall be talkin' 'bout, Sloopy! Sloopy be all talkin' now! Sloopy just talk talk talk! What goin' down, Sloopy!"

Coolio smiled. "You find out."

5:41am
A GENUINE FACE, BRACED FOR SURVIVAL

Seeing some of the junkies off to work in the morning was the second-greatest part of pulling an all-nighter. Being paid to sleep for most of the shift was number one, of course.

I don't know why, but there's just *something* about seeing the guys put their best junk-sick faces forward to struggle through yet another day. I mean, those fuckers don't just have to cope with crappy jobs like most people. Every minute of the day they're fighting the urge to run back to their dealer for another armful or a crack-rock or to just head down to the Quik-Stop for a cold one.

If that's not an effective way to make life a million times more difficult, I couldn't say what is. Maybe being crippled.

Despite this, the junkies come downstairs bright and early (the few with jobs, at least). They get their socially approved drugs from me, then head on their way. I've noticed that if I watch the junkies as they walk onto the morning streets of Pasadena, I can catch a little spasm of fear crossing their faces. Some hide it better than others, but it happens to all of them. That quick look of '*aw, shit*' as they brace for their daily ass-kicking by the world.

They can't cope with life. Wouldn't be here if they could. Existence proved too much for them. It was Them versus Life, and, for every one of them, Life won hands down.

Yet they headed back out every goddamn day to go another ten rounds with the world. And having seen them straggle back in at the end of the day, I can say that the world always comes out on top. Still, they brace themselves, swallow down their fears, and fight like hell to make it through the day. Each and every day.

If I weren't so cynical I'd almost find it inspiring.

6:58am
MY HEROES HAVE ALWAYS BEEN SERIAL KILLERS

Fidal was apparently one motherfucker who remembered his high school civics class.

"That why they shot the Kingfish, Sloopy!" he was saying to me. "He been useful to Roosevelt, but then he turn *against* Roosevelt! That what got him killed, Sloopy! That why they killed him!"

"Did he really turn against Roosevelt?" I asked. "Or did Roosevelt turn against *him*?"

It would figure that the first time I came close to having an intelligent conversation at work, it'd be with a crazed homeless guy. (The usual small talk was inane stuff like, *Me:* "*...seventy-fuckin' virgins, man! I'd crash an airplane for that!*" *Old Herman:* "*Virgins? Shit, gimme some old sluts with experience!*") And it figured that we'd have the conversation about a crazed 1930s demagogue. Hey, why not?

"Roosevelt abandon the New Deal!" Fidal's eyes were wide with excitement. "He betray its spirit, Sloopy!" Every sentence that came out of the guy's mouth had the exuberance normally reserved for screaming stuff like, '*Look out! A meteor! It's falling right at us! And it's got herpes!*'

"Roosevelt abandon the New Deal, but Huey wanna keep it goin'! Huey wanted some redistribution of wealth, Sloopy! He wanted to form his own political party! He didn't wanna go to war like Roosevelt, Sloopy!"

If I remembered my History Channel viewings, Huey Long's assassination didn't have a damn thing to do with World War II or Roosevelt. In fact, his own bodyguards probably shot him by accident. But, you had to learn to jump topics when conversing with the crazed.

"Sure," I said. "Whatever. But, Roosevelt wanted to provoke Japan into war, so he could stay President a third term."

"I dunno 'bout no *provoke*, Sloopy! At Pearl Harbor—"

"Roosevelt pushed 'em into that!" I countered. "Puttin' an oil embargo on somebody as devoid of natural resources as Japan's tantamount to a declaration of war! There were plans to firebomb Japan before Pearl Harbor. Roosevelt *had* to know that they'd—hell, he *did* know!" Or maybe it was Churchill who knew about Pearl Harbor ahead of time. I always get bloodthirsty autocrats confused. "They had cracked the Japanese diplomatic code. They knew what was coming. Or maybe that was right before they bombed Nagasaki for the fun of—"

Fidal's turn to interrupt. "You forgettin' about them Japanese invading Manchuria, Sloopy! Sloopy forgettin' all about Manchuria!"

"Fuckin' pot and the kettle!" I said. "American forces committed genocide in the Philippines during the start of the twentieth century. If they were so concerned about national sovereignty they should've been bombing France and London and Belgium and themselves. *That's* where the major atrocities had been coming from for the past hundred years!"

Fidal started laughing. It wasn't at my anti-western invective; he just had a habit of chuckling at the oddest moments. It's part of being crazy, I guess, and was probably more fun than crying unexpectedly. But this time he kept laughing. And laughing. And laughing until I considered our conversation over and picked the newspaper back up to root through the Help Wanted section.

Then he stopped laughing just as quickly as he'd started. Wiping the tears from his eyes, Fidal looked back up at me and asked, "You think them bad people, Sloopy? You think they do them some bad stuff?"

I didn't bother to lay down the paper, just in case he went on another extended laughing jag. "Well...sure," I said. "We got guys in here who did ten years in prison for knifing a single person. Politicians and soldiers kill *millions* of people and we call 'em heroes? Hold them up as laudatory examples? Christ, our presidents have always been serial killers. Every one since Madison's been a goddamn butcher! Fuck else do you call it when someone's responsible for the deaths of tens of thousands of people?"

Fidal gave me a sly look. "Tell ya what, Sloopy! We agree on somethin', Sloopy? Make an agreement, Sloopy? I was in the army for fifteen years, Sloopy, and I go all over the world."

"And?"

"Know what I learn, Sloopy? Know what I find out?"

"What?"

Fidal looked to the left and then to the right. The coast was clear.

"Everybody suck," he said.

The pronouncement was made.

Everybody suck.

Not much of a philosophical revelation, more like juvenile nihilism. As some wise soul once pointed out, hating everything just isn't the same as having an opinion. But, how much profundity could you really expect from the disadvantaged?

Take what you can.

"Mind if I quote you there?" I asked.

7:05pm
RUN PUPPY RUN

My heart skipped a beat when the phone rang. It had been quiet for hours, so a shrill noise exploding by my ear caught me off guard. Recovering quickly, I grabbed the phone and said, in a soft and courteous voice that was supposed to sound like Sean Connery, "*Christ in the Gutter and A New Start for Men*, how can I be of help to you?"

"THIS IS SELMA!" was screeched into my ear. Such a powerful, hateful voice. Fuck knows how she thought I could mistake her for anyone else. "I JUST DROVE BY AND TWO WINDOWS ARE OPEN UPSTAIRS." I automatically held the phone an extra six inches from my head. "IT'S THE SECOND AND THE THIRD FROM THE LEFT. AIR-CONDITIONING COSTS MONEY, AND THIS IS THE SECOND TIME THIS WEEK THAT—" My ear drums felt violated, like they had ended up on the wrong side of John Holmes anal-raping choir boys.

I cut her off. "I'll see to it," and set the phone back in its cradle. I glared at it for a while. *I trusted you, you fucking appliance; how could you do this to me?*

"Fuckin' bitch," I said, shaking my head. Terry looked up from doing crossword puzzles on the couch. He was using a pen, which meant that the crossword was officially ruined for all of the facility's late-risers.

"Selma called, huh?"

I rubbed at my ear. "Could you sense the evil coming over the phone lines?"

"*Naw*," said Terry. "I could hear the bitch from over here."

What Selma actually did around here, besides yell at anyone who got in her path, I really couldn't say. I avoided her too much to study her habits and behaviors. I guess that would make me a pretty lousy anthropologist.

Not that I paid too much attention to the less obnoxious, non-clergy folks around here. People came, people went, people suffered around me, and their one-dimensional selves didn't really make much of an impression anymore. They all just blurred into one big smear of frustration and failure.

"I mean, strike one for being a total bitch," I said to Terry. "Strike two for being a member of the fuckin' clergy, which means that she's trained to prey on fear and gullibility."

It's never too early for a spot of character assassination.

Chewing on the end of the pen I'd lent him, Terry suggested, "And strike three for being so goddamn fat."

I had to disagree with him there. "Being fat doesn't make you an intrinsically bad person."

"Sure it does," Terry said. "Means you're getting more than your fair share."

I laughed. "What, you want 'er to share the wealth? Pass some of that lard around for the rest of us? Should she shed some pounds and give 'em to those less blessed by gravity? You're like some weird mix of Marxist and aerobics instructor."

169

Terry put down the paper to better make his point. "It's like this," he said, "By eating so much stuff, she's stealing *your* potential to be fat, too. Just in case that had ever been a dream of yours."

Matter of fact... "Never considered that. Bitch really is a parasite of the worst sort."

And at that choice moment the 'Bitch' in question waddled in from the back hallway.

The hell was she doin' here on a Saturday?

"THOSE WINDOWS BETTER BE CLOSED," she said. Selma had a mean, bitter face. She looked like someone had ordained Jabba the Hutt and draped him in a gray wig and priestly robes. Hatred for everything around her radiated off Selma in waves, but besides that we didn't have too much in common. Her voice was loud and booming, yet still managed to maintain a nasal quality. If someone dragged their broken nails over a chalkboard while broadcasting it through a jerry-rigged amplifier, the results might approximate the aural torture that poured from Selma's mouth.

Obviously, I wasn't the lady's biggest fan. Anyone who flips out over petty shit gets tossed off my Xmas card list. Especially when they flip in my direction. I mean, it wasn't like my window-watching negligence was giving anyone childhood leukemia. The government wasn't jacking up the terrorist-threat level another color or two because our facility wasn't airtight. Easter would still arrive on time.

Over-reactive bitch. Or maybe I just hated middle-aged women. They're too old to be sexually appealing, and too young to feel grandmotherly affection towards me. No sucking my dick, no baking me cookies. What was the point to them, then?

I gave the idea of age-dependent misogyny another thought before filing it in the *Reject* pile with my old plan to market dually-packaged vodka and sleeping pills as Home Euthanasia Kits.

I eyed Selma for a second. Watched her huff and puff like the big bad wolf with a thyroid problem. "They're not closed," I replied to her implicit threat.

"WHAT?" she screeched. *Somebody would dare to not run cowering to do her will? Off with their head!*

She waddled over to the desk as Terry tried to make himself invisible on the couch. "WHY AREN'T THOSE WINDOWS CLOSED? YOU'RE COSTING US MONEY! WE'RE LOSING ENERGY AND *BLAH BLAH BLAH BLAH...*"

Tough as it may have been, I tuned her out. I could still hear her harpy screeches, still see her bulk resting against my desk, but she was now no more comprehensible to me than someone yodeling Hebrew. It's a neat trick I picked up from all those Sundays wasted in church as a kid.

Keep yappin', bitch, I smiled to myself as the spittle flew from her mouth. *Soon as the revolution comes, you and all your clergy buddies are goin' up against the wall with the politicians and CEOs.*

170

I got a mental image of Selma flopping dead over the president's corpse, causing organs and bile to be squished out like someone biting into an éclair. Thoughts like that kept me warm at night.

She hadn't stopped yelling at me, so I calmly picked up the local section from the newspaper and scanned the front page. *Hmmm*, looked like another high-ozone day. Nice to know that just living in Pasadena was killing me. I contemplated whether the air inside or outside the rehab was worse. It seemed like I just couldn't escape toxic environments.

"HEY! I'M TALKING TO YOU!"

I didn't look up from the paper. Another double homicide on the south side. Burglary and rape in the suburbs. Radio conglomerate staged a pro-war rally in Houston. "No," I said, "You were screeching *at* me. Once you feel like being civil, let me know."

I gave her a quick glance with a raised eyebrow that said, *'Not used to being spoken to like that, are ya, bitch?'* Then went back to perusing the paper.

Hit and run by the Galleria. Child abducted in the Second Ward. And through it all, Selma sputtered and fumed. I thought her fat fucking face would explode with disbelief. Lard and eyeballs flying in every direction. "I'LL...I'LL SEE WHAT GIM HAS TO SAY ABOUT THIS!"

Ooh, a sale at Mervyns! "Hopefully he'll tell you to leave his employees the fuck alone."

She leaned in on the desk, two of her stomach rolls smothering the sign-out sheet. Her breath came heavy and labored, air sucked into then blown out of her mouth with maximum force. Being angry was apparently quite the exertion for Selma. I wondered if she ever stopped to think why she had gotten so upset in the first place, and was it really worth it? People so rarely do. We're all such miserable bastards that any excuse to vent our frustrations will suffice.

"YOU CAN...KISS...YOUR JOB...GOODBYE." Then she gave me an angry stare. Guess it was supposed to be threatening.

I looked up at her. Then, never breaking eye contact, I leaned over and licked the top of the desk. "That work for ya?" *You clergy fuck!*

Selma realized that I wasn't going to be as easily cowed as her homeless volunteers. She stormed off in a huff of heavy breathing and self-righteousness.

Terry peeked out from where he'd buried himself in the newspaper. "Is it safe to come out?" he asked.

I nodded.

He jumped up from his seat and walked over to me. "I gotta shake your hand," he said.

"For standing up to some fat, old lady?" I asked as we shook. "What a brave young warrior I am!"

"More than I've seen anyone else around here do," Terry said. "Even Gim tip-toes around her."

"They *do* own the place," I pointed out. "The Christers ever get tired of us, y'all are out on your asses."

Terry laughed and scratched at his beard. "Be funny if you just broke the camel's back, there."

171

"*Eh*," I shrugged. "Wouldn't be the first time my big mouth's fucked things up for everybody. The economy being what it is, I'll just take my degree to some other dead-end McJob."

"Yeah, I know what that's like," Terry said.

I smiled up at him. "Oh, you partied your way through college and blew all your potential, too?" I should have been in grad school by this point. I should have had a real job earning real money. I should have been doing something with my life besides hanging around the wretched of the earth.

Terry walked back over to the couch and picked up his crossword puzzles. "Sort of," he said. "The last part, at least. What the hell else are we all doing here?"

7:12am
THE SERIAL PROCESSING OF THE KLEENEX PEOPLE

"See that girl over there?" Tennil pointed out the front door. I ignored him. "Hey, Ray! *Ray!*"

I looked up like I was doing him a favor by responding. "What?"

"Come look at this girl, man!" I dragged myself from behind the desk.

He pointed across the street at a young girl limping past the old colonial mansion. She had a hooded jacket and Sesame Street backpack. Looked to be late teens, early twenties. "And?"

Tennil grabbed at himself, probably without noticing. "Me and JDZ and Robert had her suck our dicks yesterday," he said. There was pride in Tennil's voice. "And then JDZ fucked her. He says it was up the ass, but I dunno."

The girl walked with a careful step. Maybe JDZ really had. "Y'all get a group rate?" I asked.

"Bought her dinner," Tennil said. "*Taco Cabana.*"

I wondered what had happened to the American dollar if three blowjobs and anal sex didn't rate anything more than a Black Bean Burrito with picante sauce. Maybe they'd had a coupon.

"Think Robert gave 'er a few bucks, too. Always supposed to tip for good service, right?" And then he laughed.

The girl turned in our direction, like she could hear the slander from the other side of the street. She started limping across the road towards the rehab.

"Hey, she's headed this way!" Tennil smiled. Christmas had apparently come early this year. "Maybe we can do 'er again! You wanna turn?"

I shuddered. "I wash my hands after I touch the same doorknob as you fuckers. No way I'm sharing dick-space with y'all." The girl limped through lane after lane of traffic, eyes on the pavement, not watching to see what might be about to run her over. It was like watching a suicidal game of *Frogger*.

"Yo loss," Tennil said. "Man, we did her behind the YMCA. I got to go first, throat-fucked that bitch, then I came all over her top. Bitch never stopped complaining 'bout that. She was all mumblin', '*my shirt...fuckin' cum on my fuckin' sweater...*' while JDZ's all doin' her from behind."

Tennil reached down to adjust himself. "Like, when she wasn't crying."

Nice. That was *my* spiritual affirmation for the day. Every shift I worked here made me fall in love with humanity all over again.

Tennil's anecdote also meant that none of these guys were going to have their lives made into movies. Two crackheads and a skuzzy Caucasian junkie taking turns with a young, weeping white girl wouldn't play too well in Midwestern America. Not without some moral tacked on to the end. Something to excuse all accidental erections that may have occurred during the viewing.

Or, maybe it would set box office records. Never underestimate the public's hunger for degradation. Christ knows we all cheer like hell when it's time to slaughter foreigners.

The girl climbed up the front steps. Slowly. Carefully.

"I got to feel on her titties," Tennil said. "Play with 'em while she was suckin' me. They kinda saggy, but not bad."

"Go away," I told him.

Tennil stepped outside to meet the girl, the beaded cornrows swinging off the back of his head. She looked up at him, not a hint of recognition in her eyes. He talked at her for few minutes, acting friendly and touching her shoulder. The girl didn't back away from his physical closeness, but she didn't respond, either. Just stood there, letting her head drop to stare at the ground.

Seeing the girl up close changed my earlier estimation of her age. Her being over twenty was pretty unlikely, despite the worn look on her face. Resting on the girl's chest was a large metal cross. It was the Catholic variety, a crucifix, with Jesus' half-naked body still nailed to the cross in all His sexy glory.

The cross Tennil wore on the outside of his shirts had no Jesus. I wondered if he had enjoyed hosing genetic material all over his professed messiah. It's not every day that a guy gets to cum on his god.

I opened the door for Tennil to come back inside. "She hungry," he said. "It cool if I go get her a plate from breakfast?" I looked at the girl through the glass door. She was just sitting there, scratching at her leg. It was a mindless, repetitive movement. Fuck knows what she was coming down from.

"Sure," I said. Tennil ran off to the kitchen, probably dreaming of soiled sweaters and blowjobs to come. I stayed and watched the girl. In my mind she took on three guys behind the local Y. In my mind she had her Sweet Sixteen party and first day of school. In my mind she was too drugged to even notice she was crying while JDZ rammed her from behind. In my mind I wondered if there was another species I could go join.

You could bet she never planned on growing up to whore herself for fast food and a little drug money. Who would? Hell, I thought I'd grow up to be a cross between Han Solo and Jesus. Guess nobody got their wish.

Tennil returned with the food. I took it from him and headed outside, closing the door behind me so he couldn't follow. The girl looked up briefly and reached for the plate. "Here ya go," I said as I squatted down to hand it over.

Tennil had forgotten utensils, but the girl didn't care. She dug into the powdered eggs and sausage with her fingers.

I straightened back up. "Don't worry," I told her, "This stuff's free of charge."

As usual, it was the wrong thing to say. She never stopped shoveling food into her mouth, but raised her eyes to glare like it had been me taking advantage of her last night. Me ramming her behind the Y. Me spraying cum all over her shirt.

Total distilled hatred.

It was the first and only expression I'd seen her make, and it was plenty.

I rushed back inside mumbling apologies.

7:18am
THE HEARTBREAK IS INTENTIONAL
THE DISGUST IS A HAPPY BONUS

Once we got to the eighth page of Solomon's meds in the Medicine Log, I gave a low whistle. Or tried to, at least. There are just some things in life that I'm no good at.

Like:

Feeling bad for people who repeatedly fuck up their own lives,

Solving for the third variable in geometric equations, and

Whistling.

Despite the signs posted everywhere about the times that meds are distributed, Solomon always caught me in the medicine room by pure accident. He'd waddle on past the open door going back to his room from breakfast and would give a start when he saw me in the med room. Like it was always a surprise to find me there.

Every goddamn time. Every goddamn day.

This day, however, was the first I'd ever seen Solomon without his headphones. He probably figured they were broke when the batteries ran down. The poor guy would now have to find another way to block out the world. I shuddered at the thought of his vulnerability.

"You givin' out them meds?" he asked. Same question as always.

"Sure am!" I grinned at him like a carnivore, engines revving on caffeine and other stimulants. My fingers fidgeted nervously with the zipper on my jacket, dragging it up then down its track. Up then down, up then down, up then down. "We got Vicodin at three apiece or four for ten, but today's big special is Rohypnol. It comes pre-crushed so it's that much easier to slip into that unattainable someone's martini."

He just looked at me. Small brown eyes almost swallowed by his fat black face.

Nobody home. Nobody ever going to be home.

"They work just as well in a 40oz," I offered.

"I come back later," he said finally.

174

"*No No Nooo*," I cried. "I've been up here three minutes without anybody stoppin' by. Two minutes from now my ass is *Gone*. Get your meds now so I can get out of this cramped little room and go home."

At the end of every night shift I was supposed to sit in the med room from about seven-fifteen to seven-thirty, waiting for some of the junkies to stop by for their morning fix of socially approved drugs. Actually, regulations say that we're supposed to be med-fetchin' from seven to half-past, but fifteen minutes seemed like a big enough waste. So, I was usually in there about five minutes at most.

The med room (or Tech Office, as it was officially known for no other reason than to make us feel better about sitting in a goddamn closet) was filled with cleaning supplies, linens, and a two-door chest containing two locks and the clients' meds.

I handed Solomon the key ring and its cudgel attachment. Considering how much I'd grown to enjoy tormenting the clients, handing them my only form of defense might not have been the greatest idea in the world. But, it was either that or actually get down from the desk and take the two steps on over to the med cabinet to unlock the goddamn thing myself.

Taking the key ring by the proffered (and correct) key, Solomon fiddled with the lock for a while before managing to outsmart it. He then reached into the cabinet and pulled out a small garbage bag filled with his meds. Typically, the clients have small plastic trays for that sort of thing, but it was apparent that no regular tray would hold all of Solomon's massive med collection. The man needed the *Magnum* size.

"Takin' the usual?" I asked him. Each different med that a client took had its own sheet in the med book. On that sheet we recorded: the amount of that medicine they were taking; the amount of that med they had before taking any; and the amount of that med remaining now that they just took a dose.

Each different medication got its own sheet. Solomon had a total of sixteen sheets.

I made sure to take the key cudgel back from Solly. "Takes a lot to keep your ass alive," I commented.

Behind that observation, especially at the end of a double shift, is the uncharitable question of whether it was worth it. Pills, after all, cost money.

"You totally win the Walking Pharmacy award for this month," I told him. "Congrats."

Solomon didn't say anything for a while. Just kept fishing pill bottles out of his sack like some pharmaceutical Santa Claus. Then, "Just 'tween you and me, I got the AIDS."

Yeah, I already knew that. Solly had AIDS. Solly was going to die. He wasn't the first client we'd had here like that. Get enough intravenous drug users in one place and chances are that some of them will have something nicely lethal. Hepatitis C was way more popular, but I'd run across enough AIDS cases since I'd been here to no longer feel shocked for the guys with that particular death sentence.

And on the 8th Day, God said, *Let life be majorly fucking unfair*, and it was.

And it was good.

Good for those of us who could stand on the sidelines joking about it, at least.

Laugh, and the world laughs with you. Cry out in pain, and everyone's going to chuckle at your sorry ass. We, as a species, get our yuks where we can.

"So…"

We cohabited in silence for a while. Solomon unscrewed the top to one med bottle after another, and I perched on the desk documenting his med intake. Perhaps it was the last Adderol I'd munched to see me through to the end of the shift, perhaps it was my desire to—*naw*, it was the Adderol.

Had to be.

What else could have squeezed out my next line?

"So…" I said. "How's that *imminent death* thing treatin' ya?"

Solomon didn't even look up at me. Just kept poppin' pill after pill into his pudgy little mouth.

"How 'bout I didn't hear dat," he said. "'Cause I don't take no shit off white boys."

I pretended to consider his offer for a while. "Deal," I said as cheerfully as possible, while a shrill voice in my head starting screaming. The voice sounded exactly like all the people I'd grown up around in the little town of Goatscrew, TX. It pops up these days whenever I'm at work and in desperate need of sleep. Or just at work. The voice screamed at me: '*You're not takin' that shit from some fat little nigger, are ya?*'

I'm shit-scared that one day the voice, and that word it uses, will spew right out of my mouth. Not only will this probably get me killed, but…but…hell, I'll admit; it's just the ensuing violence that I'd be worried about. Considering how frequently I get accused of racial bias here, actually saying '*nigger*' would probably confirm the suspicions that I was just another white devil out to pick on people for being better tanned than me.

It was a pity for so many of the guys to waste their energy on persecution complexes. Still, I guess it was easier than accepting that maybe the world really had followed Dr. King's advice and judged them '*not by the color of their skin, but on the content of their character*'…and still decided that they sucked.

"Fuckin' white folk," Solomon said, shaking his head at the pity of it all.

I nodded in agreement. "I hear ya."

Solly gave a funny look like he wasn't sure how to take me, then settled on shoving the rest of his pills into his mouth and waddling off.

'*Nigger,*' said the voice in my head.

Everything you've ever read about the South being full of bigots and race-baiters is true. Same goes for the North and the east and west coasts, too. They just don't get as much publicity about it. Human beings seem to have an inborn need to hate someone or something *en masse*. If us Texas-brand honkies didn't have the niggers and the spics to hate, and if the niggers and spics didn't have us, we'd all pitch in to find somebody else. That's what happens in a society

176

where most people's hobbies consist of watching TV and loathing anyone who's a little bit different.

Beats stamp collecting, I guess.

Down the hall I could hear Solomon returning to his room. He could block himself off in there from the rest of the world till he either got new batteries for his headphones or his immune system imploded.

I had the strangest urge to chase him down the hallway. The feeling came from out of nowhere. I wanted to burst into Solly's room and say that I was sorry. Just *sorry sorry sorry*. Not for my attempts at levity that used his impending death as fuel for the comedy fire, but sorry for the world that we'd both found ourselves inhabiting.

Not an apology, 'cause it wasn't my fault that we all suffered. Not my fault, not Solly's fault, probably not anyone's fault. It's time like this that'd it be real handy to have a god to blame.

I just had the need to tell Solly that I was sorry we lived in a world where people died horribly, died slowly. Sorry that even if Solly managed to stay off crack he'd still, at best, waste away in some AIDS hospice. Sorry that not only did people die horribly, die slowly, they also died horribly and slowly frequently enough that the survivors had to swallow their fears and give an uneasy chuckle while waiting for their own grisly demise. Sorry that we lived in a world bad enough for gallows humor to even be considered a coping option.

Then the urge passed, as quickly as it had come. I found myself staring at Solly's bag of meds, wondering where that little burst of compassion had come from. Maybe it was something I'd eaten, like all those uppers.

Walking Solly's meds back to the med locker, I gave a heavy sigh. The Adderol I'd munched was apparently wearing off. Goddamn legal pharmaceuticals. The high lasted too long for me to bother taking another. Not so close to the end of a shift. Crap. I was fixing to crash, and it wouldn't be pleasant.

God, I needed a drink.

7:22am
GOD LOVES HIS CHILDREN

When Robert's throat cancer came back, it took two weeks to kill him. One to realize just how bad he was feeling. One more to strain for his last breath in a community hospice. Scared and sharing a room with three other dying strangers, no one went to see him.

The last time I saw Robert was three weeks and four days ago. He had stopped by the facility on the way to his morning classes at cooking school. He was halfway through the semester.

You wouldn't believe the shit that go into a goddamn soup, he told me. Robert was keeping his head shaved, even though the hair had started to grow back once his chemo ended. He had decided it looked better that way. I agreed.

Once he was done with chef school he would go intern at a restaurant.

I gonna be pullin' down some big money, he'd said. *Good chef can make twenty or thirty bucks an hour.*

Not bad, I'd told him. *I'm gonna have to start coming to you for money.*

You know I give it to you, he had said.

I know, man.

"You know his cancer had to come back at some point," Todd told me. "That's what remission means."

"You're right," I said.

"Guess his momma changed her mind about healing 'im," Jack shrugged. "That's why they don't let dead bitches be doctors."

"You're right," I said.

"At least it was quick," Gim said. "It's not like he lingered in the hospital for months."

"You're right," I said.

I got three sisters and they all ministers, Robert told me one time. *Ya know, Ray, I the only fuck-up in my family.*

Got three sisters, too, I'd replied. *And I think you're okay.*

He had smiled his big, goofy smile, teeth missing in front. *Thanks, Ray*, he'd said. *That mean a lot to me.*

I had smiled right back.

I know, man.

7:27am
EVERYONE GETS THE LIFE THEY DESERVE
EVERYONE GETS THE LOVE THEY DESERVE

Almost halfway through the fifteenth hour of a sixteen-hour shift and I was getting twitchy. Yours truly had been at the rehab since the previous afternoon. I saw the day turn into night, and then back into day, without leaving the diseased confines of my workplace.

I watched the junkies. Watched the crackheads. Watched the clock. Arrived drunk. Sobered up. Suffered though a hangover.

Not a happy camper.

It was in this miserable state that I had to turn away one homeless person after another. The past few hours had seen a large number of homelies seeking entrance to the building. Much more than usual, and probably because it was so goddamn cold outside. No one who came ringing the bell or banging on the door (which killed my poor head) asked for the usual things. No begging for spare change or sandwiches or to use the bathroom. They all just wanted in. Wanted to get the hell out of the cold.

I couldn't blame them. I was inside the building and still had my leather jacket zipped up tight. It had to be freezing as all hell outside. The wind was blowing knives down the street, and it rained off and on. No one would want to be out in weather like that. Not me. Not the bums. Not anybody who didn't have a radiator shoved down their pants.

178

So, they all wanted inside. Predictably, I wasn't as hot for the idea. For them, getting inside the building represented a temporary end to their suffering. For me, it represented nothing but hassles. They wouldn't have to worry about freezing or catching pneumonia. I'd have to worry about them going where they shouldn't, getting into things they shouldn't. The homeless aren't house-broken. So, I decided they could stay out in the cold.

I made the decision. They could live with the consequences.

My lack of charity got the usual angry responses. The last three bums I told this to all responded with a variation of the last guy's line. To quote: "I comin' back, and I killin' that white motherfucker!"

He shouted this to two other bums I had turned away at the door. They had also issued threats against my life when informed that they could work on their frostbite for all I cared. In response to the last guy's declaration, they shouted a unanimous agreement. Then, they went on to discuss killing me at some length. I could hear them all through the glass front of the building. They sat on the front steps, waiting for me to get off work, and discussed killing me.

Resolved: That the honky should die as painfully as possible.
For: 3
Against: 1   (*me*, of course)

Who says democracy doesn't work?

"We oughtta *kill* that white motherfucker," I could hear them saying.

On a normal day I would have laughed this off. I've had my life threatened at work so often that I barely noticed it anymore. I'd learned to take it with a grain of salt. No one had killed me yet, so no biggie.

I told myself that bums getting upset was an understandable thing. They had nothing, led dangerous and desperate lives, and were usually some combination of crazy and drugged. Being given another reminder of how little the rest of the world cared about their well-being wasn't going to make them any happier.

"We oughtta *kill* that white motherfucker."

Understandable.

"We oughtta *kill* that white motherfucker."

Well, *typically* understandable. It suddenly became the Breaking Point.

I was tired, miserable, wanted to go home, and was *livid* at being threatened by people associated with a business that I didn't even work for. I was pissed at the Christers for running a ministry that lured the homeless here where I had to deal with them. I was pissed at the bums for threatening my life day after day. I was pissed at humanity for not committing mass suicide after I blew out the candles on my last birthday cake.

I was pissed, and I was going to do something about it.

"We oughtta *kill* that white motherfucker!"

I stalked into the kitchen, grabbed the biggest knife I could find, walked back to the lobby, kicked open the front door, and screamed, "*WHO'S* GONNA KILL THE WHITE MOTHERFUCKER?"

This was me waving a butcher knife at three bums. This was me flipping out at work. This was me menacing the downtrodden and desperate. This was me hoping that somebody rushed me so I could hack them open. This was everything horrible about the job having finally eaten my soul.

This was why you shouldn't fuck with me when I'm hung over.

"*WHO'S* GONNA KILL THE WHITE MOTHERFUCKER?"

The bums screamed and bolted. All three put as much distance as possible, as quickly as possible, between themselves and the bully at the door.

I'd never thought it possible to run so fast wearing so many overcoats. The bums shoved and trampled each other. They scrambled like hell off the porch and down the sidewalk. If someone held a Street Olympics (like the Special Olympics, but not as depressing), these guys would be the ones with cereal endorsements. They ran and tripped and ran and stumbled and kept running. One tried to push his shopping cart with him, but when it tumped into the street he left it and kept running. All his worldly possessions, dumped in the gutter, soaking up rainwater.

I watched them haul ass around the corner and considered laughing for a second, but it passed.

7:28pm
THE GOD THAT FAILED
BUT TRIED, TRIED AGAIN

I was adjusting my backpack for the ride home when the doorbell rang. Being on my way out, I clicked the door unlocked. I would be gone in seconds, so it didn't matter to me who got in here. They would very quickly become someone else's problem.

The door was pushed open. In walked the most destitute human being I had ever seen. That is, *if* the shambling wreck twitching his way towards me even qualified for the title. His hair was falling out in patches, he was barefoot, there were running sores on his arms and face, his left eye wouldn't stop blinking, and the torn t-shirt he wore was smeared with foreign substances.

The worst part was, I kind of recognized the guy.

No way his wife was going to take him back now.

"H-hey there, Ray. How you doin'?" He smiled at me. There's no way that a homeless crack addict can be anything but repulsive, so fuck knows why he was bothering to try.

I moved my backpack off the desk and lowered myself into the seat. My Sadist-sense was screaming like a boiled porpoise. This was going to be entertaining.

"*Reverend* Leroy!"

"Hi," said Corey.

I smiled at him. "I'd ask how ya been, but it's pretty apparent."

"Yeah," he said, ducking his head a little, "I been better, but—"

"But—*what*?" I interrupted. "Can't imagine any modifier drastic enough to alter your situation. Like, you're a homeless crack addict, *but* you finally got that online degree you've been after. Or maybe you're looking like hell these days, *but* Universal Studios finally bought your first screenplay..."

Corey just stared at me. His eye never stopped blinking, but the rest of him went slack. "What?"

I sighed, then cut to the chase. "Well, it's nice to see you went back to your real god," I said. "That *Jesus* shit got really old, really quick."

His face flashed anger, but it was quickly smoothed back down into a half-hearted smile. Guy even tried a little chuckle to brush over my viciousness.

Pathetic.

One hand scratching at his muck-smeared T-shirt, he whined, "Now, I dunno 'bout that. I'm still filled with the love of Christ. He never leave—"

I cut him off before he could spew any more self-denial. "*Bullshit*," I said. "You were born a crack worshipper, and you'll fucking die one. *That*...is your god." He looked down at the floor and mumbled something I couldn't hear. The human spirit is never so broken that it can't be stomped into a few more pieces.

"Now, what did you want?"

"What?" He looked back up.

"*You're* the one who came *here*," I said. "Unless it was to show off how well you're doing, I'm guessin' you want something."

I had lost ten bucks on the guy. The obnoxiously religious never last too long before they're sucking the pipe again, but *this* Reverend Leroy had relapsed and disappeared two weeks quicker than I had bet my money on. Jack had called him almost to the day.

"I..." it seemed to get stuck in his throat.

"You...*what*?"

Corey wiped at his greasy face a few times in what could have been shame. "I need a few bucks, man. Just a few. I gotta have—just a few dollars."

I felt the need to make him spell it out. "And?"

He glared at me. "Could I...please have...you got just a buck or two, man?" He shifted from angry to pathetic at warp speed. "I'm *really* hurtin'."

I looked him up and down. "I believe ya."

"Can you help me, *please*?"

I glanced past him at the few other homelies wandering around the lobby. Reverend Leroy was worse off than all of them. No way in hell his wife was *ever* taking him back now.

"*Well*..." I glanced down the back hallway, making sure no one important would catch what I was about to pull. "Ya know that you're not supposed to come beggin' around here, but..." I reached into my pocket and pulled out my wallet. A dollar was extracted from it. "I just might have something for you."

His face lit up. "Oh, *bless ya*, Ray. Thank you. Bless you. Thank—"

"I got somethin' for ya...if *you* can do somethin' for me."

Corey looked unsure. "Uh...sure, Ray. Whatcha need?"

I had a need, all right. Not for anything material, though. I needed something that only Corey could give me. Something that I never knew I needed till I worked here. Something that I never would've admitted to needing before I worked here.

"I just want you to say, and I want to hear it nice and clear," this was gonna be good, "*Fuck Jesus.*"

His eyes bulged. He put his hands up like I had taken a swing at him. "*What?*"

"You heard me."

I think, in that moment, my own soul should have gone belly-up and cried uncle.

But, of course, I don't believe in the soul.

"C'mon," I said, "Mr. Dollar wants to hear you say it...*Fuck Jesus.*"

"I can't...I...I can't do...you know I...c'mon, Ray! You kiddin', right?"

Not smiling, I slowly shook my head from side to side. The dollar was waved in the air.

Corey's gaze followed the dollar. "*Raaaay*, that ain't right, man! That ain't right! You can't do that to a brother!"

"I'm not," I said, still not smiling. "I'm doing it to *you*. And it's nothing worse than what you've done to yourself. I'm just making you chose, one more time, between your gods. Now who's it gonna be? C'mon, *Reverend*. Rock or the cross? Crack or the Christ? *Whoooo's* it gonna be?"

Corey squeezed his eyes shut. He grimaced. Then he opened them back up and said, "No thanks, Ray. You can keep your dollar. I'll keep my *Jesus*." His eyes were bright, probably for the first time in weeks, and he smiled with pride.

Still, Corey didn't leave. Just stood there in front of the desk. It's people's body language that gives them away every time.

"Fair enough," I shrugged, and laid the dollar on the desk. Corey's gaze never left it. "But what we have here is..." I reached into my wallet for a few more bills. "*Nine* more dollars to join up with the first." I placed them on the desk with the other dollar. Not close enough for Corey to reach out and grab them. I knew he'd do it if given the chance. *New Start Rule #1*, and all. "You're halfway to a pretty fat rock with ten bucks."

"*C'mon*, Ray."

"Choice is yours, man."

"Ray, this ain't cool!" His voice broke, his face scrunched up. Homeboy looked on the verge of crying.

"Ten dollars," I repeated. "Easiest thing in the world. If you're gonna have a self-destructive streak, ya might as well make it entertaining."

"C'mon, man!" I fanned myself with the money. "*Fuck* that *Jesus!*"

"*C'mon!*"

I saw his eyes begin to mist. You never sink so low that there's not some new bottom to hit.

"So...what's it gonna be?"

"*Raaaaaay!*" The tears started to flow. "I'm hurtin' so bad, man!" Corey's entire body trembled, and the snot ran from his nose just as fast as the tears leaked from his eyes.

I rolled my eyes. "And I'm startin' to get bored here, *you junkie shit!*"

There is no depth that people won't sink to. Nothing that they won't do. No excuse that they won't make for their own failings. I'd seen it all and heard it all over the past year, and I was so sick of human weakness. So sick of our excuses. And so *goddamn sick* of the disgusting, hopeless world we lived in.

"What's it gonna be, man?"

So sick of it.

"Come on, *Reverend!*"

So sick of it all, that what could I do but embrace it with open arms?

"What's it gonna be?"

Later, still enveloped in post-orgasmic bliss, I clicked the button to let Toni into the building.

"Hey, Ray baby!" he called to me.

Feet up on the desk, I gave him a casual salute. "Hey, there."

Toni dropped his backpack behind the desk and gave me a friendly hug. I actually hugged him back. I felt horribly radiant.

He patted me on the feet, but I couldn't be bothered to take them off the desk. Not any more than I could take the smile from off my face.

"What are you so happy about?" Toni asked. "You're all Mr. Smiley over there."

I gave a little shrug. "It's a horrible world, man." I tossed a wink in his direction. "Proud to be a part of it."

7:33am
ANYONE WHO LETS LIFE BEAT THEM DOWN
DIDN'T DESERVE HAPPINESS IN THE FIRST PLACE

It was finally cold in Pasadena. Something like 30-ish degrees outside, or so the junkies told me. It was too bad that I hadn't thought to bring my jacket the previous night, but on the upside, all the mosquitoes would finally be dying off. I almost wished that the change in weather could do the same for the other parasites around here. But hell, why waste energy on spite?

There was still a little time left to the shift, but I was leaving anyways. My replacement hadn't shown up, Gim wasn't here, but that didn't matter. Enough was enough.

It was time to pack up my stuff and write the same bullshit as every day on the shift report:

'*Made rounds every hour.*'

'*Nothing to report.*'

A new sheet of paper for each shit report. Trees died for this.

Both written assertions were lies. Naturally. I had been upstairs a total of once the entire eight-hour shift, and plenty of stuff had happened—everything from bum fights to relapses—but I just didn't feel like taking the time to record it.

Todd asked if I was really going to bike home in the cold. We East Texans are total pansies when it comes to low temperatures. "Wish I could just burrow on home," I said. "But I don't think that's going to happen."

Being about to leave work and its few attendant responsibilities, I disabled the lock on the front door. A horde of homelies rushed into the building. Now that I wasn't going to have to deal with them, they were welcome to come in out of the cold. This would be great news to the ones who had been huddled up against the building all night.

Their noxious scent trailed after them and made itself comfortable in the lobby. The first familiar waft of sweat, piss, beer and vomit smashed me in the nose, and I started packing even quicker. The Methodists were going to be pissed that the homelies had gotten into the building so far ahead of schedule...and that was kind of the point.

The floodgates were opened, and in flowed the tides of human refuse. I instantly dubbed it the best idea I'd had all shift.

Fending off the usual demands for my spare change (*zakat* delays the inevitable), I slung my backpack over my shoulders and cinched the straps. The backpack was heavier than when I had arrived. About three rolls of toilet paper, a stapler, and a gallon of milk heavier. I fetched my bike and rolled it out to the lobby.

Todd was standing by the front desk, talking with one of the homeless women. She had a pointy nose, warty face, and long, bony fingers coupled with a shriek of a voice. The woman was tailor-made for children's nightmares. And if her looks weren't enough, her sharp stench of rank cunt would do the trick.

Her: "My husband's in...my husband's in jail. You got a quarter?"

Todd: "Actually, I've got two dollars for you. You're going to use them to take care of yourself, right?"

Her: "My husband's in jail. I need some paper. He broke his ribs. Can you get me paper?"

Todd: "I'll see what I can do. Just make sure you stay warm out there, okay?"

Her: "Why don't you—my husband in...*you* can keep me warm."

Todd: "What?"

Her: "Why don't *you* keep me warm?"

Todd: "*Whoa*...ummm...hey, Ray...in the mood for an early birthday present?"

I shook my head as I wheeled past them towards the door.

"Sure I've done worse," was called back, "But not this sober."

The door was kicked open, and I escaped into the light.

7:47am
EPILOGUE:
THE REAL PAYCHECK AT THE END OF A SHIFT

I kick off my shoes and start stripping the moment I walk in my apartment. I'm so grateful there's a place on this madhouse of a planet where I don't have to drape myself in a bunch of ridiculous fabrics.

My shirt, shorts, boxers and socks are tossed to the floor. The rehab's stench still clings to me somewhat, but I've learned that not even bathing gets rid of it entirely. It's just something you adjust to.

Martini ingredients and a Valium wait for me in the kitchen pantry. They counteract the coffee on the days when I've had some. When I haven't, they just make me feel better.

I mix the drink, drop in the pill, and slam it while heading for the bedroom.

Then, an urge hits, and I go back for another drink. This, too, is downed quickly. Then I make myself a third, just to be on the safe side. With that polished off, I head back to the bedroom.

Feelin' tired, Ray? asks a little voice in my head.

Mmm-hmmm, I respond—in my head, of course; otherwise I'd be crazy.

My bedroom door is swung open. *Well then*, the voice says, *Everyday's your birthday, man. Here ya go.*

And curled up in the bed, beatific from the sunlight sneaking around the edge of the blinds, is my girlfriend. Short hair tousled like Medusa gone butch, stout and dark figure, clad only in a pair of large gray panties. She doesn't respond to my entrance, just keeps on breathing in and breathing out like there was nothing else in the world that would ever need to be done.

One of the more satisfying feelings is coming home to find somebody waiting for you in bed (as long as you know them and/or they're not armed, I guess). It's like being granted an official pardon for all the unpleasant shit you've done or had done to you throughout the day. Like God winked down from his gold-plated throne and let you into that special preview of Heaven normally reserved for the faithful. Like all the suffering in life suddenly became extraneous and unimportant, and how can anyone really be pessimistic when the world has such wonderful gifts in it?

There's someone, they're in your bed, they're in some stage of undress, and they're waiting for you.

Consider yourself forgiven and absolved.

I lift up the edge of the sheets and slide in next to her, matching tabs and slots, recesses and protrusions, until we've got a perfect spoon going. She still isn't awake. People never look so immaculate as when they're asleep. Perhaps it says something about us as a species that we never shine with such child-like innocence—all the hate, worry, and pettiness melted away—as when we're unconscious and drooling on ourselves, but *whatever*.

My girlfriend reaches over to pull my arm tight around her, and presses back against me. All this without waking up.

Let sleeping girlfriends lie, the saying goes, but I'm feeling selfish. I kiss a line down her back from her shoulder on in. This finally wakes her.

She turns her head to smile at me. "Hey, baby," I say gently.

"*Hey,*" she breathes back at me. Her hair falls in her eyes and she wipes it away with the back of her hand. I interlace my fingers with hers and give them a light squeeze.

"Missed you at work," I say, kissing her hand.

"*Mumble, mumble* you, too," she says.

I prop myself up on an elbow and give her a quick kiss and as big of a hug as I can. "Sorry...morning breath," she says.

Yeah, she's got a hellacious case of it (and I taste like martini), but at this point it's just another beautiful part of her that contributes to the beautiful whole.

Of course, anyone's attractive when you're about to shove yourself up them.

"I love you," I say, as I move myself into a straddling position. She smiles up at me, all adoration and trust. I reach for the bedside lube. It's a decent substitute for foreplay. "I really do."

She says she loves me back, and I can't stop smiling. Because I'm about to get laid, and because as much as I tell my girlfriend about my job, I've never told her about *New Start Rule #1*.

FINIS

186

IF THIS WAS AT THE START OF THE BOOK, YOU COULD'VE SAVED YOURSELF A LOT OF READING

"It is not true that suffering ennobles the spirit; happiness does that sometimes, but suffering for the most part makes men mean and vindictive."–Maugham

"A wretched soul bruised with adversity,
We bid be quiet when we hear it cry;
But were we ourselves burdened with like weight of pain,
As much, or more, would we ourselves complain."
--Shakespeare, *The Comedy of Errors* (2.1.35)

"There's so much suffering in the world that we'd be stupid *not* to find it funny."
--Ray, talking to himself, *again*

ACKNOWLEDGEMENTS

Despite what may seem like an atmosphere of misogyny in these halfway stories, this book wouldn't have been possible without the support and help of several wonderful women. Thanks go to Kiwi, Ariel, Sar-Sar, Marie, Mrs. Bowman, Ramie and the resident non-female, Eric.

Thanks also to Greg, who taught me the true meaning of Easter.

And I'd be a real shit if I didn't mention my folks (only half-female). They always went above and beyond their biological duties for me, and the fuck-up I became is entirely my fault and none of theirs.

DEDICACION

Este libro es por mi familia con muchos graditudos.

y

Este libro es por Marie y Nicole con muchas apologias.